D1187905

90710 000 079 811

Dave & Nick

Dave & Nick

The Year of the Honeymoon ... and Beyond

Ann Treneman

The Robson Press

First published in Great Britain in 2011 by
Biteback Publishing Ltd
Westminster Tower
3 Albert Embankment
London
SE1 7SP

Copyright © Ann Treneman 2011

Ann Treneman has asserted her right under the Copyright, Designs and Patents Act 1988 to be identified as the author of this work.

All rights reserved. No part of this publication may be reproduced, stored in a retrieval system or transmitted, in any form or by any means, without the publisher's prior permission in writing.

This book is sold subject to the condition that it shall not, by way of trade or otherwise, be lent, resold, hired out or otherwise circulated without the publisher's prior consent in any form of binding or cover other than that in which it is published and without a similar condition, including this condition, being imposed on the subsequent purchaser.

ISBN 978-1-84954-164-0

10 9 8 7 6 5 4 3 2 1

A CIP catalogue record for this book is available from the British Library.

Set in Adobe Caslon by Namkwan Cho
Printed and bound in Great Britain by CPI Group (UK) Ltd, Croydon CR0 4YY

London Borough of Richmond Upon Thames	
K	
90710 000 079 811	
Askews & Holts	
941.086 TRE	£14.99
	9781849541640

Acknowledgements

My thanks go to all who helped make this book happen, including my publisher Jeremy Robson, my friend Paul Dunn who gave me the initial idea, my fellow sketchwriters at the Commons, all my colleagues at *The Times* and, of course, politicians of all hues without whom this book truly would not have been possible. Particularly warm thanks to all my appreciative, observant, wonderful readers. These sketches appeared in their original form (all have been edited and, in some cases, augmented) in *The Times* or, in one instance the *Sunday Times*. In particular I would like to thank those who work with me at Westminster in what we call 'The Room': Roland Watson, Sam Coates, Anushka Asthana, Michael Savage and Soraya Kishtwari. It was quite the year for weddings – Dave and Nick, Wills and Kate, Zara and Mike, Ed and Ed, not to mention Ed and Justine. So, thanks also to my (new) husband Ian Berkoff. ♥

Contents

Introduction

I beg your pardon
I never promised you a rose garden
Along with the sunshine
There's gotta be a little rain sometimes
     Written by Joe South
     Most famously recorded by Lynn Anderson

So, immediately, reading that lyric we see the problem, for it seems to me that Dave and Nick did, actually, promise each other (and us) a rose garden. On that beautiful, fateful day in May 2010, they certainly exchanged vows to that effect in the Downing Street rose garden. You can call it a coalition if you want, but those of us who were there in our plush chairs – bees buzzing, birds singing, sun dappling as it will on such days – immediately realised that this was, actually, a wedding.

'This is the first coalition government in sixty-five years,' bubbled Dave, sun sparkling in his eyes, looking alarmingly like Nick. 'We have a shared agenda, a shared resolve. Today we are not just announcing a new government and new ministers. We are announcing a new politics, a new politics where the national interest is more important than the party interests, where cooperation wins out over confrontation, where compromise, where give and take, where reasonable, civilised, grown-up behaviour is not a sign of weakness but a sign of strength.'

Thus, he, Dave did take this man, Nick, to be his lawfully wedded coalition partner, to have and to hold, for poorer or even poorer (it was an austerity themed service), until election do them part (in 2015). 'This coalition can be a historic and seismic shift in our political landscape,' vowed Dave.

And he, Nick, did also take this man, Dave, to be his coalition partner. 'This is a government that will last,' he claimed, 'not because of a list of policies, not because it will be easy. There will be bumps and scrapes along the way. This is a government that will last despite those differences because we are united. Our ambition is simple and yet profound, our ambition is to put real power and opportunity into the hands of people, families and communities to change their lives for the better. For me, that is what liberalism is all about.' He added: 'I came into politics to change politics and to change Britain for good. Together [he looks at Dave], that job starts today...'

I reprint these words because vows at such times do mean something, not least because they provide an insight into the crazy things people say when they are newlyweds. But if the words flowed like fine champagne that day, it was the chemistry that I noticed. Nick and Dave, Dave and Nick, they seemed to be loving this crazy little thing called love (sorry, it's hard to keep these songs away at weddings). Of course, as the cynics pointed out, they didn't really have any other option – this was an arranged marriage, with a pre-nup hammered out in the mad, bad, crazy days after the election that elected no one. But there are arranged marriages and then there are arranged marriages. Everyone who was there could see that this was one that suited them both.

But what these sketches, edited and in some cases enhanced from my column in *The Times* over the last eighteen months, also show is that, perhaps like all new couples, they had absolutely no clue what lay ahead. What Nick referred to blithely as 'bumps and scrapes'. Hmmmm. Not quite. More like multi-vehicle pile-ups. Did Nick ever imagine, even in his darkest days, that he would become a hate figure, burnt in effigy by students furious that his version of abolishing tuition fees to the triple them? Or how backbench Tories would delight in taunting him on voting and Lords reform? Did Dave really have any idea of what coalition would mean: the compromises, the cuts, the tuition fees chaos, the criticism, the fury of his backbenchers, the endless advice from the in-laws (Paddy Ashdown, I mean you)? His first anniversary present, the AV referendum, was a disaster. Yes, it may have seemed the perfect gift – it's a paper anniversary, what could be better than a ballot paper? – and, yes, Nick had said he wanted it more than anything else but, like so many extravagant presents, it all went totally wrong. Next time, I suspect Dave will give Nick something more useful – like a tie.

Maybe it is because political journalism, like politics in general, is so male-dominated, but there is a huge amount of emphasis placed in both on facts, issues, policy. Political reporters invest endless amounts of time and effort in finding tiny fissures that could become splits, measuring shifts in emphasis that could, with enough pressure, become U-turns. Certainly the coalition has seen its fair share of U-turns – there are enough in this book to rival the practice session of any learner driver – and there have been hundreds of thousands of words written about deficit reductions, policing, education, voting reform, nuclear power, defence budgets, civil liberties, phone hacking, Libya, riots, poverty etc.

And yet, at the core of this coalition are two men. It is their relationship that fascinates me and provides the driving force of this book. I start not with their beginning as a couple but when they were one, so to speak, and how similar they seem even then, with hindsight. There's Dave making the first ever Tory jokes about low-carbon commuting. There's Nick endlessly talking about optimism. In so many ways – their backgrounds so similar, the ambitions so matched – they look like they were destined for this.

The election turned out to be their 'getting to know you' phase. The nation met Nick through the election debates, sparking the crush (short-lived) that was Cleggmania. Then, post-hung election, came those five famous days in May when Nick was flirting shamelessly with not only Dave but Gordon Brown. Indeed, right up until the very end, it seems, Nick was using Gordon to get what he could out of Dave and Co. This is the politics of courtship, of relationships, of hard realities and soft powers of persuasion. Again, this is a woman's game, played by men.

'It's not about the chemistry,' said Nick on *The Andrew Marr Show* (which acts, in so many ways, like a Relate therapy room for Dave and Nick) after their one-year anniversary and the disastrous AV referendum (which was also, I think, the official end of the honeymoon). But, actually, a great deal of it is about chemistry. I have followed Nick and Dave around the country as they do their 'live and unplugged' show. And, even when there are serious policy differences, they complement each other. Their personalities are well suited. They are relaxed, fluid, in tune. It is what the dating experts call synchronicity.

'I woke up thinking: this is so much better than the alternative!' cried Dave at the wedding, so happy, so engaging. We were seeing, for the first time, the natural grace that marks out Dave's premiership as something special. But if necessity is the mother of invention then serendipity must be its sister here too. I could also see how Dave's traditional ways were enhanced by Nick's fizziness. The Lib Dem leader has an edge that Dave will never possess. Nick is a European and a metro-sexual. He is multi-lingual, is a citizen of the world, idealistic but also sophisticated (if incredibly accident prone). Dave is English, not European, his attractions are very much rooted in England's green and pleasant land.

It is not an equal relationship (the clue's in the word 'deputy') but there have been almost no leaks or gossip about how, exactly, it works. From the very beginning, Nick was thrust into the role of political wife, muted in the Commons, reduced to the role of nodding supporter. (I would love to know what his real wife, the feisty Miriam, has to say about all of that.) In America, where coalition government would never happen but where compromise government is often a fact of life because of the separation of powers set out in the Constitution, the role of the First Lady is one with real clout. In many ways – and Nick may hate this, but there is truth in it – he plays the same kind of role: essentially supportive but with his own hobbies and passions (if AV can be such a thing, which sadly for Lib Dems, it can) which are not only indulged but encouraged.

I am sure that Dave, never a rightwinger, welcomed the way Nick blunted the sharp edges of Conservativism. And Nick must appreciate the fact that the Tories know how to get things done, unlike the Lib Dems, who love to dream but recoil from hard choices. Dave's role may be dominant (the husband in the traditional marriage) but there is no doubt that it is a real partnership. There is respect there and it is mutual. Nick has shown real pluck in backing Dave on issues such as the deficit while playing the mitigating 'good critic' role of political wife on health reform and the summer of discontent. Dave has an arrogant side to him that can be breathtaking: at times, he simply skips the detail in favour of the easy cheap shot. Nick, whose earnestness has never been in doubt, helps there too. Certainly, as the Hackgate scandal exploded, with Dave refusing to apologise, the presence of Nick steadied the ship.

It is these themes that run through these sketches, the story of the coalition but also of two men making it up as they go along. Obviously the whole point of sketchwriting is to have some fun, but it also provides a wealth of detail and context. It has been a blast to follow the corresponding adventures of Gordon, the Brothers Miliband and Georgie Boy Osborne. Then there are relatives, mad uncles, ferocious grandparents, in-laws, outlaws and, in general, the crazy world of politics. But at its heart is this relationship. It is said that no one understands a marriage that they are not in. This may be so, but we can watch it. 'You better look before you leap,' goes the Rose Garden song. Too late for that now. They're in mid-air, legs pumping, arms out, suspended over the chasm.

Ann Treneman
Westminster
October 2011

Who's Who in the Wedding Party

The Groom
David 'Dave' Cameron, young and shiny-faced leader who recast his party as caring and sharing Conservatives. Old Etonian, new optimist. Brutal, sometimes shallow, upbeat, pragmatic. Best trait: Grace. Worst trait: Arrogance.

The Deputy Groom
Nick Clegg, young and pasty-faced leader elected to make his party look semi-electable. Public school-boy, metrosexual, multi-lingual. Earnest, passionate, accident-prone. Best trait: Endless enthusiasm. Worst trait: Blind hypocrisy.

Dave's best man
George Osborne, Chancellor, full-time scorpion, key Tory party strategist. Wallpaper heir. Quick-witted, sneery, clever, arrogant. Thrives out of spotlight.

Nick's best man
Danny Alexander, a late substitute after David Laws, first choice, had to excuse himself for expense-related reasons. Tall, ginger, boring, steady. Was big in squirrel circles before he became Chief Secretary to the Treasury.

Guests

Andrew Lansley, Tory, health reform obsessive. Lugubrious, super-focused. Big on bottoms up.

Ken Clarke, jazz-loving, red-faced, big-bellied old Tory who often seems more of a Lib Dem.

Theresa May, she of the killer leopard-skin shoes and crazy *Star Trek* outfit. She's been on the Tory front bench forever. Who knew that Dave rated her so much?

William Hague, unlikely best friend of George and Dave, self-made millionaire, author, ex-Tory leader. Brilliant orator who will be relied on to give any extra speeches.

Ed Miliband, Labour, part of the famous political double act, the Miliband Brothers, whose fratricide sitcom has proved fascinating. Btw, Ed hates Nick, though Nick doesn't know it yet.

Ed Balls, Labour, attending with wife and fellow (if that is the right word) Labour frontbencher, Yvette. Ed B has, as you might have guessed, balls and is a particular irritant to Dave.

Harriet Harman, Labour, may be a non-gender-specific feminist, but she is the only one wearing a hat here. Wanted to come with Gordon Brown but couldn't find him. Stalwart frontbencher, pioneer, doughty fighter.

John Bercow, Mr Speaker, attending with his Twitter-obsessed wife Sally. The Bercows only got invited because they had to be. Everyone loves to hate John, who is short and doesn't care.

Andy Coulson. Controversial guest. Dave insisted that the former *News of the World* editor be invited, though Nick told him that he might live to regret that (guess who was right?).

Chapter One

Singular beginnings – the way they were

David Cameron and Nick Clegg are two men with an almost scary amount in common. They are born within months of each other, Dave in October 1966, Nick in January 1967, into well-off families. Nick's dad was a banker, Dave's a stockbroker. They were brought up in the Home Counties and went to the best private schools that money could buy: Eton for Dave, Westminster for Nick. Dave studied philosophy, politics and economics at Oxford while Nick did social anthropology at Cambridge. Each has had a career dominated by politics with occasional forays into the big bad worlds of marketing (Dave) and journalism (Nick). Nick was elected as an MEP in 1999, Dave as an MP in 2001 with Nick following in 2005. Both were lauded as future leaders of their parties, predictions they then duly fulfilled. Are you frightened yet? If not, read on and you will be soon. These sketches are a selection from how they found themselves in their past lives – before they found each other. ❣

Dave's Story

D-Day for the smoothie from Notting Hill

A man named Dave is born in a room full of strawberry smoothies and chilled-out love

I was there for the birth of Dave. It was 29 September 2005, D-Day, Dave day, and leadership launch day for both David Cameron and David Davis. First David D launched his bid to be the Tory leader by saying that he was passionate about change. Then David C launched his, saying that he was passionate about change.

Do you see the problem? Two Davids running for Tory leader is two too many. It is confusing and indicates a lack of choice (which, I believe, is illegal these days). So no surprises then when, at DC's launch, there was an attempt to rebrand him as 'Dave'. It's a great idea, though, actually, I think 'Fred' would have been more fun.

David Davis is a man's man and his launch was a man's man's event. It was all wood-panelling and middle-aged testosterone. No frills, no food, no fun. In contrast, Dave's launch, just down the road, seemed to be in another world entirely. Dave is always accused of being from the Notting Hill set. After yesterday I think we can drop the accused bit. Everyone was so smooth it was like being in a room of shiny pebbles. It was as though someone had gone over them all with a giant pumice stone until there were no rough edges at all.

Dave even served us brownies and strawberry smoothies. Smoothies at a political launch! Whatever next? Aromatherapy? Truly, the days of being forced to drink instant coffee served in Styrofoam cups with teeth marks already embedded in them could be numbered.

I must admit that, especially after DD's brutally abrupt event, it was all rather soothing. The theme of the party (for that is now how I thought of it) was 'chill'. The room was white and circular. The music was calming with lots of little chimes and bells and what-not. I am only surprised that we were not handed little white towels and lavender eye-pads. I felt the desire to close my eyes and imagine I was somewhere else.

Even when Dave arrived, seriously late for his own party, the dream-like atmosphere continued. The words 'passionate' and 'caring' washed round us like waves lapping the beach. He kept saying: 'There's a we in politics as much as a me.' It could be his catchphrase because, even in a dream, it makes no sense.

I hope you don't think that I am concentrating on style, not substance. It's just that yesterday style seemed to BE the substance. So far, then, this is all we know: too many Davids, not enough Goliaths. That is going to have to change. ♥

(*All headline dates refer to the day that the sketch appeared in *The Times*.)

5 October 2005
Dave takes us on an 'incredible' journey

This was Dave's big moment: his speech to the party faithful in Blackpool. He worked very very hard at making it look entirely effortless

I regret to report that I have been on an incredible journey with David 'Dave' Cameron. Yesterday he came before us in Blackpool, the leadership front runner, anxious to show us that he was more than just a pretty face. I am not sure what the point of that was: he has the elusive Kennedy factor and yesterday everybody in the hall could feel it.

Dave worked very very hard at making everything look effortless, an exercise made much harder by the fact that Ken Clarke was also on stage yesterday. Say what you will about Ken (and they do – red-faced, paunchy, walking health hazard), he has the rare gift of appearing completely natural. The main thing I want to report about Ken's speech is that he didn't use the word 'change'. Plus, he didn't tell us that we were going on a 'journey'.

Dave was studiously natural, which isn't the same thing at all. He strolled on to the stage, as if he just happened to be passing. He spoke deliberately and calmly. We were told that there would be no copies of his speech until afterwards because much of it would be impromptu. This made me snort, for the day before I had watched Dave practising his speech, entire body furrowed in concentration, to an empty hall.

'We CAN lead the new generation!' he cried now. 'We can BE that new generation.'

Then he managed to get two clichés in one sentence. 'Changing our party to change our country,' he emoted, 'it will be an incredible journey.' (Noooooo, I thought, for, like the children in the back seat, we are getting car sick in Blackpool.)

In the practice version, Dave had ended with something akin to a whoop and a sort of air punch. But yesterday, in the real version, he calmly opened his arms to the audience. I wonder how many times he had practised that inclusive hug. If mirrors could talk – and they do sometimes – what would they say about Dave?

Then, and surely this is cheating, he brought his pretty pregnant wife, Samantha, up on stage for a lot of totally spontaneous hugging. During one hug he gave her bump a little pat. It was shameless but, it must be said, rather effective. 💔

7 December 2005
The King is dead, long live the King

It may have been a leadership election but it felt like a corona-
tion when Dave, ruler of the Cameroons, accepted the crown

The coronation of Dave, King of the Cameroons, took place at a ceremony that managed to be both extremely grand and ultra-modern. At least 500 happy subjects crammed into a room at the Royal Academy of Arts. Tory MPs seemed ecstatic. 'It IS a coronation,' exclaimed one MP as he waited, wiggling in excitement.

Technically, of course, it was an election, if one organised by a party, but it did not feel like one. There was nothing grubby or practical here. It was a grand room in a grand building and it was filled with grand people: lords and ladies, fundraisers, donors. There were crowds of shiny, happy Notting Hill people. The air-kissing broke all records for a political event.

There was absolutely no tension. No one was running around, mobile glued to ear, looking desperate. The atmosphere was as bubbly as a glass of champagne. It could not have been bouncier if we had all been on a trampoline.

The Tories were here to celebrate: everyone knew who had won. Even the stage backdrop knew, for it was baby blue, the colour of the Cameroons.

The ceremony itself was simple and mercifully brief. Michael Howard said a few words about how wonderful everything was. David Davis and David Cameron came out and stood together, looking dangerously on the brink of a civil partnership ceremony. DD sported a big loopy grin. Dave had a more controlled smile, but his eyes were red-rimmed and glittering.

A huge roar erupted when Mr Cameron's total was announced. Dave kept his face open and blank, as cameras exploded in his face. DD went to the lectern to say a few words. Dave looked at us and, such is the charisma factor, it was almost impossible to look away from him. It was only when he looked at DD that we did too. DD has never sounded so gracious, as he introduced Dave as the man who would be the next Conservative Prime Minister.

Dave did his trademark no-lectern, no-notes speech. He stepped forward, which made him loom almost too large. 'I said when I launched my campaign that we needed to change in order to win. Now that I have won, we will change,' he cried. The Cameroons love these circular sentences that make no sense.

Dave made what may have been the first Tory joke about being carbon-neutral (normally Lib Dem territory). He wants to set targets for reducing carbon. 'I tried to make a start this morning by biking to work,' he noted ruefully. 'That was a carbon-neutral journey until the BBC sent a helicopter to follow me.'

Laugh? They almost exploded. The coronation was in danger of becoming a love-in.

But Dave did not relax. He may be nice but he is also ruthless. The first thing on his list? Bury Thatcherism. 'We can mend our broken society,' he promised. 'There is such a thing as society. It's just not the same thing as the State.' The next thing on the list? Attack Gordon Brown, who will henceforth be known simply as Road-Block.

The crowd adored it. It is Year Zero for the Cameroons. Then Dave hugged his wife, Samantha, kissing her no fewer than five times. You could almost hear the trumpet fanfare, as the procession began. 💔

5 October 2006
It's a happy, happy day for Dave

Dave, in his first conference speech as leader, explains how he wants sunshine to rule the day and introduces us to his great friend, General Wellbeing

Dave wants to be Prime Minister but, for the time being, it seems that he will settle for being Mr Happy. Yesterday in Bournemouth he gave his party a big hug and told them about his Sunshine Revolution. It's going to put smiles on our faces and songs in our hearts. The future's bright, the future's optimistic and, most of all, the future is Dave. We may be witnessing the birth of a cult.

'They are the dream couple,' gushed the man sitting next to me as, at the end, Dave was joined by his wife, Samantha, on the raised platform in the middle of the hall. (There are no stages in the Sunshine Revolution, only centre grounds.) But, I asked, don't you think she looks a bit reticent? 'That's good. It's English,' he noted approvingly. 'Plus, don't forget, we've had Cherie.' He shuddered as he said the name and added: 'We are ready for this.'

Dave was ready for them too. It was his first significant conference speech and he had clearly decided that he wasn't a natural tub-thumper. Nor did he go in for the theatricality of Tony Blair. Instead, he adopted a slow and laid-back style. At the very beginning, he waited for a moment and then spoke to his party as a neighbour and a friend. It was more a conversation than a speech and, in the hall at least, it worked.

There were two standing ovations before he even said a word. That seemed excessive but, then, the Tories have been in the wilderness for a long time and they are hungry. He told us that the Sunshine Revolution was not about style but about substance. He said this with a great deal of style. 'I want to deal directly with this issue of substance,' he announced, looking straight into our eyes, because he is that kind of guy.

For one thrilling moment he seemed to be teetering on the brink of a policy announcement. But, as it turned out, that was a shallow thing for me to think. For Mr Happy then explained that substance was not about policies at all. 'Substance is not about producing a ten-point plan,' he said. 'It is about deeper things than that. It is about knowing what you believe.'

Dave then told us what he believes in. These include marriage and motherhood but not, it seems, apple pie, for all food in Sunshine Land is healthy and promotes Mr Happy's great friend, General Wellbeing. The most effective passages in the hall were when he mixed the personal and the political, for Dave is skilled at that most difficult of political arts. He gave a passionate account of why the NHS is safe in his hands. 'My family is so often in the hands of the NHS,' he said in an oblique reference to his disabled son, Ivan.* 'And I want them to be safe there.'

Mr Happy loves being married. 'There's something special about marriage. It's not about religion. It's not about morality. It's about commitment. When you stand up there, in front of your friends and your family, in front of the world, whether it's in a church or anywhere else, what you're doing really means something.' At this, Samantha's face was flashed up on the big screen. She looked bemused, but beautiful. It all seemed a bit too intimate.

Then, before we knew it, Dave was shouting: 'The best is yet to come!' Actually, I think that may be *the* policy in Sunshine Land. ♥

(*Ivan, aged six, who had cerebral palsy and epilepsy, died in February 2009.)

Nick's Story

19 December 2007
Nick and Chris emerge from the secret room...

The Lib Dems, having killed off two leaders, Charles Kennedy and Ming Campbell, in quick succession, gathered just before Christmas to elect a new one. It was between Chris Huhne and Nick Clegg but, first, we had to hear from Vince...

We knew who had won – or thought we knew – by watching the wives. We had gathered in a ridiculously over-crowded room in the St Martin's Lane Hotel near Trafalgar Square. It is not healthy to be in an enclosed space with so many Lib Dems, not least because they tend to suffer from body odour. I feared the air circulation system would collapse under the strain.

The announcement was late, for the Lib Dems love their leadership elections and don't like to rush them. The room, overheating to incubator levels, was littered with photographers taking pictures of each other and broadcasters interviewing each other. In the front of the room were all the former Lib-Dem leaders, pretending to have intense conversations with each other.

Then, suddenly, Miriam Clegg and Vicky Huhne came into the room, straight from the secret room (Lib Dems love secret rooms) where they had been closeted with their husbands.

'The wives!' whispered my neighbour. At Lib-Dem events everybody loves to whisper because it adds to the intrigue.

Miriam, who is Spanish, was all smiles, her dark hair bouncing this way and that as she chatted away. Vicky, who is Greek, looked a bit drawn as she beetled over to her chair. They bussed each other as if they'd not just been in the secret room.

'Only two kisses,' we noted ominously.

For Europeans, and all Lib Dems consider themselves such, this is a paltry number. Surely, the minimum would be four in normal circumstances. But this was not normal for, as far as we could see, Miriam's husband had beaten Vicky's. They began to chat with the determination of women doing their duty while being filmed by eight cameras.

They were put out of their misery by the appearance of Vince Cable, acting leader, economist and ballroom dancer supreme. He was met with thunderous applause. Everyone loves him. Indeed, they love him so much that they are replacing him with someone worse. That's the kind of thing that the Liberal Democrats do so well.

'You can all relax,' Vince noted drily. 'I'm not intending to announce a military coup.'

This was a blow. Vince told us that the finest moment of his brief interlude as acting leader was on *Strictly Come Dancing*. As he gave the result, Nick and Chris stood together to one side, looking awkward. They have been on the campaign trail for two months and are starting to resemble each other. Indeed, they walk in tandem as if they are partners in a permanent three-legged race.

'The total number of votes cast was 41,465,' said Vince.

He said that Nick Clegg had received 20,988 votes. At the word 'twenty', there was an 'ohhhh'. Then he said Chris Huhne had got 20,474. This brought another gasp.

No one expected it to be so close. Mr Huhne, irrepressible even in defeat, bounded up. 'Well, there are close-run things and close-run things!'

Then Mr Clegg gave a speech about how he wants a new beginning. It was rather dull. But, still, he looks good. Is that enough? 💔

10 January 2008
Nick plays with the big boys at PMQs

The strategy for Nick's first big Commons test – PMQs – was clear: Nick should be Nick. It sounded simple…

I n Lib-Dem terms, it was a triumph. By that I mean that Nick Clegg's debut at PMQs was not a disaster. He didn't collapse. He didn't cry. He didn't shake, rattle or roll over. The fact that he was also a bit ordinary is beside the point. Don't forget, this is the party of the weird. For Lib Dems, ordinary is remarkable. One of the highest compliments a Lib Dem can give is: 'My, but you were ordinary today.'

Mr Clegg was nervous beforehand, his handsome face petrified, his limbs wooden and possibly controlled by strings. He had tried to break the hex of Sir Ming Campbell (and escape the comparison with Lib-Dem vaudevillian Vince Cable) by changing his seat. All previous leaders have sat on the aisle, close to the Tories and directly across from the vituperative tongue of Dennis Skinner. Mr Clegg decided to move two places over. It was almost touching that so much thought went into this.

'He's moving away from me already!' cried David Cameron, who starts the new year with a new comb-over. (I sit above him and am an expert on his thinning pate.) 'He is the fourth Lib-Dem leader I have faced. I wish him well – although not that well.'

Mr Clegg's facial muscles did not move, which I attribute to nervousness rather than Botox. It must have been hard for him to sit next to Vince, the greatest leader the Lib Dems never had. Earlier I had asked a Lib-Dem aide about Mr Clegg's strategy for PMQs. Would there be jokes? 'Nick is not Vince,' the aide said. 'Nick is Nick.' I took that as a no.

So that was the goal. Nick who is Nick wanted to be Nick. Such consistency is rare for Lib Dems. We watched and waited for any little slip. The Lib-Dem leader doesn't get to go until after the Tories. Yesterday Dave had concocted one of his 'portfolio' question sets for the PM. He began on ID cards, moved on to tax and then, oh, who knows? It all blurred together.

It is official now: Gordon Brown and David Cameron hate each other. They got personal yesterday. Mr Brown was scathing, if a little repetitive, as he attacked Mr Cameron's attack. 'Once again, all these pre-rehearsed lines. All these lines rehearsed in front of the mirror!' he cried, to screams of excitement. 'Oh yes. Oh yes. Oh yes. All these pre-rehearsed lines!'

Boys! Boys! How scary for Nick Clegg, then, to be the only leader in the room they don't hate. Yesterday they fought over him like beaux in a Jane Austen novel. 'Let me welcome you,' gushed Mr Brown. 'I said to you in our private conversations that there is an open door.' This brought screams of 'oooohhhhh' from MPs.

But Nick, who wants to be Nick, was not to be wooed. He stood up and, when hit by the inevitable wall of noise, shouted over it. He had chosen his subject well: how the poor will cope with rising fuel bills this winter. No MP, even in the fevered madness of PMQs, would dare make fun of this.

Nick stood his ground against the PM. He finished his sentences. He got his facts right. He wasn't exciting but he was solid. What a coup for Nick to be Nick all the way through. 💔

18 July 2008
'Do-vais-day!' announced Nick Clegg
over the roar of the dishwasher

Nick, having given an interview in which he claimed he had slept with 'no more than thirty women', decided to relaunch his party. But then the dishwasher got involved.

Nick Clegg, Lib-Dem leader and wannabe sex god, relaunched his party yesterday with an event called Make It Happen. As ever with the Lib Dems, it was not entirely clear what 'it' was. Still, it was intriguing. I arrived early at the venue, a rather swanky restaurant called Bank Westminster, where it (though possibly not 'it') was happening at 10 a.m.

It seemed deserted save for one TV journo on the pavement,

phone clamped to ear. Inside, I found a flask of coffee, a camera and a gaggle of Lib Dems. Forget 'it'. Was this going to happen?

Twenty purple leather chairs had been arranged in front of a Plexiglass lectern, which was, itself, in front of a plate-glass window. We (actually it was just me) looked out on a courtyard with an ornate Victorian fountain fringed with hydrangeas. It was a beautiful setting for something, though maybe not 'it'.

A few others, almost all Lib Dems, trickled in. I glanced through the glossy Make It Happen brochure. The only thing happening seemed to be lots of pictures of Nick: Nick writing, Nick speaking, Nick with children, Nick with troops, Nick with a purple tie. You get the picture (no other Lib Dem did). One of the headlines asked: 'Why does the Government ignore me?'

I was beginning to feel bad for the Lib Dems. With minutes to spare, the Yellow Peril (as they are known) fanned out to occupy half the purple chairs. What a relief. The Tories used to do this in the bad old Iain Duncan Smith days. Yesterday the Lib Dems easily outnumbered the press, which at its peak totalled eight, including three from the BBC.

Then, suddenly, Nick was before us. I didn't hear him; he must have been wearing slippers. 'Thank you very much for coming to the launch of Make It Happen,' he said without apparent irony. 'This is a really important moment for the Lib Dems.'

Pathos. Bathos. Or, possibly, both. Who would be a politician? Then, just when I thought it could not get worse, the restaurant dishwasher started up with a mighty hum. It was tidal. Actually, I'm not sure the Pacific was this intrusive. Through the thrum, I could hear only snippets of Nick saying things like 'putting people first', 'wasteful government', 'lower taxes'.

Just when I began to get the hang of it (you have to concentrate as if it is a hearing test), the cutlery began to crash. 'This Government seems to have given up,' said Nick. 'It's as if they are having a collective do (crash, crash) day.' Do what? Later, I discovered he had said 'duvet' (is this wise for a sex god?) though he pronounced the whole thing as 'do-vais-day', emphasising the 'do', which made it sound foreign. Indeed, this may be the most exotic word since Bill Clinton taught us 'ubuntu', which means 'I am, because you are'. Ubuntu Dovaisday. Now there's a slogan.

Afterwards I cobbled together the details, such that they are. The Lib Dems are going to tax the rich more (by tinkering with things like pension tax relief) and the poor less. They are going to cut government spending by £20 billion. It's all about creating a fairer world, though details are sketchy to say the least. This was their 'direction of travel'.

'It's no good wishing for this. We've got to make it happen,' said Nick, looking a bit lost.

Outside I saw a man walk by with a towering chef's hat, as high as Marge's beehive in *The Simpsons*. Crash, thrum, mad hats. What a cartoon. It was all happening here though not, perhaps, as 'it' was supposed to. ♥

18 September 2008
Welcome to the Nick-fest

Nick goes walkabout for his first proper speech as leader – but at least the toilet joke worked

Nick Clegg had to give the speech of his life – sorry, but it's true – and he was nervous. He and his pregnant wife, Miriam, were attempting the traditional walk down Bournemouth's vertiginous cliffside path to the hall. 'Here comes the bump!' shouted the photographers. As they sashayed by, supposedly in deep conversation, all eyes were on Miriam, incredibly glamorous for a Lib Dem in shimmering silver.

And what about him? 'Going downhill already,' said one hack as Nick swept by a protester who suggested the cure to the sins of the world was vegetarianism. Inside the hall, we were primed for the Great Speech by a film about Nick Clegg: we saw Nick at PMQs, in Afghanistan, Sheffield, Iraq, Dorset, with the Dalai Lama, poor people, working people, young people and lots of adorable kids.

As the Nick-fest ended and the lights came up, we could see men on stage frantically trying to dismantle the normal lectern that had a huge 'Make It Happen' sign on it. As they tugged at the plug, I felt despair. This could only mean one thing: Nick was going to do his speech 'walkabout' style, à la David Cameron. I know this is the custom among young Aborigines but I am baffled as to why our politicians are so keen. The result is usually painful for us, not to mention their Achilles' heels.

Most politicians wander round the stage looking like little boys in search of their mothers but Nick seemed almost natural. He attacked Labour as a 'zombie' Government: 'a cross between *Shaun of the Dead* and *I'm Sorry I Haven't a Clue.*' He said that David Cameron wanted to be the 'Andrex puppy' of British politics: a cuddly symbol but fundamentally irrelevant to the product. 'We know it's blue, but so are the Smurfs and Toilet Duck.'

The Toilet Duck moment led to a collective bark of laughter. The Lib Dems remain wary of this new, young, posh leader (they would so prefer Vince) but, after Toilet Duck, you could see them warming to him. He then took us, alarmingly, from the toilet seat to the seat of government. 'I can't tell you every step on the road for us as a party,' he announced, pacing. 'But I can tell you where we're headed. Government.' The audience froze, for the idea of actual government seemed unreal, but then remembered to clap.

Nick Clegg began to shout about how great a Lib-Dem government will be, which, in the hall, didn't seem quite so mad. Then he stood in the brace position and shouted: 'The Liberal Democrats! Join us and make it happen!' The place erupted but I can't think why. What was he on about? Everyone here was a Lib Dem. They were 'us'. Why would they want to join themselves again?

After the applause died down (four minutes), Paddy Ashdown called it a 'tour de force'. I'd agree it was a tour all right, at least of the stage. The speech lasted thirty-seven minutes and forty-two seconds or, a better measure these days, about two miles. ❧

Chapter Two

The Election Dating Game

The election of April 2010 was dominated by Britain's first ever TV debates and it was during the first of these that Nick Clegg, suddenly and shockingly, became the most popular man in Britain. Cleggmania gripped the nation and, for a very short time, everyone agreed with Nick. Much to the amazement of the Tories, their man Dave suddenly seemed to be found lacking, a bit too safe, a bit too traditional, not to say Establishment. Then there was the thundercloud that was Gordon Brown, who travelled from storm to storm, the worst coming on a day in Rochdale when he met a voter named Gillian Duffy and later, in his car, not realising his mike was still on, dismissed her as a 'bigot'. As the weeks, and debates, rolled by, the nation still wasn't quite sure which one of these three men it wanted to be Prime Minister and, frankly, from the following sketches, it's not hard to see why. ❦

7 April 2010
And they're off! Pop (Dave), Pop (Nick), Bang (Gordon)

Gordon Brown, a man famous for not calling an election in the fall of 2007, finally managed to do the deed. His was an auster-ity announcement while Dave partied on the South Bank and Nick held a tiny event in what appeared to be his own bedroom

I t was a no-frills announcement, positively Presbyterian in its austerity. Gordon Brown and his Cabinet looked as solemn as a sermon as they trooped out of the gleaming black door of No. 10 at 10.48 a.m. The only thing sunny was above us, in the sky, on this lovely spring day that was troubled only by a soft breeze.

The launch cost nothing, a price Gordon can afford. The PM spoke through a mike hidden in the lapel of his Sunday best suit. His hair was (suitably) grey and newly cut, as perfect as a bowling lawn. The look of pure concentration on his face as he stood before us, the Cabinet fanned out on each side, looking like the Politburo but not as much fun, was that of a little boy desperately trying to remember his lines.

He'd just come from Buckingham Palace and the Queen had 'kindly' agreed to an election on 6 May. 'I come from an ordinary middle-class family in an ordinary town,' he said, voice booming out on the amateur sound system rigged up in Downing Street. Helicopters whirred above.

So he'd finally done it. After the Election That Wasn't in the autumn of 2007, here was the Election That Had To Be. The Politburo (sorry, Cabinet) watched, looking almost glazed. Gordon, voice tolling like a bell, said things were not as bad as they could have been. Tony Blair had his theme tune of 'Things Can Only Get Better'; Gordon has his version, which is 'Things Could Always Have Been Worse'. With every word, our spirits lowered.

I'd chosen the wrong place to be. For, across the river, due south, at that very moment, I was told that Dave was having a party, complete with throbbing music and happy youngsters. Dave launched early, as he couldn't wait for Gordo to get back from the Palace. The Queen will not be amused. Still, Nick Clegg had launched even earlier, with the television cameras showing him talking to some shadowy people in what appeared to be his bedroom.

So the starting gun yesterday sounded like pop (Nick), pop (Dave) and, finally, BANG (Gordo). When we were allowed out of our pews in Downing Street I raced over to see what was left of Dave's event. But where he should have been – on the terrace, right next to the Death Trap tourist destination, directly over the Wonder Waffles stand, Big Ben in the background – there was only air. I could not scent victory, only the sickening sweet waft of waffles. 💔

8 April 2010
Who is the angriest Mr Angry of them all?

The last PMQs of the Manure Parliament was an ill-tempered affair. Not so much goodbye as good riddance

If the last PMQs of this Parliament is anything to go by, this is going to be a down and dirty election. 'In the gutter,' said one observer after watching. And the sewer, I might add. Still, at least the Manure Parliament stayed true to its awful standards: this last PMQs was riddled with propaganda, evasion and lashings of anger.

Gordon Brown had tried to stage-manage his exit with all the subtlety of a bulldozer. Almost every Labour MP who spoke had been prompted to ask a question that went something like this: 'Is it true, oh wonderful master, that you have created a land of milk and honey?' Mr Brown, preening, would turn around and admit that, yes, actually it was true. This from a man who stood in Downing Street only yesterday and launched his campaign talking about being ordinary and honest.

It must have been very irritating indeed for the Prime Minister that he could not fix the questions from the Opposition. The funniest moment came when the Tory backbencher Stephen

Hammond noted that the day before, Mr Brown had gone on the campaign trail in Kent, promising to meet real people, but had spent the day visiting staunch Labour supporters. 'Do you intend to spend the whole campaign visiting and moving from safe house to safe house?' he demanded.

Gordon swung his great clunking fist. 'By the time I had met them all, they WERE all staunch Labour supporters. They said they want to secure the recovery!' Everyone burst into laughter. Brown is the only person in Britain who uses that phrase.

His fury was stoked to the point of frenzy by Opposition leader David Cameron, who asked a series of pointed questions on helicopter funding, pensions and National Insurance (which Dave calls a 'jobs tax'). The PM evaded it all, claiming with almost pantomime drama that Tory plans not to implement fully the increase in National Insurance would plunge the country back into recession. Every once in a while, as if on some sort of hectoring loop, the PM would shout: 'Same old Tories!' Then this cry gave way to almost Tourettian barks of 'Ashcroft! Ashcroft', a reference to the Tory donor apparently responsible for all the sins of the world. The PM ended by screaming at Dave: 'To think that you were the future once!' Dave, who had the cooler head and won the exchange, merely laughed.

But the angriest Mr Angry of them all was Nick Clegg. He had to endure the usual level of vitriol for merely daring to stand up. I think that, after all this time of putting up with it, this just got to him. His last act was to point at the ranks of Labour backbenchers, tauntingly asking if they could remember the hope they had in 1997. 'Well look at them now!' he cried, voice breaking. 'Look at them now! You failed! It's over! It's time to go!'

And then everyone got up and did just that. The last PMQs of the Manure Parliament was over but the smell lingers on. 💔

13 April 2010
Was it a launch or an advert for Dignitas?

Labour's manifesto launch was a surreal event in a brand new hospital. I kept expecting someone to arrive with a stretcher...

It takes a certain amount of guts to launch a manifesto in a hospital, even more so in one that specialises in trauma and accident and emergencies. It shouts out for a *Casualty* theme. Never mind that the brand new Queen Elizabeth Hospital building in Birmingham looks a magnificent place: it is still somewhere for sick people to go. There really can't be many key political events that have taken place next to a sign that directs you to 'Outpatient Endoscopy'.

I would have loved to have been at the planning session for this event. First came the brainwave about using a hospital – which was only really possible because it's not open yet – and then the idea to put a wheat field in the hospital. You may ask why, and the honest answer is I have no idea. But someone had gone to a lot of trouble to erect a giant screen in the hospital reception that showed a wheat field with the sun rising or setting (you pick, but I warn you this is a political judgement). If I'm kind, I would say that it looked like a shampoo commercial; others might judge that it seemed more like an advert for Dignitas.

It was freezing. I think this may be because the hospital is so new that they haven't turned the heating on yet. Still, if there ever was a place to get hypothermia, this is it. There was no sign of food or drink. Everyone kept saying that this is a word-of-mouth election, but this was a nil-by-mouth launch. But again, as it was a hospital, maybe it was all part of the 'Let's play doctors and nurses' theme.

Hundreds of the Labour faithful had come to cheer on Gordon Brown and his team, as he now calls his Cabinet. When did politics become sport? Actually, don't answer that. The team arrived in five-minute spurts in groups of six. It was as if, like buses, they had to space themselves. When the whole team was in place, the Labour sound system cranked up their ten-year-old tape of '(Your Love Keeps Lifting Me) Higher and Higher' – and I knew that Gordon and Sarah (this is their song) were almost in A&E.

We all watched a Labour YouTube cartoon with stick figures named Joe, Jane, Jack, James and Jill, which is supposed to encapsulate the manifesto in two and a half minutes. Yes, that long. Then Gordon was before us and the wheat field – he really was outstanding in his field, if only for this event – telling us that the manifesto is all about the future. He said the manifesto (non-YouTube version) was written in the future tense: I checked but, actually, it was written in something I would call the present future hopeful tense.

'We are in the future business,' he boomed. I must admit that I had not realised that the future was a business or that it would be quite this strange. ❦

14 April 2010
Memo to Dave: we need more canapés and less talk

The Tory manifesto launch was a study in post-urban chic. It was all very edgy but – sniff, sniff – what WAS that smell?

The Tories held their manifesto launch in the incredible hulk of post-industrial Britain that is Battersea Power Station. 'A building in need of regeneration in a country in need of regeneration,' said Dave. I found this helpful, for it is one of those things that I could never have figured out on my own.

The first thing I noticed, upon arriving at the living metaphor (sorry, launch), was the smell. 'Do you smell rubbish?' I asked a man at the gate. He pointed at the building next door. 'It's a dump,' he said. I wrinkled my nose. I like my metaphors sterile.

I set off across a dystopian landscape of dirt and rubble – it was all a bit *Mad Max* – until I found a ramp that, like a tunnel in *Alice in Wonderland*, emerged into a totally different land. Here, inside the great hulk, we were hermetically sealed in an extremely expensive marquee that was part tent, part glass.

I identified it as Toryland almost immediately by the canapés, which managed to mix Notting Hill trendy (cranberry-streaked mini-muffins and tiny pains au chocolat) with post-industrial working-class fare (mini-bacon sarnies and sausage rolls).

It was all very post-urban chic. The wastebaskets were covered in burlap, for God's sake. In the loos there was sea-kelp moisturiser. We gazed through the glass wall at the wreck that is Battersea Power Station. Overhead, between teetering towers, birds – crows? pigeons? vultures? – wheeled. Hitchcock used this for his thriller *Sabotage* but it would do for *The Birds*. If you wanted to go outside, the Tories had hard hats and fluorescent jackets for us.

The Tory soundtrack was all about change. 'Ch-ch-ch-changes,' sang David Bowie as we trooped in for the show. The fun stopped the moment we sat down. On our seats was a little blue hardback called *Invitation to Join the Government of Britain*. It was full of tasks. They want us to run schools, join the Cabinet, fire our MPs. What about those of us who want to come home from work and slump in front of *Come Dine With Me*? No mention of us.

The manifesto, like the launch, was hard work. There were seven speakers. I accept that William Hague and George Osborne might have a say, and Baroness Warsi, if only because I like her. But Caroline Spelman? Theresa May? It was only when Andrew Lansley told us: 'You want to be your own boss, you can with us!' that I felt like shouting: 'OK, sit down!' As it dragged on, I couldn't help but wonder: how can we trust the Tories to cut the deficit when they can't even cut the speakers at their manifesto launch? Or the speeches? Dave gave one that was thirteen pages long. If I were invited to join the Government of Britain, this is what I would do: more canapés and less talk. And let's ban post-industrial metaphors too. ♥

15 April 2010
The Lib Dems leave us with a sinking feeling

The subterranean Lib-Dem launch was a murky affair in which a snorkel would have come in handy

The Lib-Dem manifesto launch was held in a circular basement room in the City, dimly lit by bendy blue neon tubes. The ceiling was very low and the acoustics were terrible. It felt as if we were underwater. Indeed, it was as if we were in an aquarium, fighting to breathe, move or hear. I only wish I had been given a pair of gills beforehand.

If I were to be kind, I would say this event was at the cutting edge of austerity chic and that it had a sort of Quaker-like simplicity. But actually it was just flat. No razzmatazz, no music, no sense of excitement, just a few MPs sitting at the front of the aquarium, looking doleful, with bubbles coming out of their mouths.

First up was little Sarah Teather, who bubbled that Labour had launched in an empty hospital and the Tories in an empty power station, but the Lib Dems were in an occupied aquarium (sorry, building), a place of work and 'rigorous financial scrutiny'. Pity it was almost too dark to read the manifesto.

The sainted Vince's halo glowed through the murk. He said Labour and the Tories had not talked about the deficit: 'This is the elephant in the room.' I looked round. No way was there space for an elephant.

'I am the elephant man,' intoned Vince unnecessarily. A vision of John Hurt in *The Elephant Man* popped up into my head. Do the Lib Dems really want to be associated with a Victorian freak show? I soon had my answer when Nick Clegg took the podium. 'Thank you, Elephant Man,' he said to Vince, who looked even grimmer. I can't remember having less fun.

There was no sign of Miriam, the wife who is, as we now knew, too busy working to be an appendage. My theory is that she and Vince have done a sort of wife swap, anyway. Who needs a wife when you've got Vince?

I could see no other Lib-Dem MPs or peers. I suppose that in these times of tight financial control, every mini-croissant counts. The Lib Dems promised they would provide the best breakfasts of the election but this hardly qualified. Can you have austerity snacking? I think they can.

Behind the lectern, Mr Clegg was doing knee bends and throwing his arms out a lot. It was hard to hear so I just read the Autocues instead. It was all about fairness and rigorous financial scrutiny. But then he reverted to political autopilot.

'We can turn anger into hope. Frustration into ambition. Recession into opportunity for everyone. This is hope married to credibility,' he said, 'optimism that is in touch with reality. It's what makes our manifesto different.'

To which I can only say, glug, glug, glug. 💔

16 April 2010
The first TV debate agrees with Nick

We all rushed to Manchester, obsessed with a volcano erupting in Iceland, to watch three men in what appeared to be a Star Trek *transporter studio. There was only one winner…*

It was Iceland's revenge. All anyone was talking about on the day of the Great Historical Debate was the Great Ash Cloud. It is a shame the debate was governed by seventy-six

rigid rules. Surely what should have happened at 8.30 p.m. was
for Alastair Stewart to throw away the rulebook and ask: So how
DO you spell the name of the volcano that has erupted? Isn't
that just the best first question ever? Would any of them have got
Eyjafjallajökull? (Don't forget the accent.)

But instead we had opening statements, some spouting, a bit
of rumbling, not a lot of fire, much less lava erupting. Everyone
seemed a bit mechanical, as if they needed oiling. The set, with
those coloured columns, looked like a bad mock-up of the *Star
Trek* transporter room. The answers to the first question on
immigration (another missed opportunity for Eyjafjallajökull)
went on for fifteen minutes. We were in a 'beam me up'
situation.

I was struck by the incessant use of first names by all three
men. Gordon looked a bit ill when he said the word 'David', but
he said it. Not, I note, Dave. That was a name too far for Gordo.
It all seemed a bit fake, given they've been hacking bits off each
other for years. Only Alastair Stewart seemed real as he barked:
'Mr Brown! Mr Brown!'

They couldn't stop telling us about their happy families. Gordo
answered a question on crime by telling us that his father ran a
youth club. Then Dave confided that his mother was a magistrate. Gordo raised the stakes by announcing that his parents had
taught him values.

Nick, rather desperately, announced that he had friends. Then
he told us that his children went to an 'excellent state-funded
school'. Enough already! I half expected them to pull out holiday
photos or finger-painting.

Then something began to happen. Gordon said that he agreed
with Nick. Dave agreed with Nick too. Nick, obviously, agreed
with Nick but tried not to agree with anyone else. Gordon kept
on smiling, which was frightening. David seemed a bit dull,
corporate and, somehow, older than usual. Nick, the spikiest of
the two, was looking, well, rather good.

In future, they should ban the closing statements. 'Thanks for staying with us,' said Nick, arm reaching out. Then Gordon thanked us. And then Dave told us to choose hope over fear. How irritating is that? In terms of drama, Eyjafjallajökull won the day though, in terms of the debate, I agree with Nick. ♥

20 April 2010
The Admiral of Downing Street
sends in the Ashmada

A Sunday Times *poll after the first debate showed Nick Clegg with an amazing approval rating of 72 per cent, ahead of Dave with 19 per cent and Gordo on (eek) minus 18 per cent. It seems that Churchill had an 83 per cent rating in 1945, leading the* Sunday Times *to run a headline that said: 'Clegg nearly as popular as Churchill.'*

For every enormous cloud of volcanic ash there is a silver lining. This is what Gordon Brown must have thought yesterday. While other party leaders (even Nick!) were grounded, forced do something wimpy like campaigning, he was leading the nation out of crisis, our man on the bridge, our man in the bunker, calling the shots, looking like Churchill.

Yes, Nick Clegg, overnight, may have become nearly as popular as Churchill, but only Admiral Brown, as I believe he now prefers to be called, can actually act like Churchill and send in the Fleet to fight the volcano. Only Admiral Brown can inspire the nation to a new Dunkirk spirit. Only he can convene a meeting of Cobra.

Ah, Cobra. How Gordon loves that word. Well, OK, so it's an acronym for something quite dull (Cabinet Office Briefing

Room A). But it sounds exciting, as if it takes place in a secret location and is attended by the likes of M or C. Yesterday Admiral Gordo emerged from Cobra looking haggard, speaking to the nation from in front of a fireplace with a Turner seascape in the background. The message was clear: he will fight them on the beaches (and by them he means David Cameron and Nick 'not quite Churchill' Clegg).

'We are seeing the spirit and the resilience of the British people at its best!' boomed the Admiral. 'Ark Royal will be sent to the Channel. Equally, HMS Ocean will be sent.' I could hear the band striking up 'Rule Britannia'. 'And we are sending HMS Albion via Spain,' he declared. Does that sound magnificent? I think it was the most prime ministerial thing that he has ever said.

He had sent the Armada or, as I guess we must call it, the Ashmada. As Gordon headed back for another Cobra meeting (you cannot have too many when fighting a volcano), Dave was reduced to rushing off to Brighton in order to have a seascape backdrop. We saw him, on a hill over Brighton, gulls swooping, looking fresh-faced. 'The idea of using the Royal Navy was actually something the Conservative Party very constructively suggested,' he claimed, sounding like a rather desperate Mr Me-Too.

Then there was Nick Clegg who, like the great ash cloud, was omnipresent. How Admiral Brown must have loved it when he heard the news that, finally, post-Albion, post-Cobra, Nick had been forced to say: 'Actually, I agree with Gordon.' ❦

21 April 2010
It's Cleggmania as Nick has an Obama moment

As the nation swooned over Nick there was only one place to be – with the man himself as he headed out to judge a tractor-building contest. Does it get better than this?

he moment that I knew that something had changed was when I asked the man next to me on the concourse at Paddington what he thought of Nick Clegg, who was walking towards us.

'The next Prime Minister?' he said, entirely seriously.

I did not laugh (a major change in itself). Really? The man nodded. Nick had done well in the debate. He was probably going to hold the balance of power after the election. 'He'll at least be Home Secretary,' he announced. Again, I did not laugh.

So to Chippenham, then, with the next Prime Minister to watch him officiate at a tractor-rebuilding contest. Oh yes, it's all glamour on the campaign trail. The Lib Dems had reserved an entire train carriage for the media pack. A week ago, the Lib-Dem press corps could fit into a phone box. The *New York Times* was there. *Time* magazine too. Someone speaking Italian. One national paper had five journalists. Was this, everyone wondered, Nick Clegg's Obama moment? Well, if it was, he was sharing it with a tractor. Well, actually two tractors (1949 Fergusons, since you ask).

'One, two, three – GO!' shouted Nick Obama as he stood in the tin barn at Wiltshire College in Lackham and watched two teams – one in green overalls, the other in blue – race round their stripped machine, grabbing bits of tractor and rushing back to stick them back on.

At this point, for unknown reasons, Nick decided to take questions from the students. What, they wanted to know, did he think of foxhunting? As he opened his mouth, a loud clang from the blue team drowned him out.

Nick tried again. Thrummmmmmm! A power drill had started up.

'It's hard to talk over this!' he shouted, words snatched as they left his mouth. 'The blue tractor is annoying me!'

He tried to tell us his policies amid the cacophony but only a few phrases managed to wiggle through. I heard 'post

offices' (CRASH) and 'milk' (BANG) and 'buses' (WALLOP).
Every time he was in danger of making sense, there was
an almighty crash. But Nick, used to not being heard, just
carried on, affable, irrepressible, boyish grin flashing like a
neon sign.

The ludicrous question and non-answer session was halted
by a bellow of '8.44!' The students burst into applause. Nick
ran over to congratulate the green team until he realised they
had lost (nine minutes eleven seconds). 'Oh, it is the blue
team!' he cried, rushing over to give them certificates that he'd
just signed.

He went out to the farmyard, press milling round like chickens being fed. Could he win? 'I'm Nick Clegg, not Nostradamus,'
he announced, adding: 'Anything can happen!'

On the way home (back on the train), the competition for face
time with Nick was intense. Finally, I managed to sit next to him
and noted, carefully keeping the incredulity out of my voice, that
people were actually using the Obama word.

'It's absurd,' he announced happily. Really? He nodded
fiercely. 'When you've been cut down to size as ruthlessly and
consistently as I have for many months, you have to have your
feet firmly on the ground. No, I have many flaws but I am
trying to keep a sense of perspective on this. What goes up, can
go down.'

Still, I say, maybe the tractor in Chippenham was the Obama
moment. 'Absurd,' he said, eyes dancing, face lit up, looking
utterly thrilled by it all. ❦

22 April 2010
Getting real? How things can
change in the nick of time

*The second debate was in Bristol where everyone tried not to
agree with Nick*

From the start, this debate was all about Nick. Would the other two agree with Nick? Or not? And what about Nick? Would HE agree with Nick (Lib Dems often disagree with themselves, sometimes in the same sentence).

So the big question was who would nick the Nick debate. Gordon got off to a classic start when he announced: 'If this is about style or PR, then count me out.' Was this Gordo's big pitch? 'Like me or not, I can deliver!' And I don't think he was talking pizza.

Nick was standing in the middle but still seemed the outsider. He didn't agree with Gordon or David (not Dave – at least not yet). Even on Europe, Nick managed to sound as if he wasn't a rampant Europhile. He told some story about how Europe took fifteen years to define chocolate. But then he began to disagree with himself by saying Britain needed Europe. 'To coin a phrase,' he said, 'size does matter!' Oh dear.

The catchphrase seemed to be 'Get real!' First Gordon said on Trident: 'Nick, get real!' Nick spat back: 'You say, get real. This is extraordinary!'

Then Dave, desperate to get noticed, said that he'd told his own party to 'get real'. 'I thought I would never utter these words,' he announced, 'but I agree with Gordon!' Gordon hated that, for he doesn't want Nick to think that he (Gordon) likes Dave at all. My, but this ménage à trois was getting complicated.

Now a woman named Mary asked a question about cleaning up politics. 'Mary,' said Nick, 'you are the boss! You are the boss!' Then Gordon started bombarding her with information about tax credits and Nick jumped in: 'Mary asked about politics and she's being told about tax credits!' Gordon looked outraged: for him, tax credits are riveting.

So who won the Nick debate? Well, certainly not Gordo. (He really is so awkward: after one pensioner named Grace asked him a question, he commented: 'Women – and you are one of them…') Dave settled down and was getting better and better. I think it ended in the Nick of time, so to speak. ❦

26 April 2010
Gordon is more on the edge than edgy

It was Sunday so I dropped in to see Gordon Brown on the campaign trail and saw a man who seemed to be having a crisis of confidence – in himself

Ijoined the 'leader's tour' for the first time and I couldn't believe what I was seeing. Gordon Brown was exhausted, late for his own speech, stumbling over his words. He reminded me of a performing bear who has seen better days, a bit unsteady and raggedy, but who, every once in a while, rears up on his hind legs and shows us what he can do.

I think Gordon may have realised yesterday that God had a point in making Sunday a day of rest. The whole Labour campaign seemed as unsteady as Sarah in her scarily high, bright red platform wedges. As she teetered up the ramp at Westminster Academy in Central London, the Prime Minister in tow, I stared at them. Those shoes were a cry for help.

But then what *do* you wear to launch a green manifesto in an inner-city school, with a huge fake wheat field behind you on a giant screen? It really was an odd event. We are told that Labour is changing its strategy and that Gordon is going to be meeting more 'real' people: the campaign would be edgier. But there were no real people here, only surreally pro-Labour ones. It wasn't edgy so much as on the edge, of what I'm not sure.

Gordon and Sarah Shoes arrived at the school to ecstatic applause (by the way, Gordon, that's a clue that they may not be real). He then disappeared upstairs, we knew not why.

Downstairs, in front of the wheat field, we enjoyed a parody of the *Trisha* talk show. (Example: Douglas Alexander, when asked about his parents, gushed: 'They are people people!') The drummer from the band Blur, David Rowntree, spoke. Ed Miliband told us about the green manifesto for, oh, a minute. Then came a motivational Twitter speaker (I'm not making this up).

Finally, it was time for Gordo, except that it seemed Gordo wasn't ready for us. I know that it's a bad pun but 'Waiting for Gordo' is an election theme. What was he? Later I was told that he had been 'psyching himself up' and rewriting his speech on the run. Isn't that worrying? This audience was about as scary as a poodle.

Downstairs, everyone was ad-libbing. Various youngsters stood up to share (what next? karaoke?) when, suddenly, thankfully, we heard ecstatic clapping from upstairs and Mr Brown and the Shoes – finally! – were among us. 'Yesterday it was Elvis,' noted Gordon, taking up position in front of the wheat field. 'Today it's Blur!' I think that was the high point.

He hardly mentioned the green manifesto. The speech – one minute faltering, the next tub-thumping – was a hardcore attack on the Tories. As the Prime Minister left, to more wild applause, with Sarah still teetering, I hoped he was going home to have a lie down. The man needs a break. 💔

27 April 2010
Running for his life, Ed keeps all the balls in the air

I spent a manic day with Ed Balls as, true to his name, he juggled balls with children and charmed the vodka man on the train

Ed Balls may be a grown-up but at times yesterday, during a rush-rush-rush visit to the Brighton marginals, it seemed unlikely. At one point, at an after-hours tennis club at Hertford Junior School, he was lying on the tarmac in the playground, aged forty-three going on ten, balancing a tennis ball on a racket. Around him, children his age (as in ten for real) were copying him.

'I think that Ed Balls is just a little bit competitive,' commented one grown-up next to me as we watched the him, large blue eyes like orbs as he concentrated on the task at hand. Somehow, he did manage the feat of arising from his back while keeping his racket level, tennis ball rolling round it. Then, he did a strange little dance, one leg kicking out behind, one arm bent, as if he might be in musical comedy. 'Ta da!' he cried as the children cheered.

There is much talk about a 'balanced' Parliament (code for hung) these days. I don't know about that but Mr Balls is certainly up for a balanced tennis ball at least. In London, the Tories were taunting him, saying that he was afraid to lose his seat. He was furious about that later but, at this moment, having just arisen from the tarmac, he had other things on his mind: the children now wanted him to go visit something most fowl.

'OK! Let's go see the injured chicken!' he cried. The kids dragged him to a little wooden hut, inside which a pathetic-looking chicken lurked. They documented all the illnesses the chicken had (broken beak, lice etc.). They then convinced him (Ed, not the chicken) to eat some wild garlic. 'ARGHHHH!!' cried the Secretary of State for Children, Schools and Families as he bit into one.

My, what a pell-mell life he leads. He had awoken at 7 a.m., discovered a Tory schools story making news and rushed out to do Sky, the BBC, ITV. Then he gave a speech, followed by a press conference ('If you flirt with Nick, you'll end up married to Dave' was the gist). He then raced, cheeks puffing, a total sprint, to catch the 1.06 p.m. to Brighton. We jumped on the train with a minute to spare. He was, if not a maniac, certainly manic.

'Ooohh! Is it yoooooouuuuuu?' cried a fellow traveller as we sat down in a seat in economy, still breathless. Thus began a surreal journey, for this woman turned out to be a serious Ed Balls fan. I began to suspect that she was a plant. Even the trolley man liked him.

'I've got your vodka,' he cried at Ed, who looked a bit taken aback and asked for a ploughman's sandwich. 'I had a plough-man's lunch once,' said the trolley man, 'and he got very angry.' Ed laughed.

It is strange because Ed doesn't come over great on television but, in the flesh, he is very personable. He will talk to anyone about anything. By the time we got to Brighton he had reprogrammed my BlackBerry so that I could have ÜberTwitter. I'd inspected his retro-Nokia phone, the one that he'd just been fined for using in his car. 'It's a fair cop,' he said.

Ed Balls is running for his life, I would say, but he is having fun with it. 💔

28 April 2010
A day in the country with the women who wrote Desire

Louise Bagshawe's chick lit heroines tend to be feisty and ambitious. After a day with her in must-win Corby, I can see where she gets them from

I meet Louise Bagshawe, bestselling chick-lit author and Tory candidate in the must-win seat of Corby, in the car park of the Olde Three Cocks pub in the village of Brigstock. She is with an older man. 'This is Lord Luke. He is my chauffeur for the election! I am going to miss this when the campaign is over.' I laugh. Leave it to a novelist to have a lord driving her round. But, I say, won't you win? 'Of course I'm going to win!' she cries. 'But I won't have a chauffeur anymore. I'll have an Oyster pass.'

She and Lord Luke then get into his Audi Quattro ('Fire up the Quattro!' shouts Louise at one point) that has a little silver dog on the bonnet because he keeps pugs. I follow them through the village, on to a country road that turns into a dirt road that ends in a farmyard. Here we meet another peer, Lord Taylor of Holbeach, who speaks for the Tories on agriculture. It turns out that he is big in flower bulbs.

We all go round the back where a group of farmers have gathered under a gorgeous old apple tree. As Louise and peers get to grips with the various issues I look round: it is idyllic, blossom falling, birds singing, cows watching from afar.

It feels a million miles from Westminster but this seat could not be more political. It is a classic two-party fight. The Labour candidate is the Health Minister Phil Hope, who had a 1,517 majority. 'This is a bellwether seat. It always goes with the general election winner,' says Louise. 'So no pressure!' Louise's heroines tend to be feisty and ambitious. I can see where they get it from.

But when I ask her to describe herself in adjectives, she chooses: loyal, talkative, optimistic (Dave, you have a lot to answer for). So, not glamorous, then? 'Look at me!' she cries. She is thirty-eight with long blonde hair and wearing a large blue rosette. I know what she means but she may not realise how deeply unglamorous most politicians are. 'My books are escapism, even for me!' she says (she talks in exclamation marks). Actually they tend to be described as 'sizzling' and have names such as *Glitz*, *Passion*, *Glamour* and (my favourite) *Sparkles*. She used to live in New York with her husband but now is a divorced mother of three and lives in the constituency.

She is fearsomely organised, always on the run. I note that her latest book is pink and called *Desire*. The blurb says: 'Passion on the run … can there be a happy ending?' Well, if you're writing the book…

(P.S. Louise Bagshawe, duly elected, changed her surname to Mensch in 2011 after getting married.) ❣

29 April 2010
How not to make an ass of yourself, by Boris

This was written on the day that Gordon Brown, in Rochdale, having just met a 'real person' named Gillian Duffy, got back into the car and, not realising his lapel mike was still active, called her a bigot and blamed everything on his hapless aide Sue. I was in Ealing in West London, with Boris Johnson, the man who wrote the book on how to work a crowd

Boris Johnson really could teach Gordon Brown a thing or two (or 300) about 'real' people on the campaign trail. Yesterday Gordon Brown proved he can't cope with meeting one woman with some very ordinary worries about immigration. God knows what the Prime Minister would have made of Ealing, in deepest West London, where Boris went walkabout amid scenes of unscripted chaos and never, once, blamed anyone else for anything, even when he was photographed with a candidate named Bray in front of a horse's ass.

Yes, truly. The rump in question belonged to a statue (*Small Work Horse*, by Judith Bluck, 1985) in the pedestrianised shopping precinct. 'Group photo!' shouted someone from Angie Bray's team, stopping with uncanny precision right next to the upturned tail.

'Boris! Is this a three-horse race?' shouted someone as everyone gurned and raised their DIY poster boards.

'It's a one-horse race!' shouted Boris.

What, asked someone, was the caption for this photo? 'Braaaay!' brayed Boris, quickly moving away from the rump. Angie (or Ange, as Boris called her) scrambled after him, insisting: 'No, that would be if it was a donkey!' Hee-haw, as donkeys (and asses) would say.

I'm not sure Gordo could have coped with even one part of that scene. First he'd have to blame someone (Sue, mostly likely). Then he would have to return to the scene to beg the horse's forgiveness.

But the truth about walkabouts and 'real' people is that they are (actually) real and so, by definition, random. Yesterday people told Boris about autistic children, illnesses, parking, travel, unemployment and, yes, their anger at immigration. So here are some tips from the Book of BoJo:

- When someone from Poland talks to you, answer back in Polish. 'Dzien dobry!' cried Boris at the Pole, who was thrilled.
- When someone hands you a mobile phone, do not throw it (habits of a lifetime etc.), but talk into it. Yesterday the owner

of the Chitter Chatter phone shop tried to give Boris a new phone. Of course, Boris rejected it (well, he had to, the BBC was filming), but only after securing a vote for Ange. (This is an ultra-tight three-way marginal.)

- When someone disagrees with you, have a bit of a good-humoured debate, then say: 'Well, I'm sorry we disagree!' And walk away.

- Have fun. When asked about the Lib Dems, Boris began to splutter: 'How can you conceivably trust the Lib Dems! Spineless protoplasmic invertebrate amoebic fibbers – Janus-faced!' (Isn't that so much better than 'bigoted'?)

- Finally, pretend you don't know where you are going. As Boris left yesterday, he walked away from his own car. 'Boris!' cried everyone as the blond-haired one looked abashed. Personally, I think he did it on purpose. Gordon needs a masterclass – now. 💔

30 April 2010
The final debate: what, exactly, was the question?

The third and final debate was held in Birmingham. It was make or break for Gordon, fresh from his Rochdale disaster, having spent the last day in almost permanent apology mode

I t was Gordon we were all watching. Would he win, lose or merely survive? On the plus side, the subject of the night was the economy. On the minus side, well, where to start? The man has had so many accidents he should be in A&E. The one thing I was sure he wasn't going to say was: 'I met this woman in Rochdale yesterday...'

They all looked grim, like undertakers on a night out. The lurid magenta and orangey backdrop didn't help; it was like they were standing inside a tequila sunrise cocktail, debating in a daiquiri.

I wasn't surprised to hear that Gordo began– because he simply cannot stop himself apparently now – with a mini-apology: 'There's a lot to this job. And as you saw yesterday I don't get all of it right.'

The night quickly turned into a fight club, a slugfest between Dave and Gordo. Little Nicky was often reduced to jumping up and down in the middle, squeaking: 'There they go again!' He kept decrying how the other two were 'political point-scoring' which was, of course, a political point. Still, that was his role and he is great at it.

Gordon painted a terrible picture of what would happen to Britain if the Tories got in. You know that figure in Edvard Munch's painting *The Scream*? Well, that figure is running from a Tory government, according to Gordon Brown.

'I will never form an alliance with a Tory government which is going to cut child tax credits,' he announced, ruling out something that would never happen anyway.

Dave retorted: 'What you are hearing is very desperate stuff from someone who is in a desperate state.'

That was personal. Then Gordo called Dave's plans 'immoral'. Dave hit right back: 'He's trying to frighten people and he should be ashamed.'

At this, little Nicky jumped up: 'Here they go again!'

A man named Raddley asked if politicians were aware that they had become removed from the concerns of real people, especially on immigration. 'Why don't you remember that you are there to serve us, not ignore us?'

It was a great question, though I can't say the same for the answers. Gordon and Dave gave fantasy answers at some length before Nicky threw out his arms. 'Where is Raddley?' he said, peering out, exclaiming: 'Of course we are there to serve you!' Of course?

So who won? There was, again, no knockout. Dave was calm. Nick was over-excited. And Gordon? He survived and, for him, that's a triumph. 💔

4 May 2010
Does Dave have Eeny, Meeny, Miny or Major Mo?

*It's the final countdown and Dave popped into a school for a bit
of Olympic sport before heading off on his big pyjama party bus.
Is this momentum or just bonkers?*

Does Dave have the Big Mo? That was the question as I
headed to Southwark to see the Tory leader do something
Olympian (of course). He claims he does but surely we
should be the judge of whether this is the Big Mo, the Little Mo
or just plain Eeny, Meeny, Miny, Mo.

Dave had come to the City of London Academy directly from
Blackpool, as you do when you've got not only Mo but also a
plane. He'd been heckled there by a Labour man who said Dave
had a 'false message'. To me, that is not a heckle but a philosophi-
cal point of view. But you can't stop to ponder such things when
you've got 365 miles to go by lunchtime.

The plan was to launch a plan for a mini-Olympics for
schools. The Tory bubble, i.e., the press and political team that
have followed Dave for the whole campaign, occupied one end of
the gym: they are over-excited by the latest gimmick, a 24-hour
political pyjama party bus trip that was to begin at 6 p.m. in
Scotland. They are going to drive down the West Coast assault-
ing (sorry, meeting) voters. But, I ask, what about sleep? I am told
that Dave will nap on the bus. That's not momentum, I think,
just insanity.

Dave arrived by car, ploughing through a few Lib-Dem
supporters. Boris came by bike ('On yer bike!' they shouted). In
the gym, about 100 kids sprinted round as the politicians watched.
I waited for Dave to join in (Tony Blair would have). He doesn't.
Dave is playing it tremendously safe; he cannot risk the headlines
if he fell over now.

So does Dave have the Big Mo? I'd go for a bit of mo but no more than Eeny or Meeny. 💔

5 May 2010

Gordon and Sarah drink too much Love Potion No. 9

It was hard to watch when Sarah and Gordon unleashed their love on us from the GMTV sofa. Bizarre doesn't even begin to cover it

It was the Mills & Boon fightback. Yesterday, in a world first, Gordon and Sarah appeared, live and in love, together forever, on the *GMTV* sofa. I have heard about joined at the hip but they were also joined at the shoulder. For most of the interview they sat so close to each other that they seemed to be sharing an arm.

They looked as if they had just drunk an entire bottle of Love Potion No. 9. Sarah gazed at him (her husband, her hero) adoringly. Gordon was transformed, just by sitting next to her, into a lovestruck schoolboy, giggling almost uncontrollably. They often held hands which is always good if you are sharing an arm.

They were going for the Cupid vote. Did Gordon get angry when the media criticised Sarah? 'Yes,' he said, giggling. 'I just think what she's done, just coming round with me, working with me, supporting me.' Then he blurted it out: 'I just love her.'

At this Sarah giggled too and their joint arm twitched. 'Thank you!' she gushed. He looked even more thrilled. (I have made none of this up, I promise you.)

They seemed to be in their own private bubble, as if they had popped into *GMTV* on honeymoon. Their interviewer Lorraine Kelly (official gooseberry) had the unenviable job of trying to get them to talk to her and not each other.

She noted that people who had listened to the debates on the radio had liked Gordon more than those who watched on television. Gordon loved this. 'Good voice for radio!' he said nonsensically, giggling and then adding: 'Good face for radio!' He and Sarah giggled.

Lorraine praised Sarah for managing to maintain some kind of 'normal' life. Sarah looked particularly beatific and said: 'One of my big jobs in this is to make sure that our ordinary family carries on.' This overwhelmed Gordon, who gushed: 'She's amazing.'

Lorraine noted that last week Gordon had met a real person – i.e. Gillian Duffy – 'with unfortunate results'.

Gordon chuckled: 'Sarah wasn't there!'

'You weren't there, Sarah,' said Lorraine. 'If you had been, would it have happened?'

'I wasn't there so I really don't know,' said Sarah, which I interpreted to mean 'Of course'.

Had Gordon called Sarah right away? (Better Sarah than Sue, I thought.)

'This is very personal,' said Gordon, a bit unsure before he blurted out, like a child telling himself what to do: 'I made a mistake – talk to Sarah!'

Sarah soothed him, saying that they always talked to each other 'when things happen' (which is one way of putting it).

I would say pass the sick bucket, except we were way beyond that. 💔

6 May 2010
Flipping heck, does it get barmier than Buckingham?

It was the day before the election and I went to see something fishy in deepest Buckingham, in the constituency of the ever-controversial Mr Speaker, Little Johnny Bercow

To Buckingham, then, to interview a dolphin, have a drink with Nigel Farage of the UK Independence Party (UKIP) and to try and find Mr Speaker. Does it get weirder than this constituency on the day before a general election? I doubt it.

It shouldn't be like this at all. By tradition, the Speaker runs unopposed at elections. But John Bercow, who used to be a Tory and is now officially no party at all, is no ordinary Speaker. He is the ultimate Marmite man; you either love him or you hate him. So, while neither Labour Nor the Lib Dems fielded a candidate here, the ever-bumptious Nigel Farage actually gave up the presidency of UKIP to run against him. And then, John Stevens, anti-UKIP and an independent, decided to run too.

Confused? Well, that brings me to the dolphin. Flipper stops traffic as he walks through the market square, a 6ft-high blue dolphin who, because he lives on land, has developed huge paws and is a bit furry. Darwin would not be surprised. The dolphin is carrying a sign for John Stevens, whom I am standing with in the square.

'I see something fishy!' cries one of his campaign aideS as he spies Flipper.

Mr Stevens, a serious candidate who may resent all the attention being paid to his mascot, grumps: 'Dolphins aren't fish, they are mammals.'

Actually, as I was about to discover, they are comedians.

'It's all about being fit for porpoise!' cries Flipper. 'We are having a whale of a time!'

The idea behind the mascot was to highlight the fact that Speaker John Bercow was a 'flipper' in the expenses crisis of 2009 (to 'flip', in that context, is to switch which home is declared, for tax purposes, as the main residence). Mr Bercow repaid £6,500 voluntarily but the dolphin doesn't seem to care about that. Sadly, I don't get to see Flipper's partner, a creature called 'U-kipper', a giant orange fish with Nigel Farage's face pasted on as a mask.

Nigel, the man, not the fish, looks tanned and ridiculously healthy despite the fact that he is running a campaign mostly based around pubs. Actually, Nigel might resent that 'mostly'. We immediately go to a pub, the White Hart, where he orders a pint of Old Hooky. 'Ahhhh,' he says after his first sip. 'The day just improved markedly!'

So why pubs? 'The pub is the hub!' cries Nigel, who says he's been to about 100 during the election. He advises the likes of Gordon Brown and David Cameron to go to more too. 'They don't mix with real people,' he says. If they did, they would know immigration is a big issue.

Now, rather bizarrely, Two Danish journalists join us. I discover that they are here to talk to Nigel not about the election but about British pub culture. Nigel announces that his motto is 'work hard, play harder'. 'I had cancer when I was young and I after that I promised that I would do it my way and have a thoroughly good time,' he beams over his Old Hooky.

I leave the pub to go look for Mr Bercow. I'd left multiple messages on various numbers but no one had called back. Now, suddenly, as I walked down the street, I am told that he has just bought a meat pie in a butcher. I race to the shop and find plenty of pies but no Bercow. Then I hear he's in a deli. I rush there and, much to my amazement, there he is, as large as life – which isn't saying much as he is rather small – talking on his mobile, a giant green and gold rosette over his heart.

'Green and gold – House of Commons colours!' he says.

In the last election, as a Tory, he'd had a large majority. Now, as a nothing, he is not complacent. He doesn't seem amused in the least by Flipper or Nigel. 'I don't regard elections as a glorified pub crawl!' he says. But, to be fair, neither does Nigel, who had objected when I'd used the term earlier. 'Pub visits, let's call them,' he insisted, his eyes twinkling.

(Addendum: The next day, shortly after the polls opened, Nigel Farage was injured in a plane crash after a UKIP banner got tangled in the tail of a two-seater aircraft. Nigel, who came third in the poll, left hospital days later saying he was 'the luckiest man alive'.) 💔

7 May 2010
Floating in the dark on the Luvvie Election Boat

I spent election night with the people who put the party into party politics

So, I asked David Baddiel as we floated on the BBC boat moored outside the London Eye, 'who do you think is the most famous person here?' The scruffy one points to the starboard side. 'I don't think, I know. Bruce Forsyth IS the most famous.'

It's 11.30 p.m. and the BBC election night party is getting interesting. It's a bit of a frothy crowd, not so much the Love Boat as the Luvvie Boat. A series of short power breaks have ended in a very long power cut and so, though we are surrounded by three huge TV screens, they are all blank. We are supposed to be at the very centre of the media election and we know absolutely nothing. We are in the dark in every way.

'No bourbon?' asks Brucie, as his manager brings him a glass of juice. Other lesser celebs come up to gush. I ask if he'd be up for hosting an election debate next time. 'I don't mind,' he said, 'I'd get a few more laughs than they got!'

He notes that no one minds being in a news black-out. 'Look! Nobody cares!' he says, glancing over at the babbling gaggle drinking a Chilean sauvignon blanc or Côte du Rhône. I hear the sound of breaking glass. Election, what election?

Just down the ramp, on shore, in the old County Hall, is the ITV party. Outside, under a patio heater, I run into a group that included Lord Jones, as in Digby, Geoff Hoon (not at his own election count for the first time in decades) and Alastair Campbell. It felt very end of an era, like a tribute band reunion.

Then Digby, nursing a large glass of red, ruined my nostalgia by announcing that, yes, he WOULD take a job as Trade Minister with the Tories but only if he didn't have to join the party. 'I know there is a rumour about that,' he said. Well, there is now.

Inside at ITV I meet the novelist Kathy Lette. 'I am the only Labour supporter here!' she announces, flashing her scary, sparkly red shoes (think Dorothy in *The Wizard of Oz* in stilettos). She wants to invite Gordon and Sarah to Sunday lunch, she says, and ban any mention of politics. Behind her, I see Piers Morgan, who now looks very Californian and therefore a bit like Tony Blair. Just as I think this, Ali C appears too. It's unnerving.

Back on the Luvvie Boat, during a rare moment of power, Andrew Neil roams round with his microphone. At one point he is interviewing David Baddiel, Dom Joly, Dame Kelly Holmes and Fern Britton. Sadly, the power cuts just as Fern is about to share her views with us.

The air-kissing is getting even more intense now. I spot only two (ex) politicians: Michael Portillo and David Howarth (Lib Dem). I ask Peter Snow if he's missing his swing-o-meter. 'We are completely in the dark!' he announced, almost dancing with excitement.

Über-scientist Richard Dawkins tells me that he voted for a Lib Dem who is an avowed atheist. The Irish Ambassador sweeps by: 'I'm going to another party to find out what's happening in the election.' No one followed. ♥

Chapter Three

A Mad Week in May:
The Pre-Nup and the Wedding

The day after the election dawned, bleary-eyed, and, though the British people had spoken, no one was entirely sure what they'd said. The Tories, at 36.1 per cent of the vote, had 307 seats. Labour, at 29 per cent, was down 91 seats to 258 and the Lib Dems, down five seats to 57, had 23 per cent. Perhaps the biggest loser was Nick Clegg, whose hopes had been raised by the nation's brief bout of Cleggmania. But now, with no party having won the 326 seats necessary for a majority, Britain had its first hung parliament since 1974. No one was sure what exactly was going to happened next. Nick, shaking off his disappointment, saw his chance and grabbed it. What followed was a crazy, hazy five days in May in which Nick flirted with Dave, then Gordon, then Dave, then Gordon, then … well, you get the idea. We were watching a pre-nup in the making and then, of course, there was the wedding.

8 May 2010
Loves me, loves me not: Clegg and the dating game

The day after the vote before, confusion reigning, the word went out that Nick Clegg was on his way to London from Sheffield to address the nation

Spare a thought for Nick Clegg. He had believed he was a contender. He had thought that the voters agreed with

Nick. But now, the morning after the nightmare before, he was merely a pretty face lusted after by the other two (real) contenders for their own selfish reasons. Thus he did the only thing he could: he played hard to get. For yesterday we saw three men playing a very public game of power dating.

The most dramatic moment of the entire campaign and election came at 10.40 a.m., when Nick Clegg emerged from his car parked at the end of Cowley Street and plunged into the mob of press that had gathered outside his headquarters in Westminster. He stood in a tiny circle of space, boom mikes and cameras bobbing perilously over the scrum, the crush overwhelming, photographers on stepladders, helicopter whirring overhead. He seemed tired but resolved.

Here, in this street, his tie orange, his mood blue, he was going to salvage something. He'd said that whoever got the most votes and seats had the 'first right' to try to govern. Then, just in case Gordon and Dave hadn't heard him clearly, Nick added that it was up to the Tories to prove that they could govern in the 'national interest'. In dating terms, this was a clear invitation. 'Dave, call me!' he was saying. But there was a warning there, too: don't leave it too late. Dave didn't. He called a press conference for 2.30 p.m.

Nick, observing this, must surely have plucked a few petals off a daisy and told his aides: 'He loves me, he loves me not.'

Our love-hate triangle now moves to Downing Street where Gordon Brown is fuming. Yes, it's true he dislikes Nick, but he hates Dave. How dare they talk of love! Such was his fury that he knew he had to do the hardest thing of all – act. Thus, at 12.40 p.m., Gordon strode out of No. 10. He looked straight into the camera (and thus into the eyes of Nick) and did all but throw himself at Nick's feet. He even told Nick that he respected him (yes he did, even though everyone who has ever dated knows that this is a bad line). Then he gushed about their wonderful new life together.

Nick, plucking his daisy absentmindedly, laughed. He may have just lost the election but he was winning the love-bombing war. Then, at 2.30 p.m., he tuned in to hear Dave declare HIS love.

The Tory leader, his tie as blue as the eyes that now bored straight into the camera (and thus into Nick) declared: 'I want to make a big, open and comprehensive offer to the Liberal Democrats.'

Dave talked about how much they had in common. They both hated ID cards. They both wanted to get rid of the 'jobs tax'. And, unsaid but lurking behind every word: they both hated Gordon! Their manifestos had much in common.

'We can give ground,' said Dave, which all married people know means total surrender. Dave mentioned his 'big open and comprehensive offer' again. Then he laid it on thick about how it was in the 'national interest' for this relationship to go ahead.

'I hope with all my heart that this is something we can achieve,' said Dave. Nick listened to this declaration. Had Dave really said: 'With all my heart'? Yes, he had! Then Nick selected another daisy from his bouquet and began to pluck its petals: 'He loves me, he loves me not...' (To be continued.) ♥

10 May 2010
A great big mess all in the national interest

By Sunday the confusion had gone viral. Suddenly everyone had an opinion and the phrase on everyone's lips was 'in the national interest'. It sounded good but what did it mean?

It was a day in which absolutely everything was done in the national interest. First, on *The Andrew Marr Show* (which I believe could emerge as the epicentre of coalition government), Baroness Kennedy of The Shaws announced that Labour must rule with a rainbow coalition.

'But Brown is not a colour in the rainbow,' noted Rory Bremner, who, in the national interest, is learning to impersonate Nick Clegg and David Cameron at the same time.

Then Michael 'Meerkat' Gove appeared, blinking frantically.

He said that in the national interest he would make the ultimate sacrifice to form a coalition with the Lib Dems. 'Are you prepared to give up your Cabinet seat?' Mr Gove stared into the camera. 'Yes!' he barked.

Next up was Lib-Dem Commander Lord Ashdown of Norton-sub-Hamdon, wearing corduroy in the national interest. I was disappointed he did not abseil into the TV studio. He kept fiddling with his ear. Was he getting messages from Nick? It looked suspicious. He sees this as a patriotic test. 'It is the sovereign command of the British people, which I must obey,' he announced. The British people (were they the ones in his ear?) had told him: 'You may not like these other guys but we now require you to talk to them!'

I raced to Whitehall to see all the guys talking to each other (no women involved, I note in the national interest). I have never seen a constitutional crisis before and I can report that, basically, it is just one big mess. No one seems to know what is going on. All we knew is that something – Talks? Coffee? Tea? Daisy-plucking? – was going on between the Blue Team and the Yellow Team behind the studiously apolitically coloured door (teal, I think) of the Cabinet Office. My, but it was cold. It felt like February on that pavement outside that door which had never been troubled by a crowd before, much less this raggle-taggle of media, tourists and the occasional British citizen.

I talked to one man sporting an 'I Should Be In Charge' badge. 'I suppose you know that we are in between Prime Ministers for the first time in decades,' he said.

So who exactly was in charge? Hard to say, but soon at least we knew who was in Number 10. Gordo, aka Mr Squatter, had arrived along with Mrs Squatter and the little Squattees via the back door in the early afternoon, direct from Scotland. Lord Mandy, wearing an open-necked shirt, was already inside. Ed Miliband was also there. This was the ancien régime, the Squatteriti if you like, gathering to plot how to hang on to power.

The only one to enter No. 10 via the front door was Iain

Bundred, the press officer also known as 'Bunders'. How very *Jeeves and Wooster* that a man named Bunders was at the heart of this.

By 5.30 p.m. the crowd outside the Cabinet Office numbered in the hundreds, cameras sticking out like barnacles. Finally I saw the sharp eyes of George Osborne flash through the windows and the Blue Team emerged to say that the talks had been positive.

Then we heard from the Yellow Team, led by Danny Alexander, the tall carrot-head MP and Nick Clegg's chief of staff.

Afterwards Danny walked along Whitehall, a huge pulsating scrum around him, looking bemused. 'Is it Tony Blair?' asked a passer-by. No, I thought, just Danny A. Who would have thought it? These are heady times for the Liberal Democrats, not to mention the national interest. 💔

11 May 2010
The hand of history, the clunking fist and a finger puppet

Everyone kept calling it the 'New Politics' but, as Gordon set out to woo Nick in earnest, it looked alarmingly like the old politics, just messier. But Nick, the one they all wanted, seemed to be loving it

It was not so much the hand of history as the great clunking fist that hit Westminster at 5 p.m. yesterday. Gordon Brown's announcement left Westminster reeling, spluttering, bleeding and, in some cases, furious. 'They are duplicitous b******s,' said one Tory MP of the Lib Dems, with truly snarling relish. The brand new MPs looked a bit like baby seals who had just been clubbed.

Which they had, of course. So much drama on their first day. There were five or six statements but Gordon's was the only shocker. There was no warning, just an aide suddenly running out into Downing Street and erecting the wonky lectern that No. 10

has used since Gordo lost the election (the smart one with the No. 10 logo, we must assume, is being kept for whenever we get a new Prime Minister).

It was a magnificent non-resignation resignation. Indeed, possibly the finest of the genre. Gordon told us that he was a loser, but a progressive loser. He was so progressive that he felt called to form a government with other progressive losers before he, Gordon, would quit (eventually). Gordon looked sombre but, surely, beneath all that dourness, this was all part of the dating game. In Mills & Boon terms, he was saying: 'Nick! Even if you love me not, Labour is the one for you!'

When Gordon returned to his bunker, we could hear the sound of clapping from inside No. 10 (so that is what the hand of history does on such a day). The Squatter had spoken and his fellow squattees approved.

So the first official day of the new politics was, to use the technical term, a total mess. It was divided into three distinct sections: morning (happy), afternoon (confusion) and 5 p.m. (nuclear).

In the morning, under the expensive fig trees in Portcullis House, the MPs' office block next to the Palace of Westminster, the new MPs really did look fresh-faced as journalists stalked them as hyenas do their prey. 'Are you enjoying the first day back at school?' asked Ed Vaizey, the affable, not to say rotund, Conservative MP for TV Appearances, as he passed by.

Cabinet ministers wandered round as if they didn't have a care in the world or, indeed, a desk. Hilary Benn had lunch in the canteen. Ed Balls raced by. Jack Straw mooched round, carrying his gym bag (it has a portcullis on it) and buying himself a cup of tea. 'I'm still the Lord High Chancellor,' he noted. But, clearly, one without much to do.

Then, in mid-morning, the Blue and Yellow teams met again behind the suddenly famous teal door of the Cabinet Office. Afterwards, as everyone left, blowing air-kisses at each other, rumours of a deal stole through Westminster like cat burglars in the night.

At 1 p.m. Nick Clegg was supposed to meet his MPs in the Grand Committee Room off Westminster Hall. He was, of course, late. This hall, with its great vaulted wooden ceiling, its fabulous stained-glass window, is a place where you can feel history: Charles I was tried here in 1649 and, eleven years later, Cromwell's head was put on display. And now Little Nicky Clegg, kingmaker, was meeting his MPs to decide the fate of the nation.

Or not, as it turned out. I felt that I was not seeing the hand of history here so much as its finger puppet. There was a poignant moment when the defeated MP Lembit Öpik appeared, a lone, not to say desperately-seeking-attention figure, to give his not very deep thoughts on it all. He ended with these chilling words: 'I'll be back.' Schwarzenegger should sue.

The Lib-Dem meeting ended with the news that the Lib Dems were also flirting with Gordo now, and soon afterwards Gordon detonated his nuclear device (this is his version of flirting).

It was evening before we caught sight of David Cameron as he met his MPs in Westminster. As he entered, we heard a thunderous rumble as Tory MPs used their hands of history to thump their desks, a Tory tribal tradition. It sounded like a stampede. 💔

12 May 2010
Constitutional crisis? What constitutional crisis!

Was Nick going to choose Dave or Gordon? The Lib–Dem leader seemed to be playing one off against the other until, finally, as twilight loomed, a decision was nigh

The deal that did for Gordon Brown all began with an innocent little Tweet from William Hague just before 2 p.m. 'Will be returning to Cabinet Office shortly to resume negotiations.'

Then the Tory team strode down Whitehall, with Michael

Crick of the BBC stuck to their side like a raucous little burr. I think that Mr Crick, whose fuzzy microphone has been ubiquitous in past days, may be the mascot of this constitutional crisis.

'They are like rock stars,' gushed Elizabeth, a pensioner, eyes wide, looking thrilled to have just seen Mr Hague (it has come to this). 'It is so frantic!'

And it was. Indeed here, outside the teal door of 70 Whitehall, it felt frantic all afternoon. The scrum grew and grew until, finally, hundreds were gathered round the door, staring at it. Hundreds of lenses were trained on it and everyone was gathered round it, in a big unruly horseshoe. Photographers on stepladders faced it, police guarded it. To the uninitiated, it would have looked as if the door was sacred and we were, in some strange ritual, worshipping it (which, actually, we were).

The Siege of the Teal Door lasted five and a half hours. Not even the resignation of the Prime Minister, which took place only yards away in Downing Street, interrupted it. For this one afternoon, the centre of power, such as there is in a constitutional crisis (known as CC from now on), was here.

Everyone who was anyone in the CC was here. There were police, protesters, cameras, random actual voters, tourists and Big Ben. And, of course, Sky television's Adam Boulton, he of the great on-air bust-up with Alastair Campbell.

'Lots of people have e-mailed me saying I should have punched him,' said Adam. But did he think so? 'No,' he said. 'I regret it.' Still, it's made him a mini-rock star, too. 'Adam! Adam! Adam! Give us a wave,' shouted the protesters.

We had no idea what was going on, as is always the case when you are at the heart of events. Behind the door, in three adjoining rooms, eight men were thrashing out a Teal Deal. At first, on this cold grey May day, it didn't seem possible that the deal would end with a change of Prime Minister within hours. The rumour that someone had seen luggage taken out the back door of No. 10 seemed quite ridiculous.

But about halfway through, about 4 p.m., it began to feel different. The crowd kept getting bigger – and noisier. The protesters from Take Back Parliament chanted unwieldy slogans. 'What do we want? Electoral reform!' they shouted. 'When do we want it? In a structured time frame!' In a structured time frame? That was so incredibly Lib-Dem. We're going to have to get used to it now.

It all felt very heady. Everyone kept warm by trying to name the new Con–Lib Cabinet (or should that be Con–Dem Cabinet? John Prescott calls it the Con–Dem Nation). The protesters were shouting: 'Danny Alexander! Danny Alexander! We just want to see you.' So here was another absurdity of the CC: now even Danny A – Nick Clegg's chief of staff – had become a rock star.

Rumours fell on us like hailstones. Gordon was going to resign. Ken Clarke was the new Chancellor. Samantha Cameron had just arrived. A man with a loudhailer shouted: 'This is what democracy looks like.' The crowd spilled over into the central reservation. It wasn't until almost twenty minutes after Gordon had resigned that the negotiators emerged. The Teal Deal had been done, the constitutional crisis was over but not the drama a few steps away.

Inside Number 10, Gordon had been waiting too. The unelected Prime Minister (aka the Squatter) knew that he was on his way out, rejected by the Lib Dems (the maths were pretty impossible anyway). He, too, was just waiting for the pre-nup negotiations to end and for Nick (of all people) to call. This he finally did. 'Nick, Nick, I can't hold on any longer,' Gordon said.* 'Nick, I've got to go to the Palace. The country expects me to do that. I have to go. The Queen expects me to go. I can't hold on any longer.'

It was a dignified end to a mess of a day. At 7.19 p.m., Gordon left Downing Street for good, on foot, walking with his children John (aged six) and Fraser (aged three) and Sarah. It was the most vulnerable, and the most human, we have ever seen him. By 8.10 p.m., Dave was seeing the Queen and then, at 8.40 p.m., he was in Downing Street, announcing that he aimed to form a coalition with the Lib Dems, his pregnant wife Sam watching.

And then he walked, for the first time, through that gleaming door, Prime Minister at last. 💔

*As reported by *Guardian* photographer Martin Argles, who chronicled Gordon's last hours.

13 May 2010
Da dum dum dum ... The Happy
Couple go down the garden path

We had no idea when we received the call for an afternoon press conference at Number 10 that 'congratulations' were in order

From the very first sight of the happy couple I knew that it was, actually, a wedding. Nick and Dave emerged from the back door at No. 10 on to a garden terrace dotted with bright green spirals of topiary. Deep in conversation, they processed by the cascading lavender wisteria (wisteria! Dave's fave*). Stride mirrored stride, smile begot smile. We could see how well they chuckled together as they came down the garden path towards us. Yes, down the garden path. You could not make it up.

We were gathered, dearly beloved, in the garden of No. 10. The hundred or so velvet chairs were arranged on the lawn, one side for the groom, the other for the other slightly more boyish groomette. The garden was a little bit of heaven with its beehive and wormery, dominated by a graceful majestic magnolia. Many of the flowers were yellow and blue, of course, perfectly co-ordinated for the politics. They had matching his 'n' his lecterns.

The grass really IS greener on this side, I can report. It almost glowed it was so lusciously alien green. The only thing missing was a small orchestra and a tremulous song by Andrew Lloyd Webber.

'Today we are not just announcing a new Government,'

beamed Dave as Nick beamed back, eyes steady, body turned towards him. 'We are announcing a new politics.'

OMG, as they say, not just a wedding but a birth too. 'I came into politics to change it, to change Britain,' beamed Nick as Dave beamed back. 'Together – that job starts today.'

Together forever! I have to say they suit each other. Indeed, both looked more relaxed together (forever) than they do with their own parties. They are both forty-three but Nick makes Dave look a bit older, which, as he is now Prime Minister, is good. I had never noticed his crow's feet until yesterday but then he laughed more than usual, occasionally throwing his head back. Everyone was talking about their hair (sorry, I wish I could say their policy on nuclear power but it wouldn't be true). Dave's mini-quiff was more coiffed, Nick's more natural.

We guests had brought only questions but, as it was a wedding, they were a bit soft. 'If the phone rings at 3 a.m., do you both have to answer it?' was one. Everyone giggled, especially Dave (or David, as Nick calls him). It seems not.

Where was Nick's office? 'He has the Deputy Prime Minister's office in the Cabinet Office,' explained Dave. 'It is pretty close together. This is not going to be a partnership where we have to book meetings.' Nick said that the Cabinet Office was like a warren. 'I have no idea where I am!' he cried, giddy with it all.

Birds were singing as they told us about their relationship. They'd set a fixed term of five years (and Parliament will follow suit), so will be renewing their vows at the election in 2015. Yes, Nick would be standing in for him at Prime Minister's Questions. 'I look forward to lots of foreign travel!' gushed Dave.

It all seemed almost ridiculously chummy. Who knew that coalitions were this much of a love-in? If they keep this up, they'll need a joint name (Clameron? Camelegg?). But they both did look transformed. At one point, Dave chortled: 'This is what the new politics looks like!' Happy days – at least for now. ❧

* In the MPs expenses scandal, Dave repaid £680 for household repairs which included the cost of clearing wisteria from a
chimney.

Chapter Four

The Austerity Honeymoon

After the wedding comes, well, the honeymoon but what was that exactly? It all felt entirely new and, in the Commons, it all looked different too. About one-third of MPs were new and the entire place looked refreshed – younger, more female, more ethnic and just a whole lot more normal. Labour was now sitting on the other side. That took some getting used to. But the Lib Dems, who looked shell-shocked, seem to have been entirely subsumed into the Tory side, reduced to two benches of yellowness. It didn't take long for jokes about the Lib Dem to surface, laughed at uproariously by everyone but them. The psychodrama fodder was endless as we all tried to understand what, exactly, had happened during those five days in May. What WAS this marriage anyway? What did it mean? How did it work? And could it possibly last? We were in unknown territory. 💔

19 May 2010
Our honeymooners dance cheek to cheek on the front bench

Dave, almost bashful, seemed thrilled to be sitting next to Nick in the Commons

The New Politics began not with a bang but a seating plan. Presentation, presentation, presentation! That is the mantra of our new rulers. The huge question of who would sit next to who on the front bench could not be left to chance. So Patrick McLoughlin, the Chief Whip, was delegated to be the hostess with the mostest, a duty he carried out with portly aplomb, clutching his crib sheet, directing traffic into blue–yellow order.

The result was that William Hague sat next to Dave, who sat next to Nick, who looked like a kid with an ice cream, boyish grin flashing like a Belisha beacon. George was away in Brussels so next came Theresa May and then Vince, who looked hang-dog miserable, his contorted body posture screaming: 'I'm a Lib Dem, get me out of here!'

Even Dave seemed a little unsure to start with. 'Prime Minister!' called Johnny Bercow, the Speaker-elect. The Commons, heaving, all aisles filled, waited for Dave, who just sat there. 'That's you!' cried Labour MPs (how strange to see them on the other side – it was like looking at one of those funfair crazy mirrors).

'This is a new era,' proclaimed Dave, who really cannot say the word 'new' enough at the moment. 'It really does look and feel different. Indeed, many of us are sitting next to people that we've never sat next to before!' To laughter, Dave turned, almost bashfully, to acknowledge Nick, who looked thrilled. They have been married almost a week now.

Clearly they are still very much on honeymoon. The other Liberal Democrats may not approve of the 'mooners. The MPs are squished into one and a half benches, a yellow island in a sea of true blue. The fact that the Lib Dems all wore their colour yesterday seemed a bit desperate. One MP had a waistcoat the colour of egg yolk that I would make illegal. Sir Ming Campbell, sitting where Dennis Skinner has for the past thirteen years, had a face of thunder (but then, he was mirroring Dennis).

Other than the seating plan, the New Politics appears to carry on exactly like the old. After months of intrigue and backbiting, the attempt to unseat Mr Bercow as Speaker failed miserably.

Mr Bercow, who was immediately irritating, thanked 'colleagues' for re-electing him. By tradition he should be dragged to the chair by two MPs but, actually, he seemed to be dragging them. What had been billed as a major revolt to oust him was reduced to two women making sorry little tu-whit, tu-whoos of protest, like baby owls trying to carry out a beheading. Needless to say, nothing happened. (If I had a pound for every rumour that Bercow is about to be removed, I would be quite wealthy.)

It was left to Sir Malcolm Rifkind (for it is he) to propose Mr Bercow. He began, for unknown reasons, with something that came quite close to a beheading joke. 'I will emulate King Henry VIII who is reputed to have said to each of his six wives, "Please don't worry, I don't intend to keep you long!"'

The star of the day, though, was Sir Peter Tapsell, the new Father of the House. At eighty, he is a magnificent shade of mahogany, as round as a hot-air balloon, as old-fashioned as a spittoon. He first entered the house in 1959 and at times refers to Mesopotamia instead of Iraq. He wore a frock coat even though he didn't have to. 'Order! Order!' he said, voice booming, a wonderfully grand old man in a brand new world. ❦

20 May 2010
Nick's power revolution might not wash

So, we all wondered, what would Nick Clegg get out of this relationship? Dave was in Number 10 but where was Nick? He didn't waste much time (trying) to tell us

To Islington, for the most important speech on political reform since 1832. Don't take my word for it: this is what Nick Clegg, our new Deputy Prime Minister, says.

The location was the atrium of a sixth-form college just off Holloway Road in North London, which may be home to the most kebab shops in Britain. (What did they do in 1832 to get a kebab? Maybe Nick would tell us.) When we arrived we were given yellow lanyards, a word beloved by Lib Dems for the bit of string that holds your ID card. But the college had run out of ID cards and so we were told to wear just the lanyards. There is a moral there somewhere, though I am afraid to find it.

As we sat, waiting for Nick, our yellow lanyards round our necks holding nothing at all, I felt that I was living the Lib-Dem dream. Nick was late. Actually Nick is always late. Apparently Clegg-time runs about fifteen minutes behind BST.

Sure enough, at 11.15 a.m., he arrived, preceded by an entourage that already numbers about twelve. Then he ducked into another room. How frustrating. It was only when I saw a Lib-Dem press officer carry out the sacred (plastic) glass of water for him that I knew the Great Political Reform Speech of 2010 was nigh.

It was very 'Power to the People'. I had hoped that Nick would just sing the John Lennon song, but instead he talked about a 'programme of empowerment'. This is harder to sing. He told us this was 'the biggest shake-up of our democracy since 1832'. He's just lucky that the Suffragettes aren't around to chain themselves to the railings over that rather extravagant claim.

It is a bit of a tradition for Nick that, wherever he gives a speech, there is noise. So the moment Nick announced 'The Power Revolution', behind me a dishwasher churned into life. I don't think Nick meant that kind of power. Nick's power revolution will 'put you in charge'. Presumably of the switch.

'Britain was once the cradle of modern democracy,' said Nick. 'We are now, on some measures, the most centralised country in Europe, bar Malta.' Bar Malta? Only a former MEP who is also a Lib Dem would care. I can hear the Libs now: 'My God, we can't be as centralised as Malta, let's have a power revolution.'

Nick told us that he was a liberal (lower case l, another example of coalition creep). 'My starting point has always been optimism about people.' Oh dear, that sounds very Dave. Perhaps they are already becoming each other.

There are three steps to Nick's power revolution:

First, he's ending the culture of spying. I glanced up at the sign that said we were all on CCTV.

Second, he's reforming politics. We've been talking about Lords reform for 150 years. 'The time for talk is over!' he said (talking). He's set up a committee that is not a 'talking shop'. This seemed unlikely. I mean, is it possible to mime Lords reform? Only Nick and Dave, being optimists, would know.

The third step is about decentralising so we avoid the Malta nightmare.

Nick ended his Great Reform Speech by enthusing: 'Power will be yours!' It seems unlikely, but what do I know? I wasn't there in 1832. ♥

21 May 2010
Proud birth of a Lib–Con love child

The birth of the little baby Lib-Con, who was an alarming shade of green, was a very public event with its two daddies looking on, proud as could be

There was something missing from the Birth Announcements in *The Times* yesterday and this is what should have been in it: LIB-CON. On May 20, in Whitehall, to Nick and Dave, a child, named Coalition Freedom Fairness Responsibility, thirty-six pages long. No brothers or sisters.

The first thing I noticed about the new infant was its colour. It would be at home on Mars. 'Is it mushy pea or guacamole?' asked a colleague. Actually, it's lime green with a hint of asparagus. Apparently one colour chart calls it Tranquil.

Basically, it's a muddy version of what you get when you mix a lot of yellow with a bit of blue: page two is just a Rothko-esque block of green. (Surely paint makers might think about calling this colour Coalition?)

The birth was at the Treasury. The NHS may be concerned by this. It took place in front of 100 civil servants and fifty press plus innumerable politicos. Midwives (midhusbands?) Oliver Letwin and Danny Alexander looked on proudly. It had been a nine-day labour, and no drugs, only drugs policies, were involved.

'In the end in politics the right thing to do is the right thing to do is the right thing to do,' said Dave as he welcomed baby Coalition. Nick looked on adoringly. They got married only last week. On that occasion, Dave said: 'This will succeed through its success.' I think these will be known as Dave-isms.

The birth was a drawn-out affair, with more speeches than a quadruple wedding. Nick spoke first: 'Even if you've read 100 party manifestos,' he said, revealing what Lib Dems do in their spare time, 'you've never read a document like this.'

I looked through the thirty-six pages with thirty-one chapters (they went from B for Banking to U for Universities, so it's not exactly A to Z). It was part in Tranquil type and part in black. To be honest, it DID look exactly like any other manifesto I've read. But Nick is not the first parent to think his child ultra-special.

I'm beginning to forget that Nick and Dave are from separate parties. Yesterday they seemed one as they doted on Little Coalition Freedom Fairness Responsibility Lib–Con (how that child is going to hate the name; maybe they'll use Co or Free for short).

Back in Westminster, MPs were throwing hissy fits. When Dave and Nick were asked about this, they seemed sanguine. 'Oh they'll get used to it,' Dave almost said.

When it was Vince's turn, he got entangled with his mike. 'As the new head of the department for technological innovation,' he said, 'we make it up as we go along.'

He speaks, of course, the truth.

Little Coalition Freedom Fairness Responsibility is going to have a very interesting life. ❣

25 May 2010
As so often with cuts, the David is in the detail

Everyone in this coalition seems to have a buddy: this was the day that George and his new best friend David Laws started hacking away at the budget

Madame Tussaud's would have been perfect for the draconian cuts announcement. Fake blood, heads on sticks, that kind of thing. Instead, at 10 a.m., I found myself waiting for the axeman in the Treasury atrium courtyard. Above us only sky. I have heard of blue-sky thinking but not blue-sky bloodbath. It seemed wrong. No one ever made a movie called *Garden Party Massacre* and yet, behind me, hundreds of civil servants had come out to watch and catch some rays.

There were two axemen. I tell you this Government is like a permanent buddy movie. Georgie 'Boy' Osborne was with his Lib-Dem fall guy, David Laws, shorter, urbane, taciturn. Georgie welcomed us to his cuts party. 'It's good to be outdoors and it's good to have a crowd!' he said, though he didn't smile. David didn't smile either, but then I'm not sure he ever has.

George bragged about how good they'd been at cutting 'with care'. 'We have conducted the fastest and most collegiate spending review in recent history.' Whatever next? Redundancy canapés? Goody bags for scrapped consultants?

I can see why George needed David Laws there. His new catch-phrase is 'David will give you the detail.' And David did. Reams of it. Mr Laws is the henchman in a perfectly ironed hairshirt. He's axed first-class travel. No minister gets his or her own car and driver. He wants them to walk (preferably barefoot, over hot coals).

Finally, the buddies were asked how easy it was to find £6 billion. 'Let me ask David to answer that question in detail,' said George. David said that, actually, it's not that hard.

That's good – just £150 billion to go. ♥

26 May 2010
Most Gracious Speech gives way to the Most Sneery

*The Queen's Speech is a beautiful and glittering event except, of
course, when the politicians insist on getting in on the act. Also:
a footnote, or perhaps a toe-note for historians, this was the day
that the Lib-Dem jokes began in earnest*

It ended badly but no one can say that the Queen did not do
her bit. She arrived, on time, in the Cinderella coach, looking ageless. She managed not to giggle when catching sight
of her new Lord High Chancellor, Ken Clarke, in full regalia,
his florid face puckering like a plum draped in cotton wool. Ken
managed, just, to hand over the white vellum without a splat but
he did not, as custom dictates, back down the stairs. I am sure
the Queen was relieved. One would not have wanted to dial 999.

It was tremendously soothing to watch. All the madness of
the election and the craziness of the coalition was put on hold.
Here, in the beautiful chamber that is the Lords, the world is full
of gold and men wearing giant playing cards. In the audience,
ladies in satin elbow gloves twinkled like stars. The tiara count
was forty-three, which is so high that you just know there must
be a recession on.

'The first priority is to reduce the deficit,' said Her Majesty,
voice tinkling like a harpsichord, never betraying that she was
un-saying all the things that she had said last time. For now it
was Nick and Dave who stood before her, not Gordon. He was
nowhere to be seen.

It was, truly, the Most Gracious Speech in every way. But what
followed, in the Commons at 2.30 p.m., was the Most Sneery. It
began, as is the custom, with two speeches by government backbenchers. Peter Lilley (yes, him) noted that it was usual for the Chief
Whip to pick one genial old codger and one oily young man. When
he asked who the oily one would be, he was told: 'We don't have one.

We've got a Lib Dem instead!' How the MPs howled. Screams of laughter, bellies wobbling like jellies. Everyone is a bit tense.

The Lib-Dem jokes (surely it is only a matter of time before there is an *Official Lib-Dem Joke Book*) continued. How, wondered Mr Lilley, should he refer to a Lib Dem? Should it be 'honourable friend'? Everyone shouted 'no' as if in panto (which they are). Or 'honourable partner'? This, noted Mr Lilley, sounded even more intimate than friend. More screams of laughter. So he settled for 'honourable ally' which, actually, sounds like they hate each other.

Dave was fantastically sneery, confident, brash. Indeed, he began jabbing away at Labour even before he read out the names of the dead in Afghanistan. When asked about the scrapping of Child Trust Funds, he huffed at Labour: 'We've run out of money. You broke the nation.'

The Libs are already cracking. Only Nick looks happy, the rest are clinging to their yellow garments for dear life. Simon Hughes asked Dave what 'his Government' was doing on housing. Dave gently reminded him it was 'our Government' now. At which point, the Lib-Dem Bob Russell started to screech at Labour: 'Failed! Failed abysmally!' Labour MPs, on great form now Gordo's gone, just laughed.

It was amusing to watch George and Nick compete over Dave. Every time Dave stood up, Nick and George each put a hand down on the bench where he had just sat, as if claiming it as his own. As I watched, Dave stood up again and I wrote in my notebook: 'TB stands up.' Yes, he reminds me of Tony Blair but then, he always said he was the true heir. ❣

27 May 2010
David Laws has a Gladstone moment

Astrologists report that this was the day that a previously unknown bright star was spotted in the sky over Westminster*

A star is born or, because David Laws does not seem quite human, perhaps I should say created via some mysterious process in the Treasury equivalent of the Hadron Collider. Given his diminutive size, this was not so much big bang as little bang but, still, it made quite the noise in the Commons yesterday.

It was sink or swim for Mr Laws. The place was packed – the new MPs are keen and Labour's are angry. Alistair Darling had got himself in a rage (yes, really, I saw an eyebrow twitch) and had demanded the Chancellor come to the Commons to explain his £6 billion in cuts. But George Osborne was busy, for he is already too important for such trivial housekeeping duties, and so he sent his little Chief Secretary to act as his human shield.

But as I watched Mr Laws, repelling insults, attacking foes, placating friends, bursting with confidence, I began to wonder if he was made of some impervious material such as Kryptonite. Not so much Superman as Super-Lib-Laws, a man who can leap ideologies in a single sentence.

'He's the biggest Tory in the Cabinet,' said a (Tory) MP admiringly afterwards.

And now he is also, it seems, Gladstone. Can you be a comic book hero and Gladstone at the same time? I don't see why not. Obviously the mutton-chop sideburns would have to go. But, otherwise, we are living in Lib–Con times: anything is possible.

The proof of this came when Edward Leigh, right-wing and slightly bonkers Tory MP, praised Mr Laws: 'I welcome the return to the Treasury of stern unbending Gladstonian Liberalism!' he trumpeted. Mr Laws welcomed these comments on behalf of Gladstone and himself: 'I hope that this is not only Gladstonian Liberalism, but liberalism tinged with the social liberalism about which my party is so passionate,' he said, stroking his party like a cat.

Every time a Lib Dem spoke, Mr Laws invoked Gladstone. Tories gushed over him while Labour foamed with anger. But the real test came when Dennis Skinner stood up, electric with hate. 'Are you aware that not a single member of the Cabinet has turned up to back you?' he spat, as MPs screamed 'OOOhhhhhh'.

I looked at the front bench. Who were these people? Oh my god, I saw Henry Bellingham, the batty Tory MP who is, incredibly, a Foreign Office minister (Africa, forgive us). Indeed the only Cabinet member was the totally beige Caroline Spelman.

Mr Skinner ranted on. 'Can there be a more pathetic sight than this Liberal Democrat, who campaigned against cuts in 2010, now hammering the young and the old and putting people on the dole?' Mr Skinner, incandescent, mouthed 'P*** off' though Hansard records this as 'Get out!' None of this fazed Mr Kryptoryite in the least. What would Gladstone say? 💔

*Little did we know that his was, actually, a falling star, for Mr Laws resigned on 29 May, a late victim of the expenses scandal

3 June 2010
Prime Minister's other half suffers in silence

To see Nick Clegg at PMQs was to see a man muted, a voice stilled, a role relegated. He was, in other words, the perfect political wife

Do you think Little Nicky Clegg is having regrets? Yesterday he sat at PMQs, next to Him Indoors, playing the freshly minted constitutional role of Prime Minister's Office Wife. I could almost see the thought bubble over him, saying: 'So who hit the mute button?' At least Dave didn't ask him to get the coffee.

It didn't help that Dave was very good at his first PMQs where he was the one answering the questions. He often spoke without notes, switching his tone from sombre (the dead in Afghanistan, the ghastly murders in Cumbria) to spiky with Labour MPs. But my eyes kept slipping over to the Silent One. Some thought he looked contemplative, but that is quite close to miserable. Perhaps he was dreaming of the day that he gets his own mini-question time – it's only three weeks away. Ring that one in red pen.

Even his inquisitor, Harriet Harman, noticed that he was suffering from Office Wife Syndrome and reached out to him in sisterly solidarity. She had been ribbing Dave about his married couple's allowance, saying a £3 a week tax break won't keep families together. 'No wonder the Deputy Prime Minister is sitting so quietly by his side,' she said. 'On this one, Nick agrees with me.' Nick, who was beginning to look like a captive in a hostage video, looked over at her wanly.

I have to tell you that the Tories seem to enjoy torturing the Lib Dems. Yesterday the more right-wing Conservatives had even infiltrated the Lib-Dem benches (they have only one and a half rows). There was Julian Lewis asking about Afghanistan. Then up popped Philip 'Genghis' Davies, who took his usual swipe at the Human Rights Act. As he denounced this, I saw some Lib Dems flinch. I don't blame them. They need their own Geneva Convention; not so much prisoners of war as prisoners of coalition. Surely they should have some territorial rights?

Sadly, there was a (small) David Laws-shaped hole on the front bench. He really was a falling star – burning so brightly and then, pfffft, gone, perhaps not forever, as his expense claims are investigated. The new David is Danny Alexander, who was so far down the front bench that he was practically in the canteen. Five years ago he was press officer for the Cairngorms National Park Authority, issuing press releases about saving the red squirrel. Now he is in charge of saving the country. What would the few red squirrels left say about that?

Finally, up jumped the Labour stalwart Ian Davidson, who shouted at Dave: 'Comrade Premier!' Dave looked alarmed, for this was a coalition too far.

'Aren't we all in this together?' shouted Mr Davidson. 'Do not a vast majority of us dislike, distrust and despise…' I looked over at the occupied Lib-Dem benches and then at Nick. I think we all knew what was coming. '...the Liberal Democrats?'

Everyone laughed. Except, of course, the Silent One. 💔

8 June 2010
Dave tells us just how bad it is

This was the day that Dave told us the news about our debt. I knew things were worse than I thought when we had to go to Milton Keynes to hear the news

So how bad is our debt? Well, bad enough that Dave had to go to Milton Keynes to tell us about it. Yes, that's right. So scary that he went all the way to suburbia and the Land of the Concrete Cows to give us the news. Here, drastic cuts are what happen when you set the lawnmower too low.

The speech was in a library at the Open University. So, shhhh-hhh. Dave likes backdrops made up of smiling people. But in our new Age of Pain, people cannot be relied upon to stay smiling. I am sure that Dave wanted the concrete cows behind him, but instead settled for four bookcases (Social Science, A-D).

'I have been in office for a month,' Dave told us and the books (which, at least, have the spine for it). I can report that Dave looks much worse. Gone is that fresh face that we loved to deface on the poster. Now he's got eye-bags and forehead wrinkles that aren't drawn on. Danny Alexander, the new Chief Secretary, was his coalition wife for the day. Danny sat in a little chair, eyes trained on Dave.

So how bad is it? Dave says our debt is massive, huge and staggering. It's so bad that every one of us owes £22,000 and if we don't do anything the total will be £1.4 trillion in five years. (Dave thinks this is frightening but he may not realise that, for those of us with credit cards, it's pretty normal.)

I waited for Dave to dish the dirt. This 'name and shame' exercise is turning us all into debt voyeurs. It reminds me of that TV show *How Clean Is Your House?*, which only worked when the home in question was a disgusting cockroach hotel. In the same way, *Dave Dishes the Dirt* has to include some horrors. It's no good coming all the way to Milton Keynes and not telling us something truly awful.

First we had to live through a lot of stuff about how none of this was his fault. Gordon's to blame for everything, including – and this is the bit I really admired – what is going to happen in the future. Dave finally got to the nitty-gritty. Defence was £4.5 billion over budget. The number of managers in the NHS has doubled. Yawn. But, then, he told us that the Department for Work and Pensions had given some families as much as £93,000 per year in housing benefit (£93,000!). This was a truly cockroachian fact.

And then Dave and Danny were gone. I asked two women near me what they thought of it all. Why, they wondered, was Danny A there? Was his presence a good use of taxpayer's money? So here's a money-saving idea, Dave. Next time you want to scare us, get a cardboard cut-out of Danny A. Come on, you know it makes sense. 💔

9 June 2010
Mr Whiplash, a Chancellor in the image of Brown

George Osborne had many years to watch how Gordon Brown used to dominate the chamber and now it looked as if he was setting out to do the same

George Osborne, as Chancellor, dominated the chamber in a way that we have not seen since Gordon Brown was in the Treasury. They have wildly differing styles but their command of the place was the same. With Gordon, it was the clunking fist. With George, it is the crack of a whiplash. Behind him the new Tories slavered.

And he is loving it, make no mistake about that. You could see that in his manner – arrogant, cocky, combative and at times petty. I have always seen him as a scorpion – and how he loves to sting.

He had a go at Shadow Chancellor Alistair Darling, still a sponge but now an angry one, who had warned that growth was as important as cuts. 'It is extraordinary,' pranced George, 'that you didn't once accept that you made a single mistake, that you didn't once apologise.' Alistair gave him his narcotic death-ray stare.

But, asked a Labour backbencher, hadn't Mr Darling been right over Northern Rock and refinancing the banks? 'Talk about refighting the last war,' snapped George. 'We spent the general election talking about those decisions and the answer is this: the British people agreed with us!' (Did they? I thought that, essentially, the British people only really agreed that they couldn't agree. Surely, if they had agreed with George, Muppet-man Danny Alexander would not be sitting next to him.)

The Labour backbencher David Winnick said that he was in the House in 1979 and saw who was hurt by Margaret Thatcher's cuts. 'That is why we are so sensitive,' he shouted. 'It's OUR people – it's the people who sent us here on the Labour benches – who are going to suffer the worst.'

There were so many ways to respond to this but Mr Whiplash couldn't resist having a flick. 'If you are so affronted by what Margaret Thatcher did, perhaps you could explain why it is every time there is a new Labour Prime Minister, virtually the first person they invite round for tea is Margaret Thatcher!' (Spookily, at this moment, Baroness T was heading to No. 10 to see our new PM.) Then there was Dennis Skinner. The Beast of Bolsover made the sole suggestion from the Labour benches on how to save money: deny the Royal Family their £7 million increase in the Civil List.

'If you are looking for cost savings,' George snapped, 'perhaps early retirement is something to consider!'

This delighted the Beast, who began to heckle him about drugs. 'Have you had any of the white stuff lately?' he cried. Mr Whiplash retorted: 'Go and take the pension – please!' The Chancellor smiled. He loves to sting, for it is in his nature.

How I wish that Gordon Brown had been in the chamber to see the man that, in so many ways, he created. ❦

10 June 2010
Dave wraps himself in the flag. Ingerland expects it

With the World Cup looming, everyone was waving the flag. Except, of course, the Lib Dems...

It was a flag-waving PMQs. Of course, we are in an In-ger-land situation but it was as if everyone was using the World Cup as an excuse to wave their own little flags. The only exception were the Lib Dems who, in the new politics, aren't allowed their own flag. Already, a samizdat Lib-Dem movement has sprung up, with members wearing bits of yellow to signal their allegiance.

Once again Nick Clegg was right next to Dave, silent and adoring. Occasionally Dave would refer to him, turning round to make a limp vague gesture at His Mute Companion. At these times Nick nodded even more fiercely. Nick was even wearing Dave's green 'coalition' tie. Truly, they are morphing into each other.

Those with flags to fly include Diane Abbott, who has to be the sketchwriters' choice for the Labour leadership. She wafted into the chamber midway through PMQs, wearing an extraordinary leopard-print maxi-dress. She looked magnificent, like a queen, and her very presence was thrilling. Harriet Harman, distracted by the queen, no doubt, asked a peculiar series of questions that ended up with a demand for on-tap CCTV.

'Let me be clear,' said Dave, which means he's going to be confusing. Sure enough, he told us he supports CCTV except when he doesn't support CCTV.

'Can I tell him what Theresa was saying to me?' said Harriet. Rarely can the use of the name 'Theresa' have caused such a hubbub. Did she mean Theresa May, the Home Secretary? 'Theresa who?' shouted MPs.

'Not the Home Secretary,' Harriet said primly. 'But Theresa from the Poet's Corner estate in my constituency. The one who KNOWS about living on an estate that needs CCTV.'

Dave – who really does need an opposition; this cannot go on – loved this. 'It is extraordinary how the party opposite is becoming more and more authoritarian. To hear Ed Balls talk about immigration, we've got the new Alf Garnett of British politics!'

Dave looked over at Ed B who, sadly, wasn't wearing a maxi-dress. 'It's one of the biggest U-turns that anyone can remember,' taunted Dave, who loves to hate Ed. 'For thirteen years, not a word about immigration. Not a word about our borders. Now they are all in a race.'

Then arose Nadhim Zahawi, the Tory for Stratford-upon-Avon. He is on a mission to get a job from Dave and misses no chance to ask an ingratiating question. 'The Prime Minister will know that I am a follower of my beloved England football team. I ask you to do a great thing for the people of England: cut through the bureaucracy and NONSENSE and fly the flag of England over Downing Street for the duration of the World Cup.'

Dave said he had investigated this. At first some said it would have a 'cost impact'. 'But I have managed to cut through that,' he said, as if he were St George slaying a dragon. 'And I can say that, at no additional cost to the taxpayer, the flag of St George will fly above Downing Street during the World Cup.'

So there you have it. I do hope Dave is going to Poundland to buy some flags for his Jag as well. After all, it's what Ingerland expects. 💔

15 June 2010
Ribbit! Quiet Man duets with a frog

*A momentous day with the Quiet Man trying to turn up the
volume*

Breaking news from the chamber: the Quiet Man is back.
And he is not just turning up the volume, but cranking
it up, big-time. We are not at vuvuzela levels yet, but Iain
Duncan Smith certainly let rip. At one point he bellowed at
Labour: 'You went on a spending spree like drunks on a Friday
night and we've all got the hangover now!' At this, Yvette Cooper's
cheeks acquired little rosy-red circles until she looked like a very
angry doll.

Tragically, his comeback at Work and Pensions Questions
was marred by the return of his oldest enemy. No, I don't mean
his own party, all of whom seem to have accepted their former
leader's reincarnation as the Tories' caring, sharing, evangelical
poverty czar. I speak, or should I say, speak but not very well, of
Freddie the Frog.

Ribbit. Ribbit. I noticed Freddie's lurking presence after the
first two words. 'Mister Speaker,' began IDS, his voice already
gravelly, on the brink of croak, a cough away from actual throat-
clearing. But all of that was to come. I hope that Mr Duncan
Smith's fight against poverty goes better than his fight against
the frog.

His big fight – not with an amphibian – was with Labour over
something called the Future Jobs Fund, which IDS has decided
had no future. Ms Cooper said that would mean nearly 100,000
jobs would be lost. 'Those figures are quite ludicrous,' huffed IDS.
'It's a silly game that is being played out.' I am sure Yvette hated
being called silly: it is the kind of insult that women take personally. But then IDS seemed to mean it personally: 'You can't, now
that you are in opposition, simply say no to everything.'

Actually, I think that he'll find that she can do exactly that. That's what's so great about opposition. Even Frank Field, the Labour maverick who is the real poverty czar, had a go at IDS over the Future Jobs Fund. But, by then, the fight against Freddie was taking precedence. IDS was taking on water like a leaking rowing boat.

As a concert rating, I'm giving him two ribbits out of a potential four. It's great to have him (and Fred) back. ❦

16 June 2010
Fear and tears over an unpalatable truth

Dave was at his best as he gave his verdict on the long-awaited Saville Report, set up in 1998 to investigate Bloody Sunday in 1972 when the Army shot thirteen protesters in Derry

There were tears in the chamber yesterday and, also, fears. But we saw true leadership from David Cameron, who talked of the Saville Report with stark simplicity, abandoning any attempt at sophistication. His words, he told us, were painful to say. For many present, they were obviously painful to hear.

'I am deeply patriotic,' Mr Cameron began, his suit black, his back ramrod-straight. 'I never want to believe anything bad about our country.' Then he said, 'But...' and the ranks of MPs grew utterly still, another rare occurrence in the chamber. 'What happened on Bloody Sunday was unjustified and unjustifiable,' said the Prime Minister. 'It was wrong.'

His words could not have been more measured if they had been accompanied by a drum beat. There was a clarity that no one could misinterpret. His apology, when it came, seemed the only thing that he could do. And it, too, rang out like a bell. Everyone's eyes were on him, including those of the Rev Ian Paisley, up in the gallery, his gravel voice mute for once.

For some in the public gallery the words of Mark Durkan of the SDLP were too much to bear. He read out the names and ages of the thirteen who died on the day, his voice breaking occasionally. He gave us the words of the great Seamus Heaney in his poem *The Road to Derry*:

'My heart besieged by anger, my mind a gap of danger,
I walked among their old haunts, the home ground
where they bled;
And in the dirt lay justice like an acorn in the winter
Till its oak would sprout in Derry
where the thirteen men lay dead.'

But, Mr Durkan said, the most poignant words were not those of a poet or a Prime Minister, but those of the relatives who could now stand at the graves and talk to their loved ones. 'When they do so, they can invoke the civil rights anthem: We have overcome, we have overcome this day...' He choked.

Directly behind him sat members of the DUP, fearful, angry and grieving for those who died at the hands of terrorists but who had had no expensive inquiries. The Rev William McCrea said there was no 'hierarchy of victimhood'. He told us of his cousin Derek, gunned down in April 1991 – 'his child was left to put the fingers into the holes where the blood was coming out'. Two other cousins were killed in 1976 – one was just sixteen, the other, aged twenty-one, had died on her engagement day. 'How do we get closure?' he asked tearfully. 'How do we get the truth?'

Mr Cameron, no stranger to grief having lost his young son only last year, maintained a careful tone of understanding and balance throughout the one hour and fifteen minutes. At the very end the Tory MP Kris Hopkins, who had served as a soldier in Northern Ireland, said how difficult it had been to listen to the statement. Only now did Mr Cameron get more personal. 'It is a difficult statement to make,' he said. 'It is a difficult statement to listen to because it's got some very uncomfortable truths for people who, like me, are deeply patriotic, who love the British Army, who love what it stands for, who revere what they have done down the ages. It's incredibly painful to say it. But we don't serve them if we don't say it.'

When it was over, there was relief, as if a long funeral had finally ended. ❦

17 June 2010
Oh, the rapture of it all! Was Dave blushing?

With the Tory lickspittle flowing, I realised how much I missed the sound of Nick's voice

This is as good as it will ever get for David Cameron. He is in a post-election, pre-Budget haze of hope. It's as if he's living in a shampoo commercial. The Opposition, obsessed with their leadership contest, hardly exists.

Indeed Dave's only real problem yesterday was that the sycophancy was so great, the love so blind, the desire to get his attention so total, that it was embarrassing – even for him.

'Can I praise the Prime Minister,' began Harriett Baldwin, a new be-pearled Tory who seemed to be channelling Uriah Heep. Labour MPs howled, but Harriett was not going to let them stem the flow of her lickspittle. She shouted: 'For his staunch support of the NHS.'

Dave preened. He refuses to take any responsibility for the economy but is happy to take credit for the NHS. Harriett, who may be new but, at fifty, should know better, asked her tough question: Would Dave come to Malvern to see the great NHS? This brought more hoots. Even Dave could not keep a straight face amid the derision. 'Don't be, ahhh…' he said to chortling MPs. 'Don't be so…' Was the Tory leader actually blushing?

Now the Speaker, John Bercow, who knows a thing or two about sycophancy, jumped to Harriett's aid, saying that it was not against the rules for a backbencher to support the Government. 'It is not that odd,' he burbled.

Dave agreed. 'Mr Speaker, we all remember you doing that very well.' The whole House rocked with laughter, for Mr Speaker is viewed by many Tories as a Labour-loving traitor. Mr Bercow, who adores being the centre of attention, jiggled up and down with mirth in his oversized *Alice in Wonderland* chair. It's as if democracy has gone on holiday.

I never thought I'd say this, but I miss Nick. Free the Lib Dem One. Yesterday he was showing signs of captive fatigue as he sat by Dave, his head nodding up and down, up and down, all the time. Dave used to agree with Nick. Now Nick agrees only mutely with Dave. It's a sad state of affairs.

Some Liberal Democrats cannot even bear to sit on their benches (Charles Kennedy has never been seen there). The official Opposition, Labour, is a shell of its former self, interested only in its own navel. Gordon Brown has not been seen since he left for the Palace. This is a man who actually wrote a book called *Courage*. Now we can track him only via his wife's Tweets. (Guess what? She tweets that she is also writing a book, called *Behind the Black Door*.)

So it's up to Harriet – (Harman) the other one; suddenly there are too many – to carry the torch for the party. Yesterday she was lacklustre as she accused Dave over the economy. 'It's not so much magic numbers,' she said, voice faltering, 'it's a Magic Roundabout he's on!'

Dave pounced. 'The figures were wrong and the jokes weren't much good either,' he said as the sycophants laughed. Forget *The Magic Roundabout*, he said, he's enjoying the Labour leadership context. 'Though it is starting to look more like a *Star Trek* convention.' The Tories adored this. 'Beam me up,' cried Dave. If only. ❦

18 June 2010
Beaker makes a mess of his big day

Danny Alexander, the man who replaced David Laws, tried
not to make a Muppet out of himself

It was Danny A's first big event in the Commons and it was, as they say, a scorcher. Mr Alexander, who looks too much like Beaker the Muppet for there not to be some shared DNA, had come to drop an £11.5 billion austerity bombshell. Labour, furious, was on the rampage.

Danny A was nervous, as any novice at running with the bulls would be. His hands shook as he told us the news, blaming it all on Labour's pre-election spending splurge, his voice almost a monotone, his delivery appalling. (Beaker, if you are reading this, sue!)

'We did not make this mess,' the Chief Secretary said in his only memorable line, 'but we will clean it up!' Liam Byrne lunged at the dispatch box. I feared he would raise it above his head and throw it. Instead, he vented his fury as only he could – by quoting Shaw. 'I think it was George Bernard Shaw who said that sometimes to succeed in politics you have to rise above your principles,' he sneered, 'and few have risen so fast and so far as you this morning.'

Danny, who looks as if he should be doing his A Levels and who wears a look of permanent surprise, blinked as if dazzled by headlights. Mr Byrne, an obsessive management consultant type who formerly rarely raised his voice, was now ranting and jabbing his finger. From the side, with his bald head and his mouth permanently open, he looked like an enraged version of the Pacman video game character.

Danny A was a traitor to Lib Dems everywhere. He had just cancelled a hospital. 'Let me ask you: what could be more front-line than this?' snarled Liam. 'In five minutes you have reversed three years of Liberal Democratic policy, of which you were the principal author. What a moment of abject humiliation!' There was more blinking from Danny A. I almost felt sorry for him. I'm sure that David Laws, watching on Parliament TV somewhere, must be flinching. Liam finished in a blaze of fury and threw himself into his seat with force, like a crash-test dummy.

Mr A chuntered that Liam had gone on a spending spree. Other Liam crimes included writing a note to his successor, David Laws, that said: 'I'm afraid there is no money, good luck.' But, Danny A now revealed, he too had got a note – from David Laws. 'His advice was rather more helpful. He left me a note that said: "Good luck. Carry on cutting with care".' Are these people for real? With all these notes, it's like a Jane Austen spoof. ❣

30 June 2010
Speaker ignores 'dwarf' abuse

No one could believe it when a Health Minister launched a vitriolic personal attack on the vertically challenged Speaker

I fear for the health, not to say career, of the new Health Minister Simon Burns. Yesterday Mr Burns went berserk – a technical term, but it was Health Questions so everyone understood – in the Commons, not against the Opposition but the Speaker. Why? Well, like all rage attacks, it was something that would seem tiny to you and me.

It all began when Mr Burns had turned round to answer a question from a Tory backbencher. 'Patients are going to be at the heart of the NHS,' said Mr Burns, his head rotating back like an owl. At this, Little Johnnie Bercow interrupted: 'Can I very gently say to the minister, can you face the House?'

Labour MPs cheered. But Mr Burns, who is fifty-seven with a florid beefy look and urbane manner about him, seemed perfectly normal (always a relative term in the chamber). But then fast-forward almost an hour when, once again, Mr Burns was busy murdering the English language, this time his whole body turned backwards.

Labour MPs complained that they couldn't hear. 'You must face the House,' insisted Mr Speaker. 'It's a very simple point. I have made it to others and they have understood it.'

Mr Burns sat down and then, suddenly, exploded, his body contorting, rocking from buttock to buttock, his head bobbing like a cork. 'Stupid,' he said. 'Stupid.'

It was a verbal Mr Creosote moment. Everyone was transfixed. Mr Burns was babbling, incandescent, apoplectic, splenetic. Among the words he fumed was 'sanctimonious'. Mr Bercow ignored him, calling another MP who asked a question on something (literally no one was listening). Then, Mr Burns made a diminutive gesture with his hands and said, clearly: 'Dwarf'.

Mr Bercow, who admits to being vertically challenged, pretended not to hear. It was left to the excitable Tory MP Michael Fabricant, looking splendid in his buttercup-yellow summer wig, to lay a soothing hand on Mr Burns's shoulder. You know things are out of control when Micky Fab is a calming influence. Many Tories feel that Mr Bercow betrayed their party, but I have never seen it spill so rawly into the open.

Mr Burns, still in a state, finally left but, during points of order, Ian Paisley arose like the ghost of his father. 'Is it in order,' he asked, 'for a member of the front bench to berate, scoff, scold and hiss at the chair whilst a member is trying to ask a question?'

Mr Bercow listened, head cocked, as if this was breaking news. He said the incident had not been 'recorded' as he had been focusing on the whole chamber. This seemed unlikely, as if he had somehow missed Vesuvius. But now Mr Speaker came over all, well, sanctimonious. 'I hope that it won't be necessary in the course of this, the new Parliament and the new politics, for that point to have to be made from the chair again,' he said primly.

In the hours that followed, Mr Burns did not deny that he'd called the Speaker a 'stupid sanctimonious dwarf' and Mr Bercow's Labour wife, Sally, tweeted: 'So much for the new politics, eh, Mr Burns.' She referred to 'nasty Tories' and 'low grade abuse'.

Her final response (she packs a lot in to one tweet): 'Mr B is Speaker so get over it!' To which I can add only: 'Stretcher!' ♥

(P.S. The following day a Labour MP noted that Mr Speaker had been 'getting short' with ministers. At this, Mr Bercow beamed with happiness (he loves attention of any kind): 'I'm not sure about that but what I would say is that I've always been short. And I'm entirely untroubled by the fact. Which is probably as well.')

2 July 2010
Clegg is bright-eyed and bushy-tailed

Nick tells us how we can be free, not least from the menace of squirrel red tape (actually, make that grey tape)

I bring you wildlife news from the launch of Nick Clegg's 'Your Freedom' campaign. For weeks now, I have been wondering what he does. I don't want to belittle his career as a fig-leaf but it is hardly onerous. Dave gets to swan around the world. George rips up budgets. Even Danny A has cancelled a few cheques. But Nick's role has seemed ceremonial – think Prince Philip, but with the extra responsibility of wearing a yellow tie – until now.

Yesterday, Nick took his first actual decision as Deputy Prime Minister. It was an amnesty for grey squirrels. I must admit I had no idea he felt so strongly about those thuggish American rats with bushy tails (sorry, but it had to be said). But then I remembered that the Lib Dems are so soft-hearted that they tried to ban the use of goldfish as fairground prizes.

The speech was at something called the Idea Store in East London (basically a library with twiddly bits and an espresso machine). At first he tried to pretend it was all about people. 'I want to talk about freedom,' he said. The State has 'crept' into our homes, our offices, our private lives. That was going to stop. Nick wants a freer society. 'Today I am asking the people of Britain to help us begin building that society.'

The fifty people of Britain in the room had no visible reaction.

Then, suddenly, without warning, he announced: 'It is a little-known fact – I discovered this yesterday – that under old laws that are still in place, failing to report a grey squirrel in your back garden is technically a criminal offence. That is one I think we could probably do without.'

Little-known fact? I am sorry but some of us are hardly off the phone on this one. Some of us have got 'Police – Grey Squirrel Sightings' on speed dial. Forget the State creeping into my private life, what about the grey squirrel in my garden? I have actually sourced squirrel recipes. As *The L.L. Bean Game & Fish Cookbook* says: 'Squirrel meat is the most delicious of all small games. Young squirrel is better than rabbit or chicken.'

Nick wants us all to log on to the 'Your Freedom' website to give him our top recipes (sorry, tips). In addition, you can watch Nick on his own YouTube channel offering tips on how to be free. William Wilberforce, eat your heart out.

Nick wants his freedom debate to be 'raucous'. Well, yesterday the Twittersphere went crazy on squirrels. The Labour MP Kerry McCarthy tweeted: 'I suspect scrapping grey squirrel law is the closest Clegg gets to implementing Lib policy on amnesty for illegal immigrants.'

As I write, the political fallout continues. For, of course, by granting an amnesty for greys, the civil rights of the reds may be impeded. Squirrel Nutkin could yet be in the chamber. Indeed, it is a little-known fact (another one) that only five years ago Danny A, as press officer for the Cairngorms National Park Authority, was writing press releases about saving the reds. In the chamber

yesterday the irascible Labour MP Barry Sheerman said that he
felt 'pity' for the DPM. 'What on earth is going on in his department?' he said. It is, as the squirrels would say, nuts. ❦

6 July 2010
Lesson in how to influence no one

*Nick unveils his plans to 'empower' people with an AV referen-
dum with Dave (who is against, of course) by his side*

It was Nick's moment in the limelight. Dave slipped in early,
next to him. The two men – still on honeymoon, incredibly,
after seven weeks – smiled at each other in their special way.
At first it went fine. Dave glowed with pride and, at one point,
even poured a glass of water for him.

Nick wants to 'empower' (ghastly word) the people by giving
them a vote on the alternative vote and new constituency boundaries. It may sound laudable but, in the chamber, there was only
carping. His reaction was a masterclass in how to lose friends and
influence no one.

Labour began by having a bit of fun. Jack Straw, who is having
a whale of a time in Opposition, said that before the election
Nick had called AV 'a miserable little compromise'. What, Jack
wondered, had changed his mind? 'POWER,' cried MPs.

Nick pretended not to hear, but it must hurt. Over the next hour
he attacked Labour MPs with a viciousness that made me wonder
if the Dangerous Dogs Act should be extended. Among his kinder
descriptions were paranoid, churlish, patronising and stagnating.

It was all very entertaining, except for one tiny detail. Nick
needs these people.

It is the paranoid, churlish Labour MPs who are going to back
him on AV – not Dave, who, no matter how many glasses of
water he pours, is against it.

Labour's Austin Mitchell said it was a shame that Nick didn't have the 'guts' to fight for proportional representation. The new constituencies would only hurt Labour. It was, he said, 'the biggest gerrymander in British history'.

Nick stung back, saying that only in the 'weird and wonderful' introverted world of Labour would this be seen as gerrymandering. Gerrymander was the word of the day. It comes from Elbridge Gerry, an American who presided over bizarre changes to legislative districts (one looked like a salamander). So what does Nick have in common with that lizard? Labour thinks it knows. ❦

7 July 2010
Dave, or 'D', acclaims Smiley's people

Our Prime Minister sets up an inquiry to tell us everything and nothing about the treatment of detainees

It was a masterful statement by Dave who, perhaps for the purposes of yesterday, should be referred to here only as D. I am sure that C approved. Indeed at one point D told us that C approved and so I think I can tell you that. In general, D told us everything and nothing.

Indeed, he is setting up an inquiry which may or may not tell us everything and nothing. I could hear the susurrating sound of a broom making a clean sweep.

The statement was called 'Treatment of Detainees' but it wasn't about that at all. It was about finding a practical way out of the moral maze that Britain finds itself in, with allegations flying round about what our spies, post 9/11, knew about the treatment of detainees being held by other countries. These had led to court cases and a loss of reputation. D said enough was enough. He wanted to pay these people off (I paraphrase) and clear the air with an inquiry. He does not want to look back.

'The point here is we want to clear the decks!' he said in his youthful, forceful way. 'We want to sort this problem out! So why not try and mediate the existing civil cases, roll them all up, deal with them, then hold the inquiry, get to bottom of what happened, set out the guidance for the future? So we will have removed the stain on Britain's reputation!'

See how he makes it sound both easy and complicated at the same time? The whole event had a marvellously old-fashioned feel to it. Somehow, like a magician who pulls a dove out of his hand, D managed to turn the whole event into a paean of praise for our spies. 'I believe we have the finest intelligence services in the world,' he said.

I felt that, in an ideal world – and D was very much painting a picture of an ideal world – 'Land of Hope and Glory' would have been playing softly.

Our spies had cracked Enigma and kept us safe in the Cold War. 'Today, these tremendous acts of bravery continue.' They died, as they lived, in secrecy. 'Their loved ones must mourn in secret,' he said.

D said that, even as he spoke, the enemy was busy. In Northern Ireland, the Real IRA was busy. In Yemen, al-Qaeda operatives were plotting. In Afghanistan, terrorists were planning to attack our forces.

'At the same time men and women, young and old, all of them loyal and dedicated, are getting ready to work again around the world,' said D. 'They are meeting sources, translating documents, listening in on conversations, replaying CCTV footage, installing cameras following terrorists. All to keep us safe.' I just knew that, out there, in the shadows where they must live, against all odds, Smiley's people were smiling. ❦

8 July 2010
Mum's the word — but Dave just can't keep it

*Harriet compliments Dave for listening to his mum and not
his new partner Nick*

Are you sitting comfortably? Then I'll begin. Or, rather, Harriet will. Sometimes — and it's entirely by accident — Harriet Harman hits Dave where it hurts. Yesterday, in her weekly bumper-car ride at PMQs, she asked about his mother and I swear I saw him flinch.

His mother Mary, seventy-five, is truly formidable. Rarely allowed out by the Tories, this is her only public comment on her son: 'He always had something to say. Even when he was five or six — and went on holiday with another family — they'd say, "For heaven's sake, can't you shut David up?"'

During the election, he couldn't shut up about how his mum was a magistrate in Newbury who loved short prison sentences. Now the coalition has declared war on them. But that didn't stop Dave from claiming the opposite yesterday. Harriet took him at his word: 'May I congratulate the Prime Minister on, instead of listening to his new partner, listening to his mother? Quite often, that is the right thing.'

Nick Clegg froze, his head in mid-bob. The Justice Secretary, Kenneth Clarke, beamed. Despite this, Harriet claimed that Ken wasn't looking so cheerful. 'Perhaps you should go down to Ronnie Scott's to cheer yourself up,' she said. But Ken, belly wobbling, looked ecstatic. He doesn't need to go anywhere to cheer up. He is a one-man *Prozac Nation*.

Dave burbled on. 'I am delighted that you have brought up the issue of my mother.' The issue of my mother? Mothers are many things, Dave, but they aren't issues. 'For heaven's sake, can't you shut up?' said a voice.

We heard again that his mother was a magistrate in Newbury.
'I have to say that one of the biggest challenges she had…,' he
said as a Labour MP shouted: 'You!' Dave stopped before trilling:
'As well as me.'

Amid hilarity, Dave ploughed on. 'One of the reasons why she
needed to hand out so many short sentences, was badly behaved
CND protesters outside Greenham Common.'

The Tories loved this. Harriet the Harperson looked unim-
pressed. 'She was there,' shouted someone about Harriet. 'I do not
know whether you were there,' noted Dave. (I think I could hear
his mother shouting in the background: 'Shut up.') 'Anyway,' he
trilled. 'If you want to have more episodes of *Listen With Mother*,
I am very happy for that at any time.'

Like hell he is. Harriet, as dogmatic as a drone, asked whether
budget cuts would mean fewer police? 'Of course there will be
difficult decisions,' tap-danced Dave to jeers. But, Harriet asked,
wouldn't fewer police mean crime would go up? Would he promise it wouldn't?

'I can promise you one thing. I will not be wandering round
my constituency in a stab-proof vest,' he pranced. Harriet looked
like, well, a mother observing a naughty child. But then Dave
doesn't need a stab-proof vest. He's got Nick. But again I heard a
voice: 'For heaven's sake, Dave…' ♥

9 July 2010
Prezza the Erminator: he is back and it's personal

*I thought it would never happen but John Prescott has indeed
embraced 'flunkery'*

He is already being called The Erminator. Others had less
kind words to describe the newly ennobled Lord Prescott
of Kingston-upon-Hull. 'Isn't he calling everyone else in

Labour a hypocrite these days?' huffed an MP. A peer, rushing in to see the great event, said: 'It's a laugh, isn't it?'

Actually, it's more than that. The little ermines of the world never thought that they would be troubled by the likes of Prezza. Yes, he likes croquet. Yes, he likes a Jag (or two). Yes, he thinks he's middle class but only two years ago, when asked about the Lords, he reportedly said: 'I'm against too much flunkery and titles. But Pauline would like me to. I tell her, "What do you want to be Lady Prescott for? You're a lady already".'

It was fitting, then, that the first person I saw, teetering on black peep-toes in the peers' lobby, was Our Pauline. She looked as if she had stepped out of *Dynasty*. Spotless white suit. Black hat like an awning. So big, in fact, that I could just see only the tips of her spidery eyelashes. Given the opinions of his lordship (as Prezza now must be called), the hat was particularly impressive. 'I can't stand her big hats,' he has said. 'She has a bloody Berlin Wall of them. I used to get a member of my staff to walk beside her at the State Opening because I was embarrassed by her hats, which you can shelter under if it's raining.'

The only thing it was raining yesterday was flunkeys. The peers flooded in to watch Prezza. Labour's royal couple, Neil and Glenys, were there. Blairites and Brownites filled the benches. I saw Dennis Turner, now Lord Bilston, who as an MP was in charge of the catering committee. New Labour, new toffocracy.

Forget the flunkery, feel the flummery and the frou-frou. The Yeoman Usher led the procession, patent-leather slippers gleaming. He was followed by a man dressed as a playing card. Then came the heavy uneven walk of Prezza, his robe just about hiding that chip on his shoulder. The reading clerk, who often flips the tiny pigtails attached to his periwig, looked as if he was struggling to keep a straight face.

Mr Pigtail read out the scroll from the Queen. 'Greeting!' His voice, so mellifluous, seemed to be speaking a different language though, for Prezza, that is normal. The clerk welcomed 'our right trusty and well-beloved John Leslie Prescott'. I couldn't help but think that, in different times, Prezza might have punched a man in pigtails who called him beloved. Prezza must 'sit among the barons'. He must 'enjoy and use all the rights, privileges, pre-eminences, immunities and advantages' of being among the barons. Somehow I don't think that is going to be a problem for the king of Dorneywood.

The moment was approaching when he had to open his mouth. A nation tensed. 'I, John, Lord Prescott,' he said, lisp banished. He'd been practising in front of the mirror. It worked. He swore allegiance to the Queen and kept God out of it. He was word-perfect. When it was done, peers gave him a hearty cheer and two claps. Prezza, toff-hater, is one of them now. Up in the gallery, Lady Prescott looked thrilled. ♥

13 July 2010
Meerkat is left counting his lists

The Education Secretary just can't seem to compile a list without any errors. Surely, this is a case of 'could do better'?

I fear that Michael Gove, Education Secretary and meerkat lookalike, is becoming addicted to lists. Over the past week, Mr Gove has issued no fewer than four lists about axed school building projects, all of them flawed. Yesterday he came to the Commons, back straight, paws up, huge eyes blinking like crazy. He was beyond himself with excitement.

He got a big orchestrated cheer when he stood up. That's not a good sign. The press gallery was full. Also a bad sign. Where hacks circle, vultures follow. We could all see that when the going gets tough, the tough get blinking. He stood up, pointing his trigger finger at his Labour opponent Ed Balls, eyelids banging up and down like pistons.

We settled in to watch the fight. It was quite a spectacle. Imagine a bullfight but where the matador is a meerkat. Mr Gove is clever, fast-talking, superior, patronising. Mr Balls charges around, head-butting away, a blunt instrument, dogmatic and powerful. They kept accusing each other of being dysfunctional. I have to say, we were looking at exactly that.

Ed shouted: 'You must now know that there is widespread anger on all sides of the House.' He'd written to Gove with questions about his flawed lists but, in reply, he'd received a piece of paper that he now waved in the air as if it were a grey bit of underwear that he had to pin out on a public washing line. 'List Number Five!' he cried.

Mr Gove snapped back: 'You say there was anger across the House! There was! The anger was about the way the Building Schools for the Future had been run by you!' Mr Gove, over-acting, back arched, eyes almost in orbit, shouted: 'I inherited a mess from you. We are clearing it up!' At this, he fell theatrically back into his seat, one leg out straight, eyes still fixed across the chamber in the same way that ballerinas, when spinning, stay focused on one point.

Indeed, he said it was entirely Ed's fault that he'd had to issue List Number Five. 'Because of the dysfunctional system that we inherited, it has been difficult to establish the absolute truth about the numbers of schools affected.' (Earlier he claimed that when things go wrong, he took responsibility. I'm sure you can see how that is true.)

As Michael the Meerkat performed, I could see Mr Balls looking at his rather old-fashioned mobile phone. Even Mr Gove's accusation that he was 'dirigiste' did not catch his attention. Soon Mr Balls stood up and announced, again with much theatricality (Equity must throw them out, they are so bad): 'It will be no surprise to know that already, within twenty-five minutes, the first mistake within this list has already been found!' Labour MPs began flashing six fingers at him (presumably anticipating List Number Six).

The Meerkat snarled at this. It is clear that the list thing is out of control. So here's my little list for Michael Gove.

How to make a list:
1. Compile it;
2. Check it until you are sure it's right;
3. Er, that's it.
I know it's irritating but is it really that hard? 💔

21 July 2010
Vince dances the quango, everybody yawns

I watched, aghast, as Vince Cable transformed into a greying econo-bore

I feel that I need to report a theft to the police. Stolen from us: the most incisive man in politics. Yesterday I watched as Vince Cable appeared before a select committee, his Benjamin Franklin half-moon specs so far down his nose that they were teetering on the edge. They served no purpose, for he read nothing out. They, like him, seemed unreal.

The Business, Innovation and Skills Committee is headed by Labour's Adrian Bailey, who has all the charisma of a librarian (apologies to all librarians). Mr Bailey asked Vince, almost tentatively, about his much-heralded cull of quangoes.

'I think we have something like seventy-eight partner organisations,' said the man who used to be Vince. Partner agencies? Do-si-do your partner if you must, but no one ever danced (even Vince, who loves to dance) with a quango. In the end, Vince said, about one-third of the partners will go.

'When will we know?' squeaked Mr Bailey.

'Announcements are being made in cases of individual bodies,' said Vince, infuriatingly vague as Mr Bailey looked grateful. I glanced round the room. The Vince groupies were already looking shellshocked. Their hero was scoring zero.

Mr Bailey handed the questioning over to the new Labour MP Jack Dromey, aka Mr Harriet Harman. 'Thank you chairman,' said Jack. I do hope Harriet doesn't hear that 'man'. She'll have to send her husband off to gender indoctrination training.

Mr Dromey and others are upset because Vince is getting rid of regional development agencies (RDAs). I settled in and waited for Vince to tell it like it is. How many times have I heard him, in Opposition, rail against these unelected expensive bodies? But now I waited in vain.

So, he was asked, did he have an Anne Boleyn strategy? The half-moon specs trembled. 'I use more neutral language,' he said.

How scary is that? Vince used to call a spade a spade, now he would no doubt call it a non-mechanical soil disturbance facilitator. He told us that RDAs would go but in their place would be something new called LEPs. I listened with incredulity. Vince used to abhor acronyms. The Vincettes were starting to flee the room.

Vince and his human shield, David Willetts, were asked about the fate of the 150,000 young people who would not get a place at university this year. Their answers were fatuous. 'We are working very hard to improve the quality of careers advice,' Mr Willetts said, while the half-moons nodded.

There was a time when Vince would excoriate such drivel. At the moment he, and some others in the Cabinet, are getting away with the parliamentary equivalent of murder. It's hot. It's the end of term. Labour is in chaos. Certainly the committee yesterday seemed in awe. I don't know why. The In-Vince-Able has become Mr Insufferable. ♥

22 July 2010
Glove puppet needs hand to stay out of trouble

Nick, standing in for Dave at PMQs, has an historic moment as he declares the Iraq War illegal

Nick Clegg stood in for Dave at PMQs – quite a feat for a glove puppet – and the chaos began even before it started. You may think this impossible, but these are the Lib Dems we're talking about.

The day started with a trumpet fanfare that Nick would be making history as the first Liberal leader to do PMQs since Lloyd George in 1922. Except someone remembered that Lloyd George wasn't actually leader then. So then the trumpets blew that Nick was the first since Asquith in 1916. But then someone remembered that PMQs didn't start until 1961.

Argghhhhh! Forget the trumpets, get out the kazoos. So, it's official then: Nick Clegg is the first glove puppet to stand in at PMQs ever.

George Osborne, next to him, kept telling him what to do, but Nick – free at last – wanted to be his own man. All I can say is – WOW! In half an hour, Nick really did change the world. His biggest moment came when he declared the Iraq War to be illegal. Just like that. I felt sorry for the Chilcot Inquiry, labouring away across the road, calling witnesses, sifting through reams of evidence, asking spies what they think.

Nick's ruling came at the end of furious exchanges with Jack Straw, who accused Nick of betraying his beliefs. Nick told him to stop bellowing and then, gathering all the breath he could muster (glove-puppet lungs are notoriously unreliable) he mini-bellowed: 'We may have to wait for your memoirs, but perhaps one day you will account for your role in the most disastrous decision of all: the illegal invasion of Eeee-raq!' (Or, as Lloyd George would have put it: 'Mes-o-po-tamia!')

A Lib Dem named Julian Huppert decried the detention of children at Yarl's Wood detention centre. What was Nick going to do? Railing against the illegal warmongering Labourites who had imprisoned children there, Nick said he was closing it 'for good'.

Cue tumultuous excitement. It took a Welsh nationalist to bring Nick down to Earth. Elfyn Llwyd noted that Nick had, in a recent interview, said: 'I am a revolutionary but I am also a pragmatist.' MPs screamed with hilarity. Mr Llwyd asked acidly: 'When you agreed to raise VAT, were you being a revolutionary pragmatist or a pragmatic revolutionary?' Nick ignored the question (for he was, of course, being only a glove puppet). Later, sadly, it turned out that Nick was wrong about E-raq and Yarl's Wood. Dave will be pleased. 💔

23 July 2010
When the cat is away...

...the mice will play, as beleaguered Nick Clegg was finding out

I bring you vermin news from Westminster. The mice are back, scampering around the tea rooms, nibbling at the fabric of our nation. In another development, almost certainly linked, Calamity Clegg has tightened his grip on power. It is now official: when Dave is on hols, the glove puppet will be in charge.

'Eek,' as the lady said to the mouse. Actually, I think we can blame Dave for both events. For we know what happens when the cat is away. And Dave has most definitely been away, eating hot dogs without mustard in America. Meanwhile, back home, Nick has been in charge – relishing it (sorry) – creating total chaos.

First, vermin news. A Tory MP announced in the Commons that rodents are in the tea room.

'Rats!' shouted Labour MPs.

'It is indeed the case that mice are seen on the parliamentary estate,' Sir George Young, the posh giraffe-like Leader of the House, said. 'And I have actually seen an Honourable Member feeding them out of...' – he seemed overwhelmed – '...kindness.'

This brought screams, although no one jumped on a chair. I don't think kindness has anything to do with it. It is just empathy. Yesterday there was much rattery about, with MPs doing their

best to create the perfect storm around Mr Clegg after his powerful performance at PMQs in which he outlawed the Iraq War
(although, later, sadly, he had to admit that he was only speaking
personally).

'Should the title Deputy Prime Minister be changed to
Deputy Prime Minister in a Personal Capacity?' asked Wayne
David, a man with two first names who should know better. One
Labour MP urged Lib Dems to adopt a dress code: blue on one
side, yellow on the other. When speaking personally, they would
turn to the yellow side. Otherwise, they would be true blue. The
Tories thought this hilarious.

This did not stop the sneermeister Dennis Skinner from
demanding Nick come and tell the truth. 'Stop this silly nonsense
about personal statements!' cried Mr Skinner, a living personal
statement.

But it was a Tory, Peter Bone, who asked the big question as
the mice cheered. Who, he asked, will be in charge when the PM
goes on holiday? The Home Secretary, the Foreign Secretary or
the Chancellor? Hmmm. Let me see, who did he leave out?

Sir George, weary now, said: 'As you know, we have a Deputy
Prime Minister.' More screams. So we do. I smell a rat but then,
it's Westminster. ♥

27 July 2010
It's time to call 101

There was an outbreak of anti-social behaviour as Home
Secretary Theresa May explained how she is going to fight crime

Theresa May wants us to have a new national crime-fighting
number – 101. It's for antisocial behaviour and non-emergency
crime. In other words, exactly what went on in the House of
Commons yesterday. I fear it will be inundated, not least by me.

Mrs May, dressed in her high-collared *Star Trek* outfit, is bringing power to the people. Police commissioners are going to be elected. She's empowering (the language alone is worth a 101 call) frontline staff. 'They will no longer be form writers, but crime fighters.' Oh no, it rhymed. I don't think I can make another call to 101 so soon.

Alan Johnson began to foam. 'This statement should be called Policing in the Twenty-First Century – How to Make Their Job Harder,' he sneered. 'You, as usual, trot out the infantile drivel about the last Labour Government, probably written by some pimply nerd foisted upon your office by No. 10.'

Infantile drivel? Pimply nerd? I looked over in the civil servant box and saw someone who might fit that description – moustachioed, bespectacled, intensely writing as if his life depended on it. This man looked born to toil in the shadows.

No longer. What's happened to Alan Johnson? Everyone used to say that he was far too nice to be leader of the Labour Party. The apple cheeks glowed, the banter flowed, he was the ex-postie with the mostie. Now it's no more Mr Nice Guy. Does 101 know? He explained that Mrs May had inherited a land of peace and harmony from him; crime had been slashed. She should be grateful, but instead she had unleashed a triple whammy. First came the cuts, then the restrictions on CCTV. And now she had the audacity to try to impose democracy on the police. Wham, wham, wham! Mrs May was a serial offender, a whamaholic.

AJ, spluttering, cheeks on fire, said that Mrs May was driven by dogma and that she was going to drive a coach and horses through police accountability. Is it even possible to do both of those things at the same time? If so, I fear it's another 101 call.

Mrs May hit back – hard. She was rather good. She even clubbed Caroline Lucas, the Green MP who is generally treated as some sort of cuddly mascot. Dr Lucas criticised the idea of elected commissioners, saying that they would be picked for their party. Mrs May snapped that police were not allowed to join any party. WHAM. She accused Dr Lucas of having a 'jaundiced view' of the British people. WHAM. It was like watching a baby-seal clubbing. Hello, is that 101? ❦

28 July 2010
Yee-haw, it's Calamity Clegg to the rescue

There is much gaiety as MPs revelled in the news that the Tories are calling the government the 'Brokeback Coalition'

The Commons was in a 'yee-haw!' mood. Rowdy doesn't even begin to cover it. The last day of the parliamentary term began with Deputy Prime Minister's Questions, starring Nick Clegg, and there was no escaping the *Brokeback Mountain* theme, the movie metaphor that is obsessing Westminster. 'On the assumption that the Prime Minister and you aren't holidaying together in Montana,' began Jack Straw, with one of his smirks.

Never mind that the two gay cowboys actually were in Wyoming, not Montana. Well, they were fictional but there is truth in fiction too. Anyway MPs were too busy yee-hawing to care about geography. Ever since it got out that senior Tories refer to the Government as the 'Brokeback coalition', no one has stopped giggling. I find the comparison odd. *Brokeback* is a sad film with a tragic ending. Surely Nick and Dave's happy smiling coalition is more a romcom, polcom, sitcom type thing (provisionally entitled *Our Two Gay Dads*)? But there is no getting away from the fact that MPs love the idea of Nick and Dave as gay cowboys. And Nick has been Calamity Clegg for some time.

Mr Straw did get around to asking if and when Calamity would be in charge of the country. 'The Prime Minister will be taking his vacation in the second half of August,' said Nick. 'He remains Prime Minister. He remains overall in charge of this Government. But I will be available to hold the fort.'

Hold the fort! MPs whooped even more. I felt we were,

almost, home on the range. Or, as the song goes, 'Yippy-yi-o, yippy-yi-a!' Still, Calamity made a pretty strange cowboy in his beautifully cut Paul Smith suit, the only metrosexual in the OK Corral who could, if he had to, take his question time in Dutch, French, Spanish or German. It just wasn't very John Wayne.

And Big John never bothered too much about the alternative vote. Calamity does little else. Yesterday he came under fire from all sides, notably from Edward Leigh, the Tory right-winger who began by calling Calamity his 'new and best Right Honourable Friend'. More giggles at that. Mr Leigh noted that, under the AV system, the Tories in 1997 would have been reduced to a 'pathetic rump' of sixty-five MPs. Mr Leigh is against AV. He wants a separate election date and a 'proper debate'.

The Western theme continued. Calamity used the word 'bonanza'. *Bonanza!* The second longest American Western television series next to *Gunsmoke*. I began to see that Calamity might be a real cowboy after all. He's not afraid of a fight. As he talked of voter registration pitfalls, the Labour stalwart Fiona MacTaggart shrieked: 'What are you doing about it?' Calamity looked miffed. 'You scream from a sedentary position,' he said, before screaming right back: 'But what did you do about it for thirteen years?' The noise level kept going up, as they shouted about the Iraq War, cuts, the size of constituencies etc.

Calamity strode though it all, as bow-legged as Big John, pistols at his side, his faithful horse (Chris Huhne?) tethered nearby. Well, I guess, in the immortal words of Big John: a man's gotta do what a man's gotta do. And this man's fighting. ❧

Chapter Five

A Marriage in the National Interest

The coalition marked its first 100 days in office in mid-August, the most dogged of the dog days, with no trumpets and a very long sigh of relief. Summer politics were a dire mix of AV and Labour leadership. In late August, the Camerons' Cornish 'staycation' was interrupted by the birth of Florence Rose Endellion Cameron (Endellion was the village they were staying in). MPs were back in September, braced for the unions' much heralded autumn of unrest, a new Labour leader and the ongoing saga of the Lib-Dem crisis in confidence. The rumour that Nick and Dave might get a quickie divorce was quickly squashed. They even had a day-trip honeymoon to romantic Nottingham. But no one could say that the couple weren't having their marriage tested as Nick ended up being burnt in effigy by an angry mob… 💔

7 September 2010
Nick is a statesman in short trousers

Dave was off on paternity leave with Baby Flo, leaving Nick to face the Commons alone as he sang the praises of his AV referendum. It didn't go well.

I don't know if Little Nicky Clegg has a recurring nightmare about the first day of school where he stands up in class, rabbiting on, as everyone pelts him with rotten eggs.

He looks down and he's naked. If so, it's not a nightmare. It's his life.

'We promised a new politics,' he said about his plans for a referendum on AV. 'Today is the day we must begin to deliver!' MPs groaned, sneered and catcalled; mockery filling the air like a noxious cloud.

Labour and the Tories have united in disgust for Nicky's brave new world of redrawn constituency boundaries, fewer MPs and a vote on AV on 5 May. He was accused of being self-serving, brutal, contradictory, hypocritical and turning his wife into a non-person. Yet Nicky, who probably believes he has been preparing for this moment all his life, seemed serene. He stood, his often quick temper in check, a statesman in short trousers.

Dave wasn't there, busy with baby Flo. It's the PM's last day of paternity leave: I bet he's really upset that he's changing nappies instead of policies while sitting on the front bench. Thus Nicky was protected and surrounded only by Lib Dems. In other words, he was virtually defenceless.

The Tory maverick David Davis was wearing a yellow tie, I assume as camouflage (DD was in the Territorial SAS, he knows all the tricks). He accused Nick of employing 'brutal simplicity' in redrawing constituency boundaries. Could the new constituencies be fought in the courts? Nick said they could; DD sat down with a flourish.

The sheer breadth of the criticism was impressive. Take this from a furious Emily Thornberry: 'Is Mrs Clegg aware that under the proposed legislation, her status as an EU citizen will mean that she is a non-person when it comes to counting the size of the Sheffield Hallam constituency?' Nick nodded eagerly: 'I will remind her today.'

Then came this broadside from the Tory John Baron: 'One of the problems with AV is the democratic con-trick it can play on voters, who can never be quite sure what they are going to get. What would you say to Labour sympathisers who voted Liberal on the slogan "Vote Liberal and keep out the Tories"?' Nick did not hit back.

Instead, he began to babble. Was it a bad dream or reality? The eggs just kept coming.

At least in a bad dream you can wake up. 💔

10 September 2010
Hacked off about phone hacking

This first debate on phone hacking was eerily prescient of what was to come. I was there to record the Oscar moments. But it is also worth noting that, the day before this debate, Nick Clegg, standing in at PMQs after Dave's father was taken ill, was asked if Andy Coulson had known about phone hacking. He said it was a police matter and then chortled: 'When Andy Coulson resigned from the News of the World *the first person to call to commiserate was Gordon Brown!' The words 'Gordon Brown' acted in the chamber like a giant whoopee cushion. 'He told him not to worry,' shouted Nick above the laughter, 'that he had done the honourable thing and he knew that he would go on to do a worthwhile job!' Later, when Hackgate proper took off, this comment was much discussed.*

The debate over phone hacking had its moments of sanity but not many. It was supposed to be about whether a committee of MPs should investigate journalists hacking into MPs' phones, but it quickly became an angry assault on the press, the police, the Crown Prosecution Service and the Press Complaints Commission.

Almost immediately it was compared to Watergate. If Deep Throat could have been watching, I'm not sure what he would have said. MPs kept saying that this wasn't just about MPs but, as so often, it did seem to be. Chris Bryant, whose phone has been hacked, urged: 'We should become, as a House, far more carnivorous!'

The Labour MP Tom Watson, red in tooth and claw, smacked his lips. He is a larger-than-life figure with a predilection for gangster pinstripes. He feared that others, including ministers, had been hacked. He said that 'something very dark' was lurking and that 'mysterious forces' were keeping it that way.

Mr Watson had what can only be called an Oscar moment. 'They, the barons of the media, with their red-top assassins, are the biggest beasts in the modern jungle,' he orated. 'They have no predators. They are untouchable. They laugh at the law. They sneer at Parliament. They have the power to hurt us and they do with gusto and precision, with joy and criminality.'

I don't want to be taken for a red-top assassin or, of course, sneer but it all seemed rather OTT. Mr Watson, who should get an Equity card pronto, added: 'The little guys, the reporters on the ground who joined up with the newspapers to seek truth, have ended up working in a LIVING HELL.' In the press gallery we looked at each other, eyes wide.

Down below, the search for truth continued. Everyone was getting a kicking. There was a *cri de coeur* from the Conservative Nadine Dorries: 'How do we know it's not every newspaper? How do we know that our phones aren't being hacked RIGHT NOW?'

I felt we were working up to some kind of amazing finale like, say, burning someone at the stake. Then MPs just grunted 'aye', and it was over – for now. 💔

13 September 2010
It's just not cricket for the malcontent Mr Crowbar

The brothers and sisters of the TUC met in Manchester, determined to foment some sort of mass uprising. Bob Crow, muscles bulging, declares war on almost everyone

I was fascinated that Bob Crow's press officer was wearing leopard-skin and a leather pork pie hat. Was there any truth, I asked, in the rumour that Mr Crow would be playing air guitar at his TUC press conference in Manchester? The Hat laughed. 'Well, I did say it was going to be a rock-and-roller of a press conference,' he said.

But when Bob arrived, he didn't look to be in a playful mood. I could see the rock but not the roll. He sat before us, talking about Millwall, looking like a bouncer on a break, drumming his fingers on the table.

Mr Crow, head of the RMT, the man who brought London to a near halt last week, looks angry. Not so much Mr Crow as Mr Crowbar. Yes, that flexible. But, then, in Manchester, he wasn't the only one talking tough. The day had begun with Brendan Barber, the mild-mannered head of the TUC, comparing the cuts to the poll tax. Outside the conference centre, the comrades gathered, war drums beating, shouting about the cuts.

The only question, it seems, is whether it is going to be an autumn, winter or spring of discontent. But Mr Crow is a man for all seasons of malcontent. Yesterday he sat, muscles bulging, tie-less in a light green short-sleeved shirt, saying workers should unite. 'We are confronting the same enemy. My view is that we do it together.'

He honed in on his newest enemy: Mervyn King, the Governor of the Bank of England, who has been invited to speak at the TUC. Mr Crowbar doesn't want to hear Merve the Swerve; he would prefer someone from Cuba or Colombia or even, as a last resort, the TUC. But not Mr Swerve. Bob is going to walk out. He is particularly irritated that Merve has been pictured in cricket whites in the TUC magazine. 'The next minute we will be playing cricket with him,' he sneered, 'to try and warm relations.'

The bankers, he said, had been part of the problem, demanding a bailout, threatening to empty the cash machines. 'They used their political power,' he said. 'The TUC better start understanding that if it doesn't start to use its power it will become a nonentity.'

He believes that, when the cuts hit, people will come out on the streets. 'What we need is the same kind of campaign that we had in the poll tax. Not going round and smashing shops up and things like that. But a campaign of civil disobedience.'

Civil disobedience? 'Going on the streets. You know. Defending ourselves. Could be anything. Batman climbing up No. 10, Spider-Man going up Buckingham Palace. I don't know. What we want is peaceful demonstrations of civil disobedience.'

So there you have it. Batman on air guitar, Spider-Man on keyboards – and Bob Crow conducting. ❦

14 September 2010
Class war dinosaurs open one eager eye

For years the TUC conference has seemed on the verge of, if not extinction, then certainly utter irrelevance. But now the dinosaurs were back and breathing fire

We are watching prehistory being made in Manchester. The dinosaurs are back, roaming if not yet the Earth, then certainly the salmon-pink carpet at the TUC conference centre. We watched yesterday as they emerged from the primordial gloop, very much alive and bellowing their hatred of the bankers and the coalition. The scariest dino of them all, Bob Crow (aka B-Rex) watched, eyes flashing, right at home.

What a difference an election makes. For years it has seemed as if the TUC was meeting for its own purposes, not so much a conference as an historical re-enactment society. But now, back in Opposition, that has changed – and how.

Political palaeontologists will be fascinated. Take Brendan Barbersaurus, their leader, previously thought to be mild-mannered, a vegetarian who lost his teeth many ages ago. Now, amazingly, he has gone carnivorous. 'What we've got is not a coalition government but a demolition government!' he roared to applause. The coalition's catchphrase 'We are all in this together' was 'insulting claptrap' (more applause).

He wants to tax the super-rich, mobilise every community, co-ordinate strikes. Then there is Dave Prentisraptur, of UNISON, mainstream, not known for being aggressive. Until now. 'Today we face the greatest test for a generation,' he cried, letting rip at the Government, the speculators, the profiteers, the bankers in general and super-rich, super-hard Bob Diamond of Barclays in particular.

It is, brothers and sisters, class war.

One beast after another castigated our Government of millionaires, our Cabinet of the super-rich who wanted to spare the bankers and blame public sector workers.

'The idea of 25 per cent or 40 per cent cuts is complete and utter lunacy,' bellowed Matt Wrack (T-Rack?) of the Fire Brigades Union. 'We will stop them in their tracks. IT WILL NOT HAPPEN!'

B-Rex warned that all trade union members would, at some point, have to decide if they were going to lie down or fight. 'If the top bankers don't get up in the morning, with the smile that Bob Diamond has on his face, the economy will run as normal,' he shouted. 'But if workers don't get out of bed in the morning, the economy will shut down. We've got to recognise the strengths that we've got!' So be warned: these beasts believe that they are the future, no longer fossils, reborn to roam anew. ♥

16 September 2010
Lady Haha proves herself to be easy meat

This was Harriet Harman's last PMQs and I was wondering: 'Where's the beef?'.

It was Harriet's last Prime Minister's Questions as Labour's non-leader leader. I think it is fair to say expectations were low, though I, until the last moment, held out a hope that she would take inspiration in her attire from Lady Gaga. Harriet Harman, dressed in meat at the despatch box would be a sight to behold. When Tory backbenchers cried, 'Where's the beef?' she wouldn't even need to answer. Surely, in meat, she would even be taken seriously on the subject of cuts.

I regret to report, therefore, that she arrived wearing clothes (yawn). But, from the start, it was like feeding time at the zoo for Tory MPs, who have spent the week foaming at the mouth about the TUC. Thus, Dave's first 'question' came from a Tory MP, castigating Labour frontbenchers for encouraging strikes.

Fresh meat indeed. 'It is the height of irresponsibility for shadow ministers to troop off to the TUC and tell them it is all right to go on strike,' cried Dave. 'They should be ashamed!' But Harriet was not ashamed. Anyone else would have gone for a dramatic day, attacking Dave over the cuts. But Harriet, proud to plod, asked him instead to condemn sex-trafficking of women and girls and, as a sign of his commitment, to sign the EU directive on this subject.

First, Dave tried flattery. She was the third Labour leader he had faced. 'I think you are by far the most popular!' he flammed to sycophantic Tory laughter. She had used PMQs to 'push issues that you care about deeply'. Was that praise or merely patronising? Harriet took it as both. She thanked him. 'Just as well,' she said, 'that I'm not wearing a hoodie.' Or a steak, I thought, as the entire chamber laughed, more in surprise than anything else. Genuine Harriet jokes are so rare that they end up in museums.

But Lady Haha then got serious. Would he sign the sex-trafficking directive? Dave said it was an 'evil trade' and modern-day slavery. But not, apparently, so evil that he would sign the EU directive. Dave, who may never be confused with William Wilberforce, was tap-dancing.

'I'm disappointed,' said Harriet, deploying the word that mothers use with such effect to instil instant guilt. He shouldn't let the Europhobes win on something so important. Harriet stopped while she was ahead (always an art).

For Harriet, this must have been a strange half-hour. We are unlikely to see a woman as PM or Leader of the Opposition for some time. Yesterday Dave said to her: 'I know we are not saying goodbye. It is only au revoir.' But it is, actually, the end of this era. There will be, at the next PMQs, fresh meat indeed. 💔

17 September 2010
Not just an economist, more a chrysalis ready to burst

Who knew that an economist could be so fascinating? Certainly not me...

I had not expected Robert Chote to be interesting. After all, he is an economist. I went to his pre-appointment hearing before the Treasury Select Committee because he is going to be a VIP to you and me. It will be Mr Chote, if he is appointed, who tells us if the Chancellor is lying. At this time of cuts and chaos, that makes him the most important person in every room he is in.

He wasn't just interesting, he was riveting. Tall, whippet-thin, wearing a suit of electric-blue shot-silk, all topped by a head of bog-brush hair that bobbed around like the dot on an upside-down exclamation mark. And did I mention the pink striped shirt, the pink checked tie and the pinky-red cufflinks? He reminded me of David Tennant, my favourite Doctor Who.

It was an hilarious job interview. It can best be summed up by saying that they loved him. Actually, that is not entirely accurate. They adored him. I'm only surprised they did not ask him if they could tie his shoes. 'This is a new chapter in the Adventures of Robert Chote,' gurgled one MP. Mr Chote's face split into a watermelon grin.

Mr Chote was told that he was the economist wanted by anyone who wanted an economist. I think you can see how tough this interview was. Mr Chote said all the right things. He talked about 'speaking truth to power'. He compared the three people at the top of the Office for Budget Responsibility (OBR) to The Three Musketeers: it helped if one was a fiscal musketeer and the other a macro-economic musketeer (forgive him, Dumas, he is an economist). He wants to avoid 'group think'.

Whatever he said, MPs nodded, as a group.

Indeed, if I could paraphrase the whole thing, it would be like this:

MPs to Chote: 'We salute you. You are brilliant.'

Chote to MPs: 'I salute you. You are brilliant.'

The love-fest peaked when Mr Chote compared himself and the OBR to the lifecycle of a butterfly. The interim OBR had been a caterpillar, he was a chrysalis and, after the office is put into law, 'a beautiful butterfly will emerge'.

When it was over Andrew Tyrie, the chairman, who also has the physique of a pipe-cleaner, said MPs would now decide whether he could have the job. 'So I can make the JobCentre before it closes,' joked Mr Chote. Hardly. He had their blessing in less than an hour: it's all go for The Chrysalis. ♥

20 September 2010
The Lib Dems have an identity crisis

They love being in power but they hate being blamed for the cuts. They love Nick, but they aren't sure they like him anymore. It's political therapy time in Liverpool

There is a Liberal-Democrat sign tacked to the door of the ludicrously large auditorium in Liverpool: 'Please be aware that special effects will be in use during this session – including loud noises, explosions and flashing lights.'

That is no way to talk about Danny Alexander, I thought, as I

watched the Giant Carrot try to explain to his party faithful why
he's cutting us, them, everyone to the bone. 'We are all in this
together,' he said. (Oh George, have you actually brainwashed
him?) He told them to be proud of the cuts because they are
guided by Lib-Dem values. Oh dear.

When Danny ended his speech, I saw one person stand and,
seconds later, another. It was a crouching, hesitant ovation of a
political party that is, quite clearly, having a massive identity crisis.

I can see why. For years they have been having their conference at the seaside (last year the big story was a beached whale).
It was all rather gentle and likeable. Now, suddenly, as if they had
been kidnapped by Alice in Wonderland, they have become very
large and very important.

Loud noises and flashing lights are the least of it. Before,
security consisted of a hairy man looking in my handbag: now
the entrance looks like Departures at Heathrow. There are men
with squiggly earpieces, 60 per cent more media and 30 per cent
more delegates. At one point, I was caught in a mini-stampede.
It's so very un-Lib Dem (it's hard to stampede in sandals).

It's power that's done it, of course. The party faithful are both
thrilled and appalled. You see it the way they say the 'p word'
– rolling it round as if it were a foreign body in their mouths.
And you could see, during the big event of the day, the Nick
Clegg question-and-answer session, that they hate and love it –
at exactly the same time.

Nick sauntered on to the stage, Euro chic in open-necked
shirt and metrosexual suit. He looked about twelve and even
more Tory than usual.

It was quite the session, explosive in its own Lib-Dem way,
almost like political therapy.

The tone was set by the first question from a party activist
named Linda Jack. She had been a fervent supporter of Nick for
the leadership. 'I said then that I would trust you with my life, so
I could trust you with my party. I still think I can trust you with
my life. Can I trust you with my party?' This brought a ripple of

laughter and applause. Nick took a deep breath. 'Of course you can, Linda,' he said, sounding forced.

No one agreed with Nick. 'Why are we being blamed for the cuts?' asked one woman plaintively. Nick blamed growing pains, the press, political language, machismo and the Labour Party (in that order).

Then came this plea from the Lib-Dem heart: 'It would be really great to hear occasionally from you and some of the other ministers that you actually don't like a policy that you are announcing.' This received sustained applause.

Nick said that was nuts (I paraphrase). 'My view – and it's my view generally in life – is that if you are going to do something, either do it properly or not at all. If you are part of a coalition Government, you OWN that coalition Government!'

The delegates clapped that too. As I said, identity crisis. ❦

21 September 2010
Welcome to Nicktopia where change is all

Nick Clegg, in his first address to his party while in power, revealed that he is agent for change with a vision for the future. It felt, I have to report, just a little bit crazy

Some called it a Tory speech but I couldn't see Dave delivering it. It was, at times, quite bonkers, almost teenage in its idealism, heady with the excitement of just being there.

And the Liberal Democrats were so thrilled to be there, too. They flocked in, packing the hall to the rafters, risking nosebleeds to see Wonder Boy.

Nick was introduced by a video that was a festival of Nickness. Nick on the election trail, with Miriam, being mobbed, smiling in that boyish way. Then Real Nick arrived, smaller than on screen, wearing a yellow tie to show he was one of them though I thought, as I often do, how he just doesn't look like a Lib Dem.

He began by buttering up (more yellow) his party. They were wonderful and, indeed, almost as wonderful as he was. 'We've always been the face of change,' he said (does that mean that change has a beard?). 'We are now the agents of change.'

But then Nick Clegg, agent for change, said that some things don't change. 'We will never lose our soul,' he announced, a statement that is usually necessary only when, actually, it's already down the back of the sofa.

'We haven't changed our liberal values,' he said, another statement necessary only when, actually, you may have.

There was one line that Dave will want to nick (as they say) for its sheer emptiness: 'This is the right Government for right now.'

Two rights don't make a wrong, I guess, but what does it mean? I guess when you are an agent for change you don't need to explain.

Nick told us of his vision for the next election in 2015. 'Imagine…' he cried (well, this is Liverpool and therefore Lennon territory). In Nicktopia, crime would be down, schools free, unemployment banished. All homes will be warm because of the Green Deal scheme. Oh, and we'll be out of Afghanistan and the banks won't be greedy.

Do you see what I mean by bonkers? 'Imagine…' he entreated us again. (Surely, Lennon would despair.) Then, in a twinkling, Nick was out of there, off to do his Deputy Prime Minister duty in New York, an agent for change, a visionary, too important to stay in Liverpool for even one more day. ♥

22 September 2010
Conference comes out of the closet: it's heaven!

With Nick out of town, Lib Dems began to have a serious good time, and how better to celebrate that with a debate on gay marriage?

As it turned out, no one missed Nick at all. Indeed, the moment he left Liverpool, the kids starting having fun. First, in the debate on cuts, they abused George Osborne ('the Grim Reaper'), benefit reforms and even Nick. 'There's a lot of left-wing thought in this party!' chortled one delegate.

Next, they gave themselves an extra-special treat and debated gay marriage. This, for Lib Dems, is very close to heaven. They consider themselves at the forefront of LGBT issues (that's not a sandwich, but Lesbian Gay Bisexual Transgender) and the motion called for LGBT people to be able to marry and, if they wanted, in church.

The debate was gay in every sense of the word. Ed Fordham is a rather dashing young candidate who told us the story of his first political meeting in Hampstead. He was asked by someone (he put on a posh accent): 'What does your dear wife think of you doing this politics lark?' Ed responded: 'My dear wife? He's over there.' At which the posh accent said: 'In Hampstead, as long as it's not an animal, we don't mind.' The delegates roared with laughter. For the first time during this conference, the audience was at ease.

Ed, fearless, moved on to religious controversies. 'Cardinal Newman! Was he or was he not in an active sexual relationship with another man? I don't care! Let's take away the right of historians to stir up trouble!' He began to bark: 'Get on with it! Come on! Stop faffing around! Get it out of the closet, dust it down and make it real!' The delegates adored this even more.

A very tall woman approached the lectern, introducing herself in a husky voice as Jenny Barnes, a transsexual. Jenny isn't planning a church wedding. 'I cannot marry a man because I'm not registered as a woman. I can't marry as a woman because I'm in a same-sex relationship.' She paused. 'Luckily, I'm an atheist!'

The highlight, though, was Brian Paddick, former policeman and mayoral candidate, who bounded up and showed us his wedding ring. He never thought that, as a gay man, he'd want to get married. 'But I never realised that I was going to fall in love with a gorgeous Norwegian man!' he gushed. 'And in January 2009 the Norwegians – who are infuriatingly logical – decided that if there was to be no discrimination between gay and straight people, why do we have civil partnerships for gay people and marriages for straight people? So we waited until January 2009 and we got married in Oslo!'

Everyone applauded. 'Congratulations!' shouted a man.

The marriage ceremony was 'intensely moving'. 'We really feel, my husband and I – that sounds weird. It's husband and husband, I have to point out! We feel we are really equal because we are married. It is important. Yet we are only married in Norway. In Britain it reverts to civil partnership and that doesn't feel the same.'

Reader, I felt I had entered a completely new world. The motion was overwhelmingly approved. That look on everyone's face was one of bliss. Without Nick, they feel free. 💔

23 September 2010
Vince confuses the comrades with capitalism lite

Vince paints himself as the scourge of capitalism, but what would Che say?

Is Vince the new Che? This was the question as we waited for the Great Sage of Twickenham to tell us about the evils of capitalism. We knew that he was going to do this because Vince had leaked his own speech so effectively that he was dominating the news for something he hadn't even said yet. But, then, all great revolutionaries are brilliant at PR. Just think of what Che did for berets. Perhaps Vince will join him in the great T-shirt hall of fame.

Upon arrival, Vince was given an immediate pre-ovation.

He was wearing a suit and no beret. I began to doubt he was a Marxist – not enough hair.

'Conference,' began Vince. 'Comrades!'

His audience laughed though for true proletarians this would not be a laughing matter.

Vince began by giving himself a Castro-sized pat on the back. He was the man who had infuriated the banks, the right-wing media and all rich people in general. He was the scourge of the bourgeoisie. 'I must be doing something right!' he cried. The Lib Dems clapped with joy. He is a cult personality here.

'But I am told that I look miserable,' he said, looking miserable. 'I'm sorry, conference, but this is my happy face.' Cue more adoring laughter.

Get on with it, I thought. Chit-chat killed the revolution. But now he told us that he wanted to introduce dancing classes for the coalition. There was just one problem: 'My partners think I have two left feet.' More ho-hos … dialectical materialism would have to wait.

'But what is it like being in bed with the Tories?' Vince now asked, as relentless as drive-time radio. 'First of all it's exhausting.' Ooooh.

Carry on Che! Lib Dems, who adore all things nudge-nudge wink-wink, giggled. Vince pretended to recoil. 'Hold on, I wasn't going in that direction,' he protested. 'It's exhausting because you keep having to fight to keep the duvet.'

It was a relief when – finally – he started talking about the economy. Vince/Che wants to shine a light on the 'murky world' of corporate behaviour. 'On banks, I make no apology for attacking spivs and gamblers who did more harm to the British economy than Bob Crow could achieve in his wildest Trotskyite fantasies,' he thundered.

He does not approve of all things laissez-faire. 'Capitalism takes no prisoners and kills competition where it can, as Adam Smith explained over 200 years ago,' he insisted. For reasons unknown, the Lib Dems clapped at the words 'Adam Smith'.

But then, ominously, Vince added: 'Competition is central to my pro-market, pro-business agenda.' I have to say this was sounding perilously like capitalism, albeit capitalism-lite.

There was, however, one more tantalising moment. 'There has to be a revolution...' he cried, before adding, '...in post-sixteen education!'

So I suppose the revolution's on hold for now. Vince was the Marxist who didn't roar. 💔

26 September 2010
The shock, the hug and the 'I love you, bro'

Everyone thought they knew which Miliband was going to win the Labour leadership. But then, after an evening of endless bar charts, the unthinkable happened

THE moment that his victory was announced, Ed Miliband had eyes for only one person – his brother. They locked each other into a hug of hugs, the older brother pounding his brother's back a little too hard, at least eight times.

The rictus grin on David's usually mobile face said it all. At one point he ruffled his younger brother's bog-brush hair, something he must have done hundreds of times before in their lives.

From that moment their lives would never be the same again, a genuinely dramatic ending to a contest that has gone on for four long months. Even the last hour had been painful, a political version of water torture as we had to endure self-congratulatory videos and a snail's trail of speeches, including one by Gordon Brown (he lives!). The soundtrack was excruciating – Gordo came out to 'I'm a Soul Man' (I rest my case) – and, when we finally got down to the business of counting the votes, so were the bar charts.

Bar charts. Oh yes, Labour really does know how to throw a party. It was really a very strange event – thousands of people gathered in a dark hall watching a screen with giant bar charts. Surely David Attenborough should be there, whispering, trying to explain to real people about this strange mating ritual.

The numbers were announced by Ann Black, NEC chairwoman, charisma count zero. The five candidates had just been clapped into the hall from the pen where they had been held, human rights infringed and, more importantly, mobile phones removed, not allowed to phone a friend or, even more important in politics, an enemy.

From the start I had been seeking signs of who won, which is a bit like trying to see a black cat on a moonless night. No one even knew who knew the result. When Harriet Harman came out and greeted Neil Kinnock, a Mili-E man, with double kisses, I thought – ah, there's a sign! But then did Harriet even know? No one even knew that.

Except, of course, Ann Black who has, I can tell you, no future as a bingo caller. She recited the numbers, endless lists of percentiles. After the first round (Dave with 37.78 and Ed with 34.33), she said: 'There are quite a few more rounds to go!' The entire room was on the edge of its seat. As one bar chart gave way to another, there were 'oooohhhs' and 'ahhhhs'. Then finally, on the last number, whoops erupted.

After The Hug, The Speech which was, sadly (because I don't like to spoil the party), just a little bit terrible. Ed stood looking like a thin and tall panda, dark-circled eyes staring out at the hall. His first word as Labour leader was 'conference'. Not a great start.

He praised each of the candidates as if he were an *X Factor* judge. But when he spoke of his brother, it was as if they were in the room alone. 'David, I love you so much as a brother,' he said. 'I have such extraordinary respect for the campaign that you ran, the strength and eloquence that you showed.'

Everyone in the hall was aware of David sitting there, smiling through the pain. Up there on the blood-red podium set, Ed kept saying, 'I get it.' Well, he has got it now. He seemed to be in shock. Afterwards he stood there gangly, awkward, not knowing what to do, his brother watching. ♥

28 September 2010
'No more soap opera?' Sorry, David, that won't do

Forget policies. All anyone in Manchester was talking about was the Miliband family psychodrama.

The moment that David Miliband bounced on to the stage, all eyes in the hall were on him and his brother. To our right sat David. To our left Ed. You have to admit, the seating plan made sense. It may have been the foreign affairs debate but it was, really, a family affair. We were about to get our daily hit of The Brothers, the soap opera gripping Manchester.

The entire hall was wondering: what would David do? On Sunday morning David had left the security zone to get away from it all but, then, at about 6 p.m., I came out of the conference and saw a media scrum vibrating around a tall, slim, bendy straw of a man, gripping his wife's hand as if his life depended on it. David had returned to the security zone – it feels totally cut off in here – as valiant loser.

And now, the morning after the morning after, which still must feel pretty raw, here he was on stage. Labour seems prone to coupledom – Ed and Yvette, Harriet and Jack – but only David and Ed are so alike, down to the strange little macchiato fleck of white in their identical black bog-brush hair.

Bounce! David was out of the chair, taking control of centre stage with one long stride. Ed shot up like a rocket, clapping, and the whole hall followed. Whoops. Hollers. This hall voted for David, don't forget. Their man was now, finally, before them.

'The party asked me last night if I would just say a few words,' said David, 'and as it happens, on my computer are a couple of files marked 'Saturday, version seven', 'Tuesday, version twenty-three'. I've got a couple of speeches to draw on!' David cuts quite a figure these days – so slim, so *Mad Men*, in dark suit and white shirt. He used to be goofy – remember the banana? – but now he is grown up, graceful, fluid.

'I am really, really, really proud – I'm so proud – of my campaign,' he said. 'I'm so proud of my party. But above all I'm incredibly proud of my brother.'

Ed began to glow. His big brother, who had been protecting him his whole life, was doing so again. David's hand was on his heart now. 'Ed is a special person – to me. Special person to me. Now he is a special person to you. And our job, our job, is to make him a special person for all the British people.'

We were riveted. It was totally corny, not to say un-British (men, talking about feelings, whatever next?) but, actually, soap operas are corny, aren't they?

David made a fine speech on foreign affairs before returning to the human drama: 'I say today no more factions, no more soap opera!' Giant surfer waves of applause crashed as he went to hug his brother. I think I saw Ed's lips say: 'Great speech' but it should have been: 'Can you write me one like that?' What a drama. And it's not over. Can Ed give a speech as good? Will David stay or go? Stay tuned. No more soap? Don't be silly. 💔

29 September 2010
Tuesday night fever is eye-popping fun

It was Ed's Speech Day and the Labour Party was still coming to grips with the fact that they really had elected him

He looked so young up there, a too-tall teenager with great panda eyes and sticky-up hair. Everyone said that it was the speech of Ed Miliband's life, but when you look sixteen that doesn't seem so long really. Behind him sat rows of youngsters, placed there, I must assume, to make Ed look like a grown-up. It didn't work.

It shouldn't have been surprising that Ed M was up there but it was. I suspect that, until yesterday, the Labour Party didn't quite believe they had elected Ed. But now they were at the leader's speech and they were being addressed by a sixteen-year-old and it was most definitely not his brother David*, who was sitting to the side, a man (not a boy) who looked as taut as a trampoline.

Everyone thought the speech would be terrible but it wasn't, especially for a sixteen-year-old. Though, predictably, it was all about his new generation. I've heard of reinventing the wheel but this was reinventing The Who, and at some length. Ed wasn't just talking 'bout his generation, he was going on and on and on about it for almost an hour.

'People try to put us down,' he said (I paraphrase). But they shouldn't because the new generation had new politics, optimistic politics and caring politics.

'People try to put me down.' he said (I paraphrase). He told us who he was, about his parents who escaped the Holocaust and inspired him and David. It was a political household. When he had stolen David's football, his older brother got his revenge by nationalising his train set. David laughed at that through gritted teeth.

The panda eyes are really very special. They act as sort of a facial form of italicising: when he wants to emphasise something, he pops them out, giving a 3-D effect. The mouth is also tremendously mobile and, at times, travels in a different direction from his face. Ed has perfected the long blink, a sort of mini-swoon, where, for a moment, you think he may lose consciousness. His gestures need work but my favourite is when, in reaction to applause, he points up in the air, for no apparent reason, exactly like John Travolta in *Saturday Night Fever*. It is very disco.

He reviewed the names he'd been called during the election. 'Wallace out of Wallace & Gromit…' The eyes popped out. The

oldies in the audience laughed (they had heard of Wallace). 'I
can see the resemblance,' he admitted, but then frowned: 'Forrest
Gump? Not so much.' He paused. 'And what about Red Ed?' His
eyes fluttered. Oh my God, I thought, he's going to faint. But
then he came back to life. 'Come off it!'

I'm not trying to put him down but, if I'm honest (and, of
course, his generation is) it was too long. He finished to an instant
standing ovation. Justine, his partner, eight-months pregnant,
stayed in her seat as he swayed on stage, one arm raised, finger
pointing up, John Travolta-style. 💔

* P.S. By the end of the week, David Miliband had fled Manchester
for his home in North London, appearing on the doorstep as
a man in a blue flowery shirt with a perpetually grinning wife.
'I'm not dead!' he had protested after his decision to be on the
backbenches.

5 October 2010
Welcome to the Land of Oz-borne

*The Tories met in Birmingham, their first conference in power
since 1996, and yet, still, they didn't seem quite ready. It was all
a bit grim, until George began to sing.*

It was the kind of speech that Judy Garland would have loved.
Oh, not the depressing bits. The dire finances. The chopped
benefits. The austerity. But for every pound of pain yesterday,
George Osborne gave us a bit of poetry, a dash of inspiration, a
burst of song, until we were very close to being somewhere over
a rainbow, if not a song.

I really do not know what overcame him. Usually George
relishes the role of bad cop, the one who beats up the Tories, telling it like it is, looking stern, dimpled chin, refusing to smile. And

certainly yesterday everyone who packed in to all four tiers in the Symphony Hall in Birmingham was expecting the absolute worst.

The build-up went on forever. First there was a mini-concert by a brass quintet. I have heard of blowing your own trumpet but this was blowing two trumpets, a trombone, a French horn and, boom-boom, a tuba. But the audience adored it.

Not so much the three Treasury ministers who followed, giving speeches of stupefying tedium. Next up was Sir Stuart Rose, who told us that George's deficit plan was not just any deficit plan, it was a Marks & Spencer-endorsed deficit plan. It felt, like those advertisements, a bit cloying.

Enough already! It was time for the man himself, who strode out to an instant pre-ovation and told us how bad things were: Labour hadn't fixed the roof, had left us on the brink, had crashed the car. It was terrible (and that was just the clichés).

But he said that he had stopped the madness. 'Vigilant at all times we remain,' he cried. He praised himself (a trumpet being close to hand) about how he'd already stopped the rot. There was no panic, no danger of a 'deathly spiral' of higher interest rates. 'Our victory is the very absence of war,' he intoned. 'Now, together, we must win the peace.'

What did it mean? Was it a haiku? The audience applauded it all, the war, the peace, the deathly spiral. I suspected that he could say anything – for instance, 'sausages' – and get a clap. He proved this by saying 'Nick Clegg' and, bolder still, 'Danny Alexander'.

He told us hard truths, home truths, straight truths. He brought out the axe, chopping this and that, all for the greater good. 'We are all in this together,' he chanted (for that is his catchphrase). The audience kept on clapping (were they hypnotised?). Then George, abruptly, left behind his land of pain and ushered us into the Utopia – let's call it the Land of Oz-borne – just beyond reach. I could hear the swell of an entire orchestra. 'Just over the horizon,' he cried, 'lies the Britain we are trying to build.'

He was releasing his inner Judy now. Just over the rainbow was a hopeful country, a united country, a prosperous country.

Just over the horizon was a land governed by Munchkins (he may not have said that) with imagination, fairness, courage. Somewhere over the horizon, he sang, was a Britain that is a beacon for liberty. We were all with him now, holding our beacon, over the rainbow, way up high.

George, deficit diva, finished to tumultuous applause, his axe briefly idle. ❦

7 October 2010
Dave has a double vision

The Tories always end their conference with a set-piece speech by the leader. This year new dad Dave seemed rather taken with that Marvin Gaye and Kim Weston song

Breaking news from Dave: it takes two, baby. Oh yes. To make a dream come true, just takes two. Indeed, to do anything apparently, it just takes two.

It's an interesting theory – though Noah got there first – and I was going to say that it just takes two to do a sketch but, actually, then I realised it took me and you and Dave on stage for almost an hour. That's three. And then there is Samantha (four!) who looked lovely, of course, even as Dave nuzzled her ear and winked at George O (five!).

It was not the speech of a lifetime but it did the job, fine for a lunchtime. Dave explained that he'd had a vision the day after the election. 'I went to bed about 7 a.m. in a hotel, wishing like everything that I was at home with Sam and the little ones, not knowing where it was all heading,' he said. 'I woke up two hours later and I felt sure of the answer.'

See, two hours. It just took two and Dave knew what he had to do. 'The country wanted leadership, not partisanship.' He paused. 'Try the big thing. Do the right thing.' Try the big thing, the XXL thing, the big jumper thing that swamps you thing. Dave talked constantly yesterday about how we had to become big.

He told us to build the big society with big-society spirit. For when we do the big thing, we do not just become bigger but also more powerful. We are not just 'flotsam and jetsam' (another fabulous duo) in the currents of wealth and power. We are not 'small people but big citizens'. I had no idea what he was on about but I knew that it was big. 'It takes two,' Dave told us, doing little knee-bends at the lectern. 'It takes two to build that Big Society.'

He told us to seize the opportunity – to learn to drive. 'I know the British people and they are not passengers – they are drivers,' he cried. So, passengers, move over. Your country needs you to learn to parallel park. When we aren't driving we should be leading projects, setting up schools, starting businesses. 'Society is not a spectator sport,' he announced.

Dave was joined by Samantha but not Little Flo (for that would be three). They dashed round to the Marvin Gaye and Kim Weston track 'It Takes Two', baby, their dream coming true. ♥

12 October 2010
Afghanistan claims another victim

It was the week after conferences and, back at Westminster, it was complete change of mood with the grim news from Afghanistan about aid worker Linda Norgrove

David Cameron walked towards us almost an hour late, his face set, his manner subdued and unapproachable. Normally he would be chatty, not to say pugnacious, but this, clearly, was not a normal day. We had no idea why he was so late to his first press conference of the political season. We'd been told that he would be here in fifteen minutes, then fifteen more, then twenty. No explanation was given but we could see for ourselves that it was serious, though none of us could have guessed just how.

So now he finally was here, in this wood-panelled top-floor room at Downing Street, speaking without preamble in a slow, measured way, each word given individual weight.

He told us he wanted to make a statement on the death of Linda Norgrove in Afghanistan. He explained how the rescue operation had been authorised. We knew that there must be something coming. He seemed out of reach, as if talking from behind glass. Two Union flags, new to the press conference set, flanked him, making the occasion almost presidential. Even when he told us, it was hard to take in. General David Petraeus had contacted him to say 'that Linda could have died as a result of a grenade detonated by the task force'.

He never used the obvious words, though I'm sure the phrase 'friendly fire' popped into the minds of everyone watching. He had just been talking to Linda's father. We all clocked that he had gone from the agony of that conversation to this room with almost no time in between.

No wonder he seemed, as the questions came, suppressed, more deliberate, slower than usual. Shell-shocked is the phrase I would use for the Prime Minister. It is the first time that we have seen him like this, almost physically absorbed by tragedy, taking on the full weight of what had happened on an order given by his government. He has read the honour roll of dead from Afghanistan many times in the Commons but this, clearly, was different. This felt personal. In the past two years he has had to endure the death of his young disabled son Ivan and, just last month, the unexpected death of his father. He knows, in a raw way, bereavement.

Later, Mr Cameron came to the Commons to listen to a statement on Dr Norgrove's death by William Hague. The PM sat, absorbed in thought, eyes on a distant place. Across from him sat Ed Miliband, taking his place as Leader of the Opposition for the first time. I do not think Mr Cameron even so much as glanced at him, politics-as-usual suspended for the day. ❧

14 October 2010
Ed makes his debut at PMQs

It was the Younger Miliband's first PMQs. He was on his own now – his brother nowhere to be seen – and no one knew quite what to expect

Red Ed, arriving at PMQs to cheers of hope rather than expectation on his side, was nervous as he sat down, pulling up his socks, blowing his nose, glugging water. The circles around his panda eyes were as black as the dark side of the Moon, no doubt a result of practising in the mirror all night long.

He looked, despite the eyes, very young, that flick of white in the bog-brush hair serving only to accentuate this. The good news for him was that expectations were not so much low as below ground. The bad news was that he was flanked by the deadly duo of Tweedledull and Tweedleduller that is Harriet Harman and Wee Dougie Alexander. Could Ed be Tweedle-even-duller?

Opposite, Dave danced round, gleeful as he took a planted question on Ed's election. 'Will you join me,' asked a Tory, 'in congratulating Opposition members in their choice of leader even though he is not on the front bench and he didn't win?'

How Dave chortled. How the Tories giggled. Ed forced his dough-filled cheeks to lift into a smile. I'll bet brother David, viewing from home, that knife sticking out of his back still troubling him, cheered. Actually Mili-D may not have been watching, preferring the Chilean miners drama to this minor one.

Ed arose and, once vertical, the nerves vanished. He stood, utterly still, hands laid flat on the despatch box. The panda eyes closed and, for a moment, I thought he might pass out. He has the longest blink in politics, unnerving for all watching. He seemed to be in slow motion, lugubrious, his words strolling round his mouth twice before emerging, clad in little pillowy duffle coats.

He asked, quietly, about the child benefit cuts. How many families where one parent stayed at home would be affected? Dave danced. 'ANSWER!' cried Labour backbenchers. Dave said it was wrong for the poor to subsidise the rich. Didn't Ed agree? The panda arose. 'I may be new to this game but I think I ask the questions and you should answer them.' Labour MPs cheered: Ed had not fallen over yet.

Why should a family on £45,000 with one person at home lose out when a family on £80,000 with both partners working would not? 'It doesn't strike me as fair. Does it strike you as fair?' he asked the Prime Minister, who danced round the answer.

'I'm afraid it's nought out of two for straight answers,' said Ed gravely, a teenager ticking off his elders.

Relief spread over the Labour benches like jam on a cream tea scone. Dave became unusually shrill, accusing Ed of being transparently political. 'It is just short-term tactics,' cried Dave. 'It's not Red, it's Brown.' No, Dave, it's awful, that joke, worthy of Gordon himself. Dave isn't used to losing PMQs but yesterday, much to everyone's surprise, he did. Could we be seeing the birth of Ed the Cred? Stay tuned. 💔

19 October 2010
Tiny biscuit offensive crumbles into the void

Alan Johnson launched himself as Shadow Chancellor at a strange event with a variety of tiny munchies and a speech that was just as filling

I emerged from Alan Johnson's first speech as Shadow Chancellor feeling short-changed and not a little annoyed. Almost exactly four years ago I went to the same location – the glass box that is the KPMG headquarters – to hear another relatively new Shadow Chancellor named George Osborne. I emerged annoyed from that also (well, it's my job), but I can tell you that Mr Johnson was much worse.

This is why: Mr Osborne made a speech, answered questions and then tried to wriggle out of answering them. He took some risks, put himself out there, had a go. But Mr Johnson hardly felt present as he read out what seemed to be someone else's speech. He took no questions and so, obviously, had no answers. It was like touching a void.

The event had all the awkwardness of a first date. Do you remember Labour's prawn cocktail offensive? I can report that, under Red Ed's regime, it has become a tiny biscuit offensive. We had to negotiate a spiral staircase to get to the biscuits. Except that hardly anyone did. What if you gave a major policy speech and no one came? Exactly this.

We were ushered into a smallish room with sixty chairs and a bright blue backdrop. No Labour signs, no Labour rose. Just deep Tory blue. About half the chairs were full, but it was all media. I could not find one City person who was not from KPMG – and even they were few in number. The Shadow Chancellor was introduced by someone from KPMG who seemed to be, more or less, Head of Stuff. Two Shadow Treasury ministers slipped in at the last moment, presumably so that they did not actually have to talk to anyone.

AJ, his red cheeks the only Labour thing in the blue room, looked as if he wanted to be anywhere but there. He read the speech, which had some good lines, with the unbridled enthusiasm of an actuary. He said that the Government's deficit plan was built on myths. 'Since the election we have seen another myth emerge: having been in semi-retirement since the 1980s, TINA has reappeared,' he said. The coalition were using TINA (There Is No Alternative) as an excuse for its draconian cuts but, actually, he noted, TIAA (There Is An Alternative).

Other than that, it was most unmemorable. Gordon Brown boomed, Alistair Darling droned but Alan Johnson, at least yesterday, was just reciting words. It ended without applause. Thus a void met a void. Mr Johnson began to walk towards us before remembering that he was too grand (or scared) to take questions.

'Farewell,' he said, exiting stage-right, a man frightened by his own Shadow job. ♥

20 October 2010
Dave says we will never surrender our time zone

David Cameron's statement on the Armed Forces was so confusing that it was hard to tell very much, except the time, by the end of it

Commander-in-Chief Dave launched a remarkable military operation – codenamed Operation Flannel – in the Commons yesterday. First he attacked his own forces from land and sea and air, cutting and trimming, slashing and burning. He blamed it all on the official Opposition, who, more or less, voluntarily surrendered. Far more deadly was the unofficial Opposition (the Tory Party), who were subjected to a Dave charm offensive.

The result? A truly impressive smokescreen of bamboozlement that swirled around the chamber, almost hiding what had just happened. Through the murk I was hardly able to see Trident, now postponed, or the two aircraft carriers that, after Dave's strike, had no aircraft on them. Through my spyglass, I could only just discern that their vast decks were now being used by what appeared to be piratical skateboarders.

Operation Flannel began with Dave telling us why Britain was great. We have the sixth-largest economy and the fourth-largest military budget. 'We have', crowed Dave, 'a time zone that allows us to trade with Asia in the morning and the Americas in the evening and a language that is spoken across the globe.'

Wait a minute, as they say in Greenwich. Our time zone makes us great? Well, at least Dave hasn't cut that yet. Nor has he trimmed even a syllable from the English language. It was, as I'm sure you can see, a triumph.

Ed Miliband came over as a rather tiresome polytechnic lecturer but he did have one rather good question. 'Is it really the case that the best strategic decision for the next decade is for Britain to have aircraft carriers without aircraft?'

Siren alert! Dave, acting quickly, got out the dry ice. 'Let me address very directly this issue of the capability gap,' he said, smoke pumping out of his nostrils. 'There is not a gap in our flexible posture. With our air-to-air refuelling and our fast jet capability we have the ability to deploy force around the world.' Wow, I thought, we've even left our time zone.

'But', said Dave, 'I accept there is going to be a gap in carrier strike.' A gap in carrier strike. So that is what they call an aircraft carrier without aircraft. Mind the gap, as they say. But he wasn't going to, as Labour had, 'push these things off to the future'. 'You've got to make the tough decisions now!' cried Dave, his epaulettes rising up to salute him.

Sir Peter Tapsell, a majestic galleon of a man, accused Dave of postponing Trident as a sop to the Lib Dems. Dave charged, smoke billowing until I could see nothing, only hear his voice bellowing: 'We are on track to replace Trident. It's the right decision!' Or, as the armchair generals would say, the right indecision. 💔

21 October 2010
George the magician makes cuts disappear

George Osborne presented the government's Spending Review with much drama, but what was he doing with an amphibian in his throat?

This was George Osborne's moment – actually sixty-two moments, not that I'm counting – and he knew it. He may hate the deficit, but he adores the power: six months ago the only things that he could cut with confidence were his own nails;

now he is the man entrusted with the national scalpel, carving away £81 billion from our budget.

'Today's the day when Britain steps back from the brink!' he began, using the language of the penny dreadful instead of international finance. He spoke as if the nation were amassed at Beachy Head, peering anxiously over the cliff.

This got a huge groan from Labour MPs, who know a bit about coming back from the brink, followed by a Tory roar of approval. The Lib Dems, silent, just looked confused.

It was quite the occasion, sixty-two moments of pure George, the man with the voice of the boy. At times, I was not sure that he was going to make it, the frog in his throat so persistent that I could not help but think it was a Labour voter. The chamber was packed, the atmosphere rambunctious. At the end of the chamber, overlooking all, stood Iain Duncan Smith, feet apart, a Victorian father figure. (Was it his frog? Had IDS given his personal amphibian the day off as part of his welfare cuts, only to have the wretched thing hop over to George?)

George would have given much thought to how he would portray himself. At the Tory party conference, he told us: 'You don't get to choose the times in which you live, but you do get to choose how you live in them.' Others may regard him as the Grim Reaper on Axe Wednesday, but he sees himself as the one bringing sanity to our finances, the antidote to Gordon Brown.

What irony, then, that the man whom he reminded me most of yesterday was Gordo. There was the arrogance, the confidence, the cleverness and the magical sleights of hand. For instance, did you know that no one lost their job? Instead there will be a 'reduction in the total public sector headcount'. (And no, that has nothing to do with lice.)

This was the day when the Sorcerer's Apprentice came into his own. George took his place in the Magicians' Circle, brandished his saw, put his lovely assistant (Danny Alexander) into a box and sawed him in half. It should have been carnage but, abracadabra, it wasn't. 'A stronger Britain starts here,' croaked George. How

George will hate that frog. The amphibian world must brace itself for a cut in tadpole benefit, ASAP. ❧

22 October 2010
Honeymooners are in it together, even if we're not

The Prime Minister and his Deputy seemed to be a proper couple now as they set out to make Nottinghamshire swoon

Dave and Nick took their double act on the road to Nottinghamshire yesterday. It was their first outing as a couple among 'real people'. Sweet, really, that they had chosen an audience from Heart radio. 'It's great to be out here in the heart of the country,' trilled Dave, live and unplugged.

The happy couple sat on two bright red stools in the middle of the school auditorium. 'Thank you, Val Doonican, for the stools,' cried Dave, who may have been a little overexcited. Nick laughed at that. When Dave sat, Nick stood. When Dave stood, Nick sat. They are a proper couple now, connected by invisible strings, finishing each other's sentences. If the politics thing doesn't work out, they could tour as a comedy act, The Honeymooners.

This was not a pre-selected audience and no questions had been submitted. Nick talked more, Dave looking on adoringly. (Gordon had Sarah, Dave and Nick have each other.) 'I just want to say,' said Dave after a long peroration from Nick about prison, 'I agree with Nick. I do! I was in Wandsworth Prison recently – in a professional capacity, I might add – and prison isn't working properly at the moment.'

Nick seemed a little oversensitive about the fact that some say the cuts will hurt the vulnerable. 'I understand that people are very fearful, and fear is a very powerful emotion and it kind of sweeps everything else aside,' he said (is he in therapy?). 'But I ask you to have a little bit of perspective.'

This turned out to be how, actually, he and Dave were helping the poor, not hurting them. Dave nodded understandingly. No one else did.

Then came the biggie, the one that Nick knew was out there waiting for him. How did he feel about breaking his pledge on tuition fees? 'I feel really bad, really bad,' he said to clapping. 'I feel really bad. I own up to the fact that I signed a pledge that I now feel that I can't deliver. I would love to live in a world where every single promise I ever made was delivered.' He began to babble about regrets (he has a few).

Dave couldn't bear to see Nick suffer so. 'I've had to do the same thing with child benefit,' he cried. 'I said before the election that I wanted child benefit to carry on as it is.' Then he realised that it couldn't stay as was. 'Sometimes it means you have to eat the words that you said,' said Dave, his jacket off.

They became evangelical. Every question, be it on teaching, aid, the Big Society or carers, received a mini-sermon about how fair they had been. I began to realise that this event was not for our benefit, but theirs. It was to make them feel better. (Top tip: next time, bring guitars.) Nick wishes that we could see the problem. 'You are dealing with a crisis that is very difficult to touch, to feel,' he said. The crowd was friendly but not convinced.

The honeymoon act could go on and on. We may not all be in this together, but those two sure are. ♥

27 October 2010
The bike shed calls as Nick's
patience goes up in smoke

Nick Clegg, so often caricatured as David Cameron's fag, will have needed a smoke or two after a tempestuous day in the Commons at his own question time

Nick Clegg, not-so-secret smoker and butt of all jokes, will have wanted a fag after his appearance in the Commons. I think we all think we know him better after his appearance on *Desert Island Discs*, where one of his songs was 'Waka Waka' by Shakira. 'This is your moment,' the lyric goes, 'No hesitations. Today's your day. I feel it!'

Well, I felt it too yesterday, Nick: one blast of contempt after another. The first came from Chris Bryant, the Labour starlet who is a man in perennial search of a headline. He attacked Nick for 'niggardly' proposals on welfare reform. The poor would not be able to live in inner London. The proposals were iniquitous, social engineering and 'sociological cleansing'.

Nick popped up, looking about twelve with his new haircut. This is your moment, I thought. Today's the day! 'We all indulge in a bit of hyperbole,' he said, 'but to refer to cleansing will be deeply offensive to people who have witnessed ethnic cleansing in other parts of the world!'

Labour MPs emitted screams of protest. 'It is an outrageous way of describing...' shouted Nick, who brought his fist crashing down on the despatch box. 'No!' he barked. 'I'll tell you exactly what we are doing!' He was capping benefit at £400 a week for a four-bedroom home. Was that wrong? 'I don't think so!' he shouted, answering his own question, which is always a bad sign.

Time for a cigarette, obviously, but instead he got a question about teenagers smoking but not voting at sixteen. He turned on Labour, snarling that they were 'wholly, wholly inconsistent' on votes at sixteen. Labour MPs screamed right back.

Clearly, whatever Shakira says, this wasn't his day. Nick was then accused of wrecking lives, making people homeless, hurting the poor, gerrymandering the country. I knew it was a matter of time before he was accused of killing people. Sure enough, the Labour MP from Gateshead accused him of promoting early death. 'Do you at all regret promoting smoking as your single greatest luxury?' he demanded.

Oh honestly, I thought, but Nick prostrated himself without, of course, promising to quit. Then he was accused of something heinous (being a Tory) and asked to apologise over tuition fees. Reader, he grovelled, though only about tuition fees, and then he ran off to find a bike shed. ❦

2 November 2010
Dave plays at happy families. It won't last

The Prime Minister returned from the Euro-summit insisting
that he was now leading Europe on all things budgetary

Triomphe! That is how Dave characterised his achievements at the EU summit. It seems that he had, single-handedly, stopped the 'crazee' 6 per cent increase in the EU budget. Then, again in a single bound, he had managed to keep the rise to 2.9 per cent. The fact that he'd originally wanted a freeze was a mere trifle. What mattered was that Dave had stopped the crazees. He was the only sane thing in the utterly insane EU world.

It was a breathtaking performance. He was in ebullient form. I don't know what our Prime Minister is on, but I think we should all get some. The chamber was packed: Euro-statements are almost a form of blood sport here. Talking of sport, the newly named Ginger Rodent – now an official minority, I believe – was there with a new haircut. Across from him sat his enemy Harriet 'Gunner' Harman, squirrel-hater and apologiser.

'Can I say to the Prime Minister,' said Ed Miliband, 'in words that my grandmother might have used, I admire your chutzpah!

'Isn't the truth about it that you wished that you could come back and say, "No, no, no", but in your case it's a bit more like "No, maybe, oh go on then – have the 2.9 per cent after all!"' This Maggie parody brought screams.

Only the Tory Eurosceptics looked on stonily. In contrast, the Lib

Dems looked mellow in their omnipresent yellow. These were Dave's new and old friends, noted Ed: the PM was in a 'tricky predicament'.

Dave disagreed. 'If mine was chutzpah, that was brass neck! Well, to put it in a way that maybe you would understand, we are just one big happy family!'

Ed, purveyor of fratricide himself, looked wary as Dave trumpeted: 'It's brotherly love on this side of the house, it really is!'

Well, up to a point. The Euro-haters looked really quite miserable as Dave held a love-in with his new Lib-Dem friends. Charles Kennedy spoke to him as 'one long-standing pro-European now to another'. He welcomed Dave's 'constructive engagement' with Europe. It would, he was sure, 'receive solid support'.

Dave thought that hilarious. 'Said without a hint of mischief!' he chortled. (The Euronerds got even glummer.)

Next up was Sir Menzies Campbell: 'As another of your new friends, may I remind him that in 2010 family life takes many different forms in this country.' MPs had no idea what this meant but still went 'Whoo whoo' for they thought it might be vaguely dangerously trendy. 'But can I also commend your pragmatism?'

Dave looked wary. 'In terms of broader family,' he said, 'I don't quite know. A wise uncle, I suppose, to give me good advice.' The Euronerds hated that even more. Ah yes, just one big happy-go-sulky family. I think we've got a spectacular feud ahead of us. ❦

2 November 2010
Night flight of the Lesser Spotted Gordo

Gordon Brown's relaunch in the chamber was a strange and short nocturnal affair

We have been waiting for Gordo for so long that it was a shock to see him. But there he was, entering the chamber at 10.14 p.m., carrying his moral compass. It was the second time he'd been there since leaving Downing Street, but the first time was a mere flit through. This time he'd alerted everyone he'd ever met that he was going to speak. Often during an adjournment debate there are three people there: last night there were about 200.

Gordo had left nothing to chance. He'd even arranged for ten or so Scottish MPs to serve as his 'doughnut', a parliamentary oddity where MPs clump around another MP to show that he is not alone. There was a mini-panic when part of Gordo's doughnut, arriving before him, sat in the wrong place. So when Gordo scooted along the third bench back and sat down, they had to scuttle along behind him, like hermit crabs in search of a resting place.

The whole event was, as the Tory minister Peter Luff put it, a 'footnote in parliamentary history'. Gordo will have hated that. He has seen himself as many things, saviour of the free world among them, but never as a footnote. His face was impassive as he sat, nervous, hands constantly moving to his hair, his leg, and finally wrapping around his body.

This was his 'relaunch'. I say this because it could not have been a coincidence that it happened on the same day that he announced he is to campaign for democracy in Burma.

Indeed, in what may be the strangest announcement ever made by a former Prime Minister, he revealed he would be 'guest-editing' his wife's Twitter feed to highlight the injustices of the Burmese junta. Back in the Commons, though, his topic was closer to home.

It was his first speech from the back benches since 1985. The Lesser Spotted Gordo has been a very rare sight since April. The man who wrote a book on courage has seemed strangely unable to muster enough to appear in public. He missed the Budget, the Comprehensive Spending Review, PMQs, the Strategic Defence Review and many sessions of Scottish questions. And now here he was, practically in the middle of the night, relaunching.

It was a speech-ette, really, as it lasted all of four minutes and was, essentially, an intervention in an adjournment debate secured by a neighbouring MP to insist that the maintenance on Britain's two new aircraft carriers (which won't have aircraft for some time) should be carried out at Forsyth shipyard, rather than in France.

Gordo began, as if it was PMQs and not a footnote in the middle of the night, with tributes to the Armed Forces. He quoted Winston Churchill. He mispronounced Portsmouth as Ports-mouth. It was almost nostalgic to listen to that great booming voice filling the chamber. He spoke eloquently about the dockyard and its place in history and its need for the contract. He sat down, poppy proud on his lapel, his voice still reverberating. Our wait was over. It all seemed most surreal. ♥

4 November 2010
Snap! Dave is caught flashing the cash

It was a candid camera moment when Dave was revealed to have put his personal photographer, Andy Parsons, onto the public payroll

Smile, Dave, you've been papped at PMQs. Remember Fergie and that toe-sucking moment? Well, this was the parliamentary equivalent. Granted, it was a long-range shot by an amateur (Ed Miliband) with a 'Fun Flash' disposable. The result was grainy but, by the end, we were left with the unmistakeable image of a Prime Minister caught in the act of employing his own photographer with our money. It was quite toe-curling.

Ed began by pretending that he didn't even have a camera. He asked about Afghanistan and tuition fees. Most photographers with a Fun Flash wouldn't use a tripod, but Ed was taking no chances. We now know that he was setting up his shot, getting the Prime Minister to talk about broken promises and 'hard choices'.

Dave didn't seem to suspect a thing. 'Along goes the Miliband-wagon!' shouted Dave, arms bouncing along in the air as if we were singing along to the bouncing ball.

'Now,' began Ed, laboriously, lugubriously, 'you talk about hard choices. I cannot believe that you are talking about hard choices this week, because who have you chosen to put on the Civil Service payroll? Your own personal photographer!'

Dave looked up, guiltily, straight at the camera. Snap! George 'Axeman' Osborne, next to him, curled his upper lip into the perfect aristo snarl. Snap!

Labour guffawed (well, Dave's face was a picture). 'There is good news for the Prime Minister,' teased Ed. 'Apparently he does a nice line in air-brushing!'

This brought a rueful look from Dave.

'You can picture the Cabinet photo,' said Ed, standing back, hands framing the front bench. 'We're all in this together, just a little bit more to the right, Nick.'

More screams as Nick (snap!) gave us a world-weary look. 'Is it really a wise judgement,' demanded Ed, 'when you are telling everybody to tighten their belts, to put your own personal photographer on the Civil Service payroll?'

Dave turned to show us his best side (the right, of course). 'Honestly,' he harrumphed, 'is this what your leadership is reduced to?'

Ed giggled. Dave – now being bombarded with shouts of 'Cheese!' – said he was cutting the communications budget by two thirds. 'We will be spending a bit less on replacing mobile phones in No. 10 Downing Street!' Spookily, Dave accused Ed of using 'lame sound-bites'. This was what Gordo used to accuse him of week after week. You know those pictures where one face morphs into another? Dave, don't let it happen with you and Gordon.

Ed's questions were done, but a new Labour MP asked what public-sector workers facing the axe would think of him hiring his 'personal vanity photographer'. I think it was the word 'vanity' that did it for Dave. Indeed, he's so vain he might think this sketch is about him. He threw his papers down as Labour MPs shouted, 'Cheese!' Or, as we say in my family, 'Money!' It gives 'flash the cash' a whole new meaning.

(P.S. On 16 November, Dave took his official snapper off the public payroll, an event that, sadly, was not captured on camera.) ❦

5 November 2010
Abbey days are here again for George the cad

ITV had a huge hit with Downton Abbey, *an upstairs, downstairs costume drama set in an Edwardian country house in 1912. Surely George was born to be in it, too?*

I think we can all agree that George Osborne, if he appeared in *Downton Abbey*, which he might, would be an aristo cad. He really is an operator. Yesterday, at the Treasury Select Committee, he should have got a shellacking. Instead, he rewrote the script. 'I take my hat off to you as a professional politician,' said George Mudie, the Labour politician whose accent will forever cast him as one of the servants.

George raised an eyebrow. As a scorpion, he recognised the sting in that tail and took it as a compliment. George wears power like a shiny suit. Alistair Darling had his eyebrows and an air of solidness. George has a sneer – a perfect snailshell curl of the left side of his upper lip – and an air of danger. But he has every intention of ruling our world. He came bearing gifts (all cads have manners, I believe) to the committee. The first was a top-secret ultra-private CONFIDENTIAL letter from BAE Systems to the Prime Minister about the appallingly expensive aircraft carrier deal. As he dangled this in front of them, the committee actually began to salivate.

He pronounced his Comprehensive Spending Review a great success. 'I have learnt that setting clear dates several months in advance is a good idea,' he said.

Michael Fallon, an MP who is also vice-chair of the Tory Party, purred. 'So when is the Budget?' he asked. George was like a cat presenting a dead mouse: 'The answer is 23 March, 2011.'

That's over four months' notice. 'Put that in your diary!' I was reminded that shellac is a type of varnish that gives wood a lustrous sheen. I was watching George shellac the committee. George was asked who the most difficult minister had been. 'I was going to say wait for my memoirs,' he said, 'but most of these political memoirs are so boring I'm not sure I'll bother.'

I yearned for Maggie Smith to pop up and say something imperious. We got the next best thing, a question from the waspish Andrew Tyrie, the chairman, over whether George had exaggerated the threat to Britain when he said that we were on the 'brink of bankruptcy'. George hated that. 'I came to office in the middle of a European sovereign debt crisis.' We were 'on a bed of nitroglycerine'.

'There was an acronym at the time,' said George. 'Piigs.' He said the word, which refers to the initials of highly indebted countries, with disdain. 'And there was another acronym: Stupid. And the U in Stupid referred to the United Kingdom.' He said this with a flourish. He had rescued the UK from being stupid. We knew who was the hero in this drama. 💔

9 November 2010
Civil servants put on ice as Dave shifts their horizons

Dave and Nick invited 100 of their closest colleagues to a freezing cold atrium to explain, in 'plain English', how they were having a power shift and moving the horizon

It was a completely bonkers event even by this Government's standards. Everything about it – the setting, the temperature, the language – was off the chart. At 9 a.m. yesterday Dave and Nick invited 100 top civil servants, plus the Cabinet, to the giant fridge that is Dunbar Court atrium in the Foreign Office for a pep talk on their departmental business plans. It was so full of nonsense that it makes 'Jabberwocky' look sane.

'Welcome to this wonderfully chilled room,' boomed Dave. Chilled? Actually, I think even bottles of chardonnay would have found it nippy. The only thing missing were the huskies and the polar bears. The civil servants, who had queued for ages to check their coats, shivered. Rule Number One in the Age of Austerity: keep your coats on, it's cold in here.

Dave was extremely beamish, as Lewis Carroll might say. His plans are a revolution. It's all about a power shift and a horizon shift. Also, in Dave World, there are no more targets. Instead, there are milestones. (I am not making this up).

Dave says that it's about using 'plain English'. I am sure you will agree that 'power shift' is plainly nothing to do with voltage. Instead, Dave is running an extension cable from Whitehall (this may explain the lack of heating) to all of us. So get ready to plug in; I am hoping to use it to recharge my mobile.

Also, and you can't get plainer than this, Dave's shifting the horizon. That one with the sunsets is the wrong one. Ditto the one with the sunrises. Now earth meets sky. In future, who knows? Dave insists that Mother Nature (don't forget that she's also lost her child benefit) has got it wrong, and he wants her to come up with a new horizon – and it has to be cheaper, too. Also, more plain English, Dave says centralisation is wrong. 'The idea that it's only the people at the top who have the answers is an incredibly negative view of the world,' said the man who had just ordered a new horizon.

Dave wants all departments to report to him every two weeks on progress on their decentralisation milestones. One civil servant (probably ex by now) referred to this as 'tight central control'.

So, what's the word for that in plain English? Well, there are a few, but perhaps 'brillig!' is the best. ♥

11 November 2010
Nick has a very bad heir day

*Outside the students were protesting against higher tuition fees
and poster boy Nick Clegg. Inside, the man himself was having
a sense of humour failure*

Nick Clegg, bad heir day. This was the day that Cleggers, as
Dave calls him, came into his own as an official hate figure.
Outside Parliament, thousands of students marched in
protest against higher tuition fees. One poster said 'Nick Clegg,
Tory Boy'. Another showed flying yellow Liberal Democrat
'hypocrite' pigs. Two students held a bedsheet on which was
scrawled Nick's vow: 'I pledge to vote against any increase in
tuition fees', but they had signed it off 'Mega LOL'.

There was mucho mega laughing out loud in the Commons,
too. Harriet Harman, who knows a thing or two about being a
hate figure, kept it simple. 'In April,' she deadpanned, 'you said it
was your aim to end university tuition fees. Can you update the
House on how your plan is progressing?' Mega LOL from Labour.
The Tories tried to hide secret smiles. The Lib Dems looked grim.

'Uh,' said Mr Clegg.

'Uh! Uh!' mocked Labour MPs.

Mr Clegg, who should know that hesitation is fatal, scrambled:
'This is an extraordinarily difficult issue.' Labour MPs mocked
again. Mr Clegg said that he had been 'entirely open' about the fact
that he has not been able to deliver his policy. But the new plan,
which actually triples tuition fees to £9,000, was 'progressive'.

'I'm glad you think it's so fair,' said Harriet. 'In April you said
increasing tuition fees to £7,000 a year would be a disaster. What
word would you use to describe fees of £9,000?' Mr Clegg gave
us all a little lecture on being progressive.

Harriet asked why he had gone along with a Tory plan and
launched into a tortuously laboured (ha) joke: 'We all know what

it's like,' she said, 'you're at Freshers' Week, you meet up with a dodgy bloke and you do things that you regret.' Uproarious LOL. 'Isn't it true that you've been led astray by the Tories?' she teased.

Mr Clegg now suffered a complete sense of humour failure. His answers were defensive and delivered with a moral tone so high that it was doing the pole vault. Everything he'd done was for the greater good. He was like a born-again preacher who, when caught in a brothel, claims he's there for spiritual purposes.

Harriet pointed at the Lib Dems and, like a bad conscious, cried: 'You must honour your promise to students.'

Nick tried to go on the attack but it didn't work. Labour MPs kept up the pressure on tuition fees until, finally, he was asked a question about Danny Alexander, whom Harriet, making a rare memorable joke, had called a 'ginger rodent'. 'The poor Chief Secretary to the Treasury is picked on all the time,' protested Nick. 'Any form of discrimination against rodents or ginger-headed folk is wrong.' Oh dear. Nick defends rats. I think we know why. Mega LOL. ♥

19 November 2010
'S**t happens' is Dave's new motto

The Prime Minister was on a roll as he explained why it's always time for a change now

I am writing this straight from a Dave-a-thon. It began at the glittering awards dinner for *The Spectator* magazine where Dave made a speech. Then, the next day, with a fresh shirt and a quick reapplication of make-up, Dave performed for 150 minutes before the Liaison Committee without so much as a powder room break. You don't spend that much quality time with the Prime Minister without learning something.

First, Dave is getting funnier. He arrived post-dinner (roast loin of venison and baby fondant potatoes – I tell you, it's auster-ity all round), saying he'd been with Little Flo. 'I came into power saying it's time for a change,' he announced. 'Little did I know that would become a nightly instruction.'

Someone near me leant over: had the Prime Minister just made a nappy joke? He had. And there was more risqué material on the way.

Dave was on a roll, making a series of Tory in-jokes, after which he announced by way of explanation: 'S*** happens.' Everyone looked at each other. Had the Prime Minister just said 'S*** happens'? He had. First a nappy joke and now this. Yes, I know they are related. It is a first.

I thought of this as Dave spoke before the Liaison Committee for, really, I think that 'S*** happens' could be – and actually is – Dave's motto. I don't know what it is in Latin and so, from now on, I shall refer to it as SH. Whether the subject was Ireland, defence, transport, police or cuts, Dave embarked on long answers that could have been summed up as SH.

Dave does not have the grasp of detail that both Tony Blair and Gordon Brown had. They did it without a briefing note, barely drawing breath. Tony was charming, Gordo a steamroller. Both were always right about absolutely everything.

Dave isn't always right (SH) and listens much more. After a question on higher education, he said ruefully: 'If Two-Brains Willets cannot answer that question, I don't know how much hope there is for me.' He still can see himself as others do. At one point he was quoting himself and stopped, saying: 'Quoting your own speeches is the first sign of madness.'

The PM is a team-builder. He told us with pride of something called The Quad (him and Nick Clegg, George Osborne and Danny Alexander). The Quad meets to come up with strategy and talk things through. Dave kept using the words 'collegiate' and 'collective'. This was the 'Quad Process'. A big word for the PM is 'proper'. This is the highest accolade he can bestow on anything. The Quad, for instance, is a 'proper process'.

By the end of 150 minutes, almost everyone had fled the

room, exhausted by a long SH discussion of Afghanistan. Dave announced that he wanted a debate on a Bank Holiday for the Royal Wedding. He beamed. Good news. At last. 💔

23 November 2010
George tells us that he told us so

With the Irish banks in crisis, the Chancellor came to tell us what he is going to do about it. He sounded alarmingly European.

I'll bet George Osborne never thought he'd be standing up in the Commons defending a decision to use our money – proper money, pounds and pence money – to bail out a country that uses the poncey old euro.

But there he was doing just that with Ireland. Why? "'I told you so" does not amount to an economic policy,' he claimed. Then, frankly, he told us so. Indeed, George told us that he had told us so many times on the euro and on the Lisbon Treaty. Plus, he'd told us so on the European Financial Stability Fund and on the euro mechanism.

Don't worry if it's confusing, it's supposed to be. The fact that George has become so fluent in euro-speak is, arguably, just as worrying as the bailout. George may claim that 'I told you so' is not an economic policy but, yesterday, it seemed gloriously close to being just that.

Of course, as soon as he told us so, everybody else in the chamber told him so. Or tried to.

Alan Johnson, who continues not to impress as Shadow Chancellor, agreed with him on Ireland but then told him so on our deficit, his cuts and growth. George sneered that Labour economic policy was a 'blank sheet of paper'. It wasn't clear if this was better than 'I told you so'.

Red Ed, back from paternity leave, looked as blank as, well, his flagship sheet of paper.

The Tories didn't seem to mind the bailout, but they hated the fact that it involved the weedy old euro (read that with a sneer). Andrew Tyrie, desiccated chairman of the Treasury Select Committee, said that the public would be 'shocked' to be bailing out a eurozone country.

Douglas Carswell, a professional euro-hater, said: 'We might be outside the euro as a currency union, but doesn't the small print of the Lisbon Treaty make us, in effect, members of the euro as a debt union?' George told him so about being against the Lisbon Treaty. 'But I've got to deal with the world as I find it today,' he announced, though this is patently untrue.

Bernard Jenkins, matinee idol Tory backbencher, noted: 'When I say I told you so, it's not just about staying out of the euro. It's I told you so, we shouldn't have ratified the Maastricht Treaty!' At this, a Labour backbencher shouted at him: 'What about the Versailles Treaty?' George said that he had told us so on Versailles (sorry, Lisbon, but it's all in Europe). He wasn't going to bring us out of Maastricht either. Everyone looked disgruntled, as if they had eaten a pincushion. George is, and I can say this so I can say that I told you so, becoming dangerously European. 💔

24 November 2010
Sacré bleu! Theresa has chosen
the path of most Resistance

The Home Secretary, not known for being playful, had a mad Michelle moment in the Commons

'Allo, 'Allo. Yesterday the Home Secretary, for a brief but entirely too long moment, slipped into the character of the French resistance fighter, Michelle Dubois, during the immigration statement.

'It is the position...' said Theresa May in her normal voice before suddenly leaning forward, neck encircled by giant pearls, feet clad in leopard-skin kitten heels. She lowered her voice in what was perhaps meant to be sexy, but ended up sounding a bit like a frog-horn.

'I listen very carefully,' she said. 'I will say this oonlee wonze...'

Mais oui! This brought squeals of delighted laughter, even though she had not listened that carefully or she would have known the quote is just: 'Listen very carefully...' And sorry to be a pedant, but this was a statement on the non-EU immigration cap, which therefore excluded Michelle and all the cast of *'Allo 'Allo* on the grounds that they are French and, of less importance perhaps, not real in any way.

In the Commons, everyone was thrilled, not least Ed Balls, her chief tormentor. For almost an hour, Ed had been orchestrating a campaign to hector her on whether she had dropped the Tory election pledge to lower immigration to tens of thousands a year by 2015.

But 'Michelle' had been coy, saying only that it remained her aim to reduce immigration. She would not, despite repeated goading, repeat the date. Ed, eyes popping, jumping round like a restless child, thought it was a U-turn.

'You are in a state of quite extraordinary excitement,' said Mr Squeaker, who is, of course, a character himself in every way.

Ed's eyes strobed. But then Michelle, listening very carefully and saying this oonlee wonze, confirmed that her aim was to do this by 2015. This brought Tory cheers.

Mr Balls, now resembling a jumping bean, popped up after the statement. 'I, of course, commend your chairing,' he said, greasily, to the Speaker. (At times the dialogue in the chamber is beyond parody.) Mr Balls said he had just witnessed 'a U-turn on a U-turn'. (An O-turn?) Inexplicably, Michelle was flirting with Ed: 'I think that the Home Secretary...' This brought whoops. Ed looked thrilled. 'After thirteen years in Opposition,' said Michelle, 'as you'll discover, you make these mistakes.'

I think we all know what René would say to that – and it isn't 'You smart woman!' And then, with only an au revoir, it was over. ❣

26 November 2010
It may be a joke, but is it any pun?

A funny old day in the chamber filled with happiness, Henry VIII, curry, diarrhoea and dwarves

David Cameron wants to start measuring our level of happiness and can I suggest that he start by examining Eric Pickles, who would score twelve out of ten. The man is on Cloud Nine, which, given his size, is a feat that defies the laws of physics. Mr Pickles was on pun-tastic form yesterday, much to the irritation of his arch enemy, the Labour femme fatale, Caroline Flint.

They were the best show in town, a Beauty and the Beast pantomime for the Christmas season. Actually, we may have to revise that to Beauty and the Buddha, for Mr Pickles sits on the front bench, pudgy hands folded over his girth, an expression of deep bliss on his face. The comely Ms Flint, who is ten times better in Opposition than she was in Government, has made it her goal in life to wipe the smile off his face. She thinks his cuts are ruining local government. He thinks they are transforming it with much-needed efficiency reforms.

Ms Flint, long, black hair falling like a curtain round her face, began by hurling at him the fact that the High Court had ruled that he had acted unlawfully in scrapping regional housing plans. This brought the flick of a smile from Mr Pickles. Even the hanky held captive by his top pocket perked up.

Ms Flint said that Mr Pickles had been 'compared to Henry VIII'. Mr Pickles beamed and, at that moment, I could actually see him, in roomy doublet and hose, sitting at the head of a long oak table groaning with food. The smile irritated Ms Flint, who then mocked him as 'Your Majesty'. His smile broadened.

King Pickles now revealed a new policy on puns as he reported his activities: 'And, at the 2010 British Curry Awards, the Government [i.e. Mr Pickles] paid tribute to the spice industry's £4 billion turnaround – a real bhuna for the British economy.'

The courtiers tittered. 'From bin collections to small business tax relief,' said Mr Lime Pickles, 'we will do our utmost to ensure that Britain's curry industry is second to naan.'

'Uhhhhhhhh,' groaned the chamber. David Blunkett, who was supposed to ask a question, stood still, his hands covering his face. 'I can hardly follow that,' he said to hilarity.

Well, I can, for next up, at Business Questions, came something even higher on my happiness index than puns. It happened as Tobias Ellwood, a rather implausible Tory, was trying to curry (sorry) favour with the Speaker. 'Mr Speaker, you are the anecdote to verbal diarrhoea…' he announced.

'Order!' cried Mr Speaker unhappily. Actually, the whole happy index thing may be a sore subject for Little Johnnie Bercow. Only the day before at a press gallery lunch, the Prime Minister, incredibly, had told a dwarf joke about him. Yes, the Prime Minister! As you may remember, last month a Health Minister had become infuriated by Mr Speaker and had called him a 'sanctimonious dwarf'. Mr Speaker, who is vertically challenged but doesn't care, ignored it. But now the Prime Minister himself was piling in, telling this little story to journalists. It seems that someone has backed into Mr Speaker's car.

'I'm not happy,' says Mr Speaker as he surveys the damage.

'Well, which one are you, anyway?' came the response.

Everyone had laughed at the lunch. I'm not sure how happy Mr Speaker was when he heard about it. But, in the chamber, he was being rather kind to Mr Ellwood, who had just made the unfortunate diarrhoea comment: 'The word for which you were vainly searching was probably "antidote".'

At which point, Sir George Young, leader of the House and

totally unflappable, said: 'If I may say so, Mrs Malaprop would
have been proud of him.' Isn't it wonderful? On the happiness
index, it's a ten. ♥

30 November 2010
Everyone is talking a load of Howard Flight

*Forget the double-dip recession, this was a double-dip presen-
tation on the economy that was topped off by some very fine
Cockney slang*

An historic day. The interminable Pre-Budget Report has
been replaced by what supermarkets would call a Bogof
(buy one, get one free) offer. First we got a press conference from Robert Chote, a charismatic economist (two words
that rarely appear together). Then we had George Osborne in
the House. Plus, and I give this equal weight, we have had our
first recorded incidence of Howard Flight's name being used as
rhyming slang.

Mr Chote, the head of the independent OBR, has the task
of telling us if the Government is lying about the economy. The
press conference was packed and I saw that Rupert Harrison, the
tall and handsome chief adviser to the Chancellor, was there as an
official spy, taking notes.

Mr Chote's staff seem to be in awe of him. 'Robert will be
with you in thirty seconds,' panted one of the claque of young
men in intellectual-type spectacles who worked for him.

Indeed Robert was, dark blue silk suit impeccably cut, bog-
brush hair trimmed to reflect a reduced growth forecast for next
year. Robert gave no opinions, only bar charts, some of which
boasted psychedelic colours, with hilariously arcane titles.

There was no drama in the figures, though the sound system
did its best by emitting a long, ear-splitting screech just as the

fetching Stephanie Flanders of the BBC was to ask a question. As the fingernail-screeching, crow-cawing noise ended, Robert said to her: 'You've asked that question before.' Everyone laughed, a noise never heard before at an economics press conference.

Mr Chote's figures seem to rule out a double-dip recession but this was, certainly, a double-dip presentation. Mr Osborne, in the House, was incredibly smug, though, to be fair, he had much to be smug about. He created the OBR and appointed Mr Chote and, though it was all independent, the figures were so in line with Government thinking that it was almost spooky.

'The Plan is working,' trumpeted George (his capital letters) who is not shy about telling us how he's saved us from disaster and now is, of course, saving Ireland as well. At some point in the long list of his achievements (it's a reverse prize-giving, where he gives himself all of them), a delicious shout came from the Labour backbenches. 'He's talking a load of Howard Flight!' chuntered Stephen Pound, official jester.

This brought a titter. I believe it is the first such reference to the Tory peer, who was told to apologise this week after saying that cuts in child benefit would discourage the middle classes, though not those on benefits, from 'breeding'. It's in Hansard now. So it's official. 💔

1 December 2010
Nick's itsy bitsy teeny-weeny policy mankini

Nick, on his way to Kazakhstan, seems a bit over-exposed on tuition fees

Nick Clegg made a quick stop in the Commons on his way to a top-level meeting in Kazakhstan, of all places. Borat believed Kazakhstan was the greatest country in the world ('All other countries are run by little girls,' as the anthem goes).

I cannot think of Borat without also imagining that startlingly lime-green mankini. I do hope that Nick has packed his version of it (yellow, of course). Certainly, yesterday in the Commons, he might as well have been wearing one, for his tuition fees policy left him just as exposed.

Outside, it was a typical Siege Tuesday in Westminster, with students protesting in the snow and choppers whirring above the thin blue line. Inside, Nick had convinced some top Lib Dems (no longer an oxymoron) to come to his Question Time as a sort of thin yellow line. The Ginger Rodent was there but, sadly, no Vince, as he was too busy explaining to TV cameras why he may abstain on his policy to allow £9,000-a-year fees.

Harriet 'Boadicea' Harman demanded to know how Nicky would vote: 'Are you going to vote for, abstain or vote against, as we are?' Nick 'answered' by asking about Labour's policy. 'Is it a blank piece of paper? Is it a graduate tax? We have a plan. You have a blank sheet of paper!' he crowed.

People would judge him by this, warned Harriet. The only principled stand was to vote against. If he abstained, it was a 'cop-out'. If he voted for, it was a 'sell-out'.

Nick taunted right back: 'Since you don't want to discuss your policy...' Yes, well, it is not her question time, but I guess that when your policy is an itsy-bitsy teeny-weeny tuition fees mankini, you've got to be tough.

Next up was Chris Bryant who, as a man who appeared on the internet in his underpants, needed to be there to see this. 'Surely you are man enough to stand up and sign up for what you voted for in the general election?' Little Nicky patronised him (it's one of the many things Dave has taught him), calling Chris 'terrifically excitable'.

The session began to degenerate into something between a siege and a brawl. The Labour MP John Mann, self-appointed global moral authority, demanded: 'A man tours the country telling people if they vote for him he'll abolish tuition fees. Then, when he has the power, he increases tuition fees. What's the best description of the integrity of such a man?'

The Man punched right back: 'This must be the same integrity which led the Labour Party to introduce fees, having said they wouldn't in 1997, and to introduce top-up fees having said they wouldn't in the 2001 manifesto.'

David Winnick, the veteran maverick Labour MP and one of Nicky's main tormentors, asked the big question: 'If you are so confident on tuition fees,' he demanded, 'why don't you go and speak to the students who are demonstrating outside?'

Nick, who believes that the best defence is an offence, mocked Ed Miliband. 'Your own leader, I heard on the radio, said he was tempted to speak to the students and then, when asked why not, he said that he had something in his diary. He must have been staring at a blank sheet!'

Brave words, though we all knew that the real reason Nick couldn't go outside was that it was a bit nippy for that itsy-bitsy mankini. ❦

2 December 2010
Eeyore fights it out with Tigger

Things go from bad to worse for a flailing Ed Miliband

Fly me, I'm Dave! That was the feel of PMQs, which was, let's face it, a mere stopover for our Prime Minister as he jetted in and out of Zurich where he's hanging out with Becks and Wills for the World Cup bid. At PMQs it was as though he were still flying, if by the seat of his pants, elated and on a high.

Then there was Ed Miliband. Actually, make that Ed Milibad. He seemed to be travelling on the world's longest down escalator.

For reasons unknown, his chosen subject was the economic forecast from the OBR, which was, by general agreement, a resounding success for the Government. But Ed, like a seagull picking at the remains of a packed lunch, insisted that it was nothing of the sort.

'I know you are determined to talk the economy down!' cried Dave, speaking in exclamation marks. 'But even you will have difficulty in finding depressing statistics in the OBR report!'

Not so. But Ed's outlook was, like the weather, too dreadful to be believed. Gosh, it was awful, like watching Eeyore fight it out with Tigger. Tory MPs mocked him over his lack of policies, waving blank pieces of paper at him. Ed looked back just as blankly.

Then he commented, almost as an aside: 'You have been doing the job for the last three months and people are beginning to ask, "When's he going to start?"'

Ouch. 'It is no wonder,' snapped Ed, 'that the Foreign Secretary describes this gang as the "children of Thatcher".'

Of course it was supposed to be the ultimate put-down. Dave looked entirely unfazed. He popped up, insouciant, almost lounging on the despatch box. 'Not waving but drowning,' he commented to yet more Tory joy.

Ed looked miserable. Dave, relaxed, was entirely at home. 'My mother is still with us so she is able to testify that what you have just claimed is not literally true,' he said, unnecessarily. 'But let me say this; I would rather be a child of Thatcher than a son of Brown.'

It brought the House down. Dave looked elated and, for a moment, it was as if he were flying. Dave, at his best, has a grace that is wonderful to watch. Ed Milibad watched, shaking his head. Next to him Harriet Harman mouthed the words, 'Son of Thatcher'. And, yesterday, heir to Blair too. 💔

3 December 2010
Alien creature that holds MPs in its grip

MPs were outraged by the horrendous wrongs inflicted on them over their expenses by the new Independent Parliamentary Standards Authority

O h the horror, the horror. The expenses debate was like one of those schlock B-movies, *The Revenge of the Wronged MPs*. While the rest of Britain shivered and shovelled, MPs gathered to emit a collective scream of pain about their expenses. They told terrible tales. There was a claim for a £338 shredder that had not been allowed. One MP had to send a photo of a photocopier (why not a photocopy?) to prove that it existed. Some have had to borrow cars from friends. Can it be more ghastly? 'I am not moaning!' cried one MP.

But they were. They were moaning for Britain but, most of all, for themselves. For the past six months, they have had their expenses regulated by the Independent Parliamentary Standards Authority, which they call The Ipsa, as if it were the creature from the black lagoon. They hate it and yesterday they tried to do to it with words what Hitchcock did in his shower scene.

The charge was led by the urbane Adam Afriyie, the Tory MP for Windsor. He accused The Ipsa of being judge and jury, regulator and regulated. Its systems were so time-consuming that it was nothing less than a threat to democracy. Yes, he actually said that. Don't laugh. Almost everyone in the chamber agreed.

The Ipsa was creating a system where only the rich could be MPs. For the rich did not have to put in receipts, they already owned shredders. 'If a member does not have sufficient resources to subsidise themselves,' claimed Mr Afriyie, 'they are then ensnared in a vice-like grip designed to bring them into disrepute with every single receipt that's produced.'

Don't you like 'vice-like grip'? The Ipsa was a giant creature, its huge hairy hands gripping and squeezing the life out of MPs, intent on wrecking democracy and disallowing shredders.

Ann Clwyd, the senior Labour backbencher, spoke softly but urgently. All MPs had been smeared by the actions of a few. 'During my election campaign, someone came up to me and shouted, "Thief!"' she told a rapt House. 'If I had been a man, I would have run after him and punched him in the face.' But since she was not a thief but an MP, she then used parliamentary privilege to name and shame an Ipsa employee, whom she accused of leaking 'juicy bits' to the press.

More revenge from Tory Roger Gale. He accused The Ipsa of living in the lap of luxury. The Ipsa rent alone was £348,000 a year. The men at the top of The Ipsa had 'inculcated' a 'climate of mistrust'.

'Let's now call a spade a spade,' said Mr Gale, though, actually, he was calling them something much dirtier.

Mr Gale knew MPs in Kent who didn't live near stations and, because of that, they couldn't claim money back (don't try to understand, you have to be an MP). MPs would not be told where to live by luxurious spades! He issued a warning of what would happen if The Ipsa did not change: 'This House, this democracy, will either be the province of the very rich or juvenile anoraks!'

John Mann, a Labour MP who is almost insufferably sanctimonious, got up. 'I am just wondering which I am!' he asked. 'I'm not rich! I've got no inherited wealth!' MPs glared at him. He was letting the side down. Mr Mann told them that if The Ipsa was independent, that meant it was, actually, independent. This had them fuming and fulminating. It is obvious that MPs will not rest until the horrible alien creature is slain or, even better, shredded. ♥

7 December 2010
MI5 was watching Katia? So were a lot of male MPs

I tried to concentrate on this very tiny but very fascinating scandal-ette involving a leggy blonde Russian researcher, but Jude Law – and Spoonerisms – kept distracting me

I blame MI5. The Commons was infected by the kind of spooky coincidences that tend to happen when spies are involved. I couldn't actually see any spies but then, if I could, they wouldn't be spies, would they? I did spy Jude Law, or his doppelgänger, in the VIP gallery, but I tried not to stare, as MI5 may have been using Jude as a distraction.

It was Home Office Questions starring Theresa May, who has just ordered the detention of Katia Zatuliveter, the leggy blonde Russian parliamentary researcher who worked for Mike Hancock, a Lib-Dem MP (of course). We are told that MI5 had been watching Katia for some time. I suspect a few other men in the still male-dominated Commons may have joined them.

Mrs May was saying nothing. I glanced at her shoes, which she often uses to send out coded messages. They were black kitten heels. What did that mean? Everyone in the chamber glanced surreptitiously at each other. She told us that she was reviewing computer security. She blamed it on WikiLeaks. We all wondered if she was really talking about something else.

Another distraction loomed when Nick Herbert, the Police Minister with stentorian tendencies, fell victim to the Spooner virus that had infected the heart of Government (I speak, of course, of the BBC, where *Today* presenter James Naughtie had called Culture Secretary Jeremy Hunt something beginning with 'c'). Now Nick Herbert had just been asked about cuts to front-line policing. 'I don't accept that those are c****,' he said, immediately correcting himself. But it was too late. Everyone was laughing. A Labour MP shouted: 'Thank you, James Naughtie!' The Speaker interrupted, saying to Labour MPs: 'Your hearing is playing tricks. You didn't hear what you thought you heard.'

But, of course, I did hear what I had heard. I thought about blaming Julian Assange or the Lib Dems (who, between them, are responsible for all the woes of the world at the moment), but decided that would be a distraction. It had to be MI5.

I glanced up and saw Jude Law and vowed to stay alert. Wait! What was this? Theresa was getting up to go. Click, click went her kitten heels even as the Labour MP Chris Bryant raised a point of order about (whisper) Katia. 'I hope that you will stay a little brief moment longer,' he pleaded. Click, click.

Mr Bryant noted that the Home Secretary had taken 'action'

on the researcher. 'I am sure you wouldn't want to comment on that as it is still *sub judice*,' said Chris to the Speaker, 'and I understand that person is appealing…' This brought titters. Mr Bryant added hurriedly, 'that decision'. Yes, he did say that. At least I don't need an asterix to report it.

It would, he said, be a very important matter if an agent for a foreign power were employed in this House. If the Home Secretary had something to say, he hoped that she would say it. The Speaker sighed and said: 'Somebody once said of you that your mind climbs mountains without any molehills.'

What did that mean? And did the Speaker really mean to mention 'moles'? Now Ben Bradshaw, the highly excitable former Labour minister, demanded that the Speaker investigate Spoonergate as well. Was this the result of a pact, a dare or a virus? Or, I wondered, moles? Yes, I know it doesn't make any sense. But then nothing does in le Carré. ♥

8 December 2010
A Tory Santa bearing gifts for the Opposition

Ken Clarke doesn't care that the only people who love him are Labour and, yes, Lib Dems

Charles Dickens grew to hate politicians during his time in the parliamentary press gallery, but how he would have delighted in the figure of Ken Clarke yesterday as he danced, bluff and red-faced, belly wobbling, feet shuffling, around his nicer and kinder sentencing policy. From appearances, it was as if Santa had been given the prisons brief.

This is what the hang-'em-and flog-'em Tory backbenchers fear the most. They look at Ken and see their greatest nightmare – a Tory who is being backed by Labour and (possibly even worse) the Lib Dems.

Yesterday, the Libs heaped praise on Ken, and Sadiq Khan, his Labour shadow, could find almost nothing to disagree with. Finally, he announced that Ken's new policy was 'a bluff on crime and a bluff on the causes of crime'. Ludicrous.

Ken hugged Sadiq close (well, as close as that belly allowed) and then gave a robust and merry account of how everyone else agrees with him. 'This morning, I was praised on Alastair Campbell's blog!' he chortled. Why, even Newt Gingrich in America thought he had the right idea. Indeed, boasted Ken, members of all three parties agreed with him!

Ho-ho-ho. But then, from the back benches, arose a spectre of discontent, a ghost of the Tory past, Philip Davies. He pointed to all the career burglars and violent criminals who were not sent to prison and reoffended anyway. 'How can you accept the figures that say too many people are going to prison? Most people in this country will look at those figures and conclude that too few are going to prison!' Ken did a little dance. 'It's not possible to generalise in this way!' he claimed. Mr Davies sat, arms crossed, and shaking his head.

But now, what was this? An apoplectic spectre, if there can be such a thing, in the form of Edward Leigh. He noted, in disbelief, what he had just heard a Tory Secretary of State say – that prison was simply an expensive way of giving communities a break. 'I'm sorry,' he said, 'but communities deserve a break! They deserve a break from being burgled!' Could Ken promise that thieves would be put behind bars? Ken's feet in his slip-on suede Hush Puppies began to shuffle a little slower as he tried to reassure Mr Leigh, to little avail.

But now arose Priti Patel, a new and by far the most comely member of the law-and-order ghost brigade. Would Ken reassure her that dangerous criminals such as paedophiles would go to prison? 'So our streets are kept safe for our children?' she asked.

Ken bowled back. 'Yes!' he cried. 'It's sometimes quite difficult to debate law and order in this country! I have occasionally

to listen to a kind of Looney Tunes debate about whether I am
starting by releasing murderers, rapists, burglars or paedophiles.
Serious criminals should be in prison. I have never met a sane
person who wishes to disturb that.'

Oh dear. The jolliness was wearing thin. Had Santa just
accused one of his own of being loony? I think so. Ho-ho-hum. 💔

10 December 2010
Inside like a siege, outside a peasants' revolt

*In Parliament Square the protesters shouted 'Shame on you' as
MPs voted on tuition fees. For the Lib Dems, split three ways,
it was moment of anguish*

The body language of the Lib Dems said it all. The votes
were being counted and the chamber was heaving, the
wells crammed with MPs, jostling and craning. Simon
Hughes, the deputy Lib-Dem leader, was sitting on the bench,
which makes a change from the fence he'd been on all day (maybe
he had splinters). He'd just rejected an overture from Red Ed
Miliband to vote 'no' with him. The fence may be uncomfortable,
but it was his home.

Nick Clegg, hate figure or future guru, depending on your
view, stood in front of the Lib-Dem benches, locked in fawning
conversation with one of his loyalist MPs. It is the first time I had
seen Nick smile all day. He'd been there at the very beginning
of the debate to hear Vince Cable give a Nutty Professor-type
speech, hands shaking, argument rambling. Nick had fled afterwards, returning five hours later to vote.

Tim Farron, Lib-Dem president, young, blond and ambitious,
had voted 'no'. Now he meandered round, looking for a chum.
Nick turned his back to him as Tim circled, until he'd done an
entire shun pirouette.

The top three in the Lib Dems had voted three different ways and none of them was talking to each other. For a party that loves to bond, it had been a terrible day as they had wrestled with their consciences, which grew until they were like boa constrictors coiling round.

Labour MPs shouted when the result was announced, for they'd cut the Government majority of eighty-three to twenty-one. They pointed at the sparsely populated Lib-Dem benches. For a brief moment, a pensive look occupied the Prime Minister's usually mobile face. It was his coalition Government's first big test and he'd won, though it didn't feel like a celebration.

Outside, students had enlisted the statue of Winston Churchill in their struggle, as they occupied Parliament Square. The cold, crisp air smelt of cordite and vibrated with sound – whistles, chants, shouts, tubas. As I came out of the vote, I could hear them chanting: 'Shame on you! Shame on you!' From the inside, it felt like a siege; from the outside, a peasants' revolt.

The best speech of the day, by far, belonged to John Denham, the Shadow Business Secretary. When he was in Government, John bored for Britain. But yesterday he was tough and eloquent. Where Vince had been fumbling, overcome by Labour MPs giving him the full blowtorch treatment, John was listened to in something, at times, quite close to silence.

'I was a minister once who resigned on a point of principle,' he said (the Iraq War), speaking directly to the Lib Dems. 'After you've done it you realise it wasn't half as bad as you thought it would be. The self-respect you gain far outweighs any temporary loss of position, power or income. This decision matters so much to so many people, I say to the House, if you don't believe in it, vote against it.'

They listened in silence. In the end, the ministers stayed firm but, make no mistake, it was the hardest day for them. ❣

14 December 2010
Ed tries his chat-up lines on the Lib Dems

Ed tries to get Lib Dems who don't agree with Nick to agree with him. But is a mutual hatred society really a good dating gambit?

It felt like the strangest first date in history. Ed Miliband has been Labour leader for almost three months but, at Westminster, we have seen him only at PMQs. Otherwise, it has been like touching a void. Now, here he was, holding his first press conference, newly media trained, trying to control his panda eyes and geek tendencies.

His big idea was to appeal, through us, as a new mate for Lib Dems who, like him, are appalled by Nick Clegg. But I'm not sure a mutual hatred society is such a great dating strategy (though, of course, it can work). I tried to imagine what a wavering Lib Dem would think of this event and this is what I came up with:

- Can you really date someone who looks so much like Wallace? It must be those big round eyes and the lopsided mouth (he talks out of one side, his right, our left). Besides, I'm not sure the Lib Dems would really want to answer to Gromit.
- He has terrible chat-up lines. He was talking about how he, unlike David Cameron and Nick Clegg, hadn't broken his promises. 'I talk of under-promising and over-delivering,' he announced. Can you imagine a Lib Dem trying to explain Red Ed's allure: 'I just love the way he under-promises.' (And, can I note, isn't promising to under-promise still a promise?)
- Ed really is a geek. At one point he noted, rather desperately, that the progressive political tradition also included the likes of Lloyd George and Keynes, who weren't 'Labour people'. 'I agree with Tony Blair on that one. He made a speech in 1995 where he talked about this,' he said. Too much information.

Now we know Ed has TB speeches filed chronologically in his brain. That really is rather scary.

- He hates Tories more than he dislikes Clegg. Ed says 'Tory' as if it were a dirty word. When asked why Dave did not understand ordinary people, Ed jumped in: 'Because he's a Tory!' The real reason he dislikes Clegg is that Ed thinks, at heart, Clegg's a T***.

- Good points include a minor sense of humour. Someone noted that he once said the Lib Dems should be destroyed. 'I think the word was extinct, actually, to be clear. Sorry to be pedantic.' When asked about his 27 per cent approval rating, he said: 'Obviously, I'd like to thank those 27 per cent.' Obviously.

- Can you ever trust a man who killed his brother? Indeed, Ed's relationship with his brother still seems fragile. Yesterday he was told that David had told his local paper that he may return to frontline politics. At this, Ed said: 'I've always said to him, as my brother, my door is always open. But, as the leader of the Labour Party, my door is always open.' How off-putting is that? Then Ed made it worse (which is, actually, hard to do): 'I will look at my copy of the *The Shields Gazette* and see exactly what he said.' But not, of course, pick up the phone.

As dating games go, it's fraught.

Red Ed, clearly, has baggage but some Lib Dems will still be intrigued. ❦

17 December 2010
Plenty of wind and gas, but no spark

Chris Huhne, human drone, drives everyone, including Hansard, to the brink

They say that lightning never strikes twice but it has never even struck Chris Huhne once. Surely it is illegal to have an Energy Secretary without even a spark of the stuff? I really do think that if you rubbed two Chris Huhnes together, even for days on end, you wouldn't see even the tiniest flick of fire.

Yesterday he droned on about his electricity strategy at such length that even Hansard reporters, famously tolerant, kept imploding.

'Oh, my God,' one muttered, as Mr Huhne embarked on another tract about low-carbon pathways.

'Chunter, chunter, chunter,' shouted Labour MPs.

Mr Huhne, his monk's bald spot glowing with his Cancún tan, kept droning about his modelling strategy for 2050. 'On and on and on and on!' shouted the Labour MP Kevin Brennan.

But Mr Huhne, powering on pure ego (surely a renewable resource) would not stop. It took an MP making a point of order about how Mr Huhne wouldn't shut up to make him shut up, but even then he sat down reluctantly with only one half of one buttock on the bench.

'WAFFLE!' shouted a Labour MP. Mr Huhne, undeterred, began to tell us how his policy was going to be 'grandfathered' and thus give us stability. At this I actually thought people were going to cry.

'You have to find a way to sit down now and again,' chided one of several Labour MPs, who got up to complain that the subsidy for low-carbon sources that Mr Huhne was proposing amounted to a subsidy for nuclear power, a concept that he supposedly opposes.

'It could not be clearer that there is no subsidy that attaches to nuclear power,' explained Hr Huhne, as if talking to people who need things explained very, very slowly. 'The subsidy attaches to low-carbon generation, and the reality is that nuclear power is a low-carbon energy source but the subsidy…'

The idea of a subsidy that wasn't a subsidy made the chamber go, well, a bit nuclear. 'That is a subsidy by any other name,' announced Stewart Hosie, a Scottish Nationalist MP. 'Who do you think will feel most betrayed by this U-turn?'

Mr Huhne never allowed himself to look even remotely

ruffled. He understood his sophisticated reasoning. Why couldn't others? But now Caroline Lucas, the only Green, expressed her displeasure. And a Liberal Democrat popped up to ask: 'Shouldn't you explore a levy on nuclear to balance any hidden, if unspecific, windfall subsidy to existing nuclear power stations?' Mr Huhne emitted a sigh. This seemed to enrage Paul Flynn, the cantankerous Labour MP: 'On what day in May were you bewitched by the Pied Piper of nuclear power in learning to love a stealth tax?' Mr Huhne countered with another drone. Finally, a Labour MP noted: 'There will be no shortage of wind or gas while you are in post, that's for sure!' And, you know, Mr Huhne looked chuffed at what he saw, perhaps, as a compliment. ♥

21 December 2010
There's snow crisis here, really

The snowstorm hit us with a vengeance, throwing the country's air and rail into chaos. Inside in the Commons, the Transport Secretary was up to his knees and still digging

I am going to issue an extreme weather warning to Philip Hammond, the Transport Secretary, or, as he was dubbed in the House yesterday, the No-Transport Secretary. You may be Snowman Phil but you are, most definitely, not walking in the air. You are up to your knees in snow and you are still digging.

Phil seemed just a little bit complacent yesterday in the Commons. The road and rail network had performed 'broadly satisfactorily', he said.

There had been 'some disruption' on the trains but the roads had been OK since Saturday. I began to wonder if the No-Transport Secretary had been anywhere over the weekend.

He did admit that, when it came to Heathrow, there were lessons to be learnt. It was 'a very real challenge'.

So there you have it: a very real challenge. I wonder when, in Snowman Phil's world, a challenge becomes a crisis. Obviously not yet.

Phil is tackling this with a kind of elegant languor that you almost have to admire. He has, he told us, not breathlessly, been talking to colleagues from other departments 'on a daily basis' since Friday. But he had – and this is real hold-the-front-page stuff – issued a 'Snow Code' to tell people how to clear their pathways without fear of legal problems. I am not making this up, though at times even I can't believe it's true.

Maria Eagle, his small but explosive Labour Shadow, laid into him. If things were going so well, why were people stuck at railway stations? Why were people in their cars for thirteen hours? She accused him of being in charge of the Department for Chaos.

Phil hated that. 'I think after a heavy dump of snow, we've had a heavy dump of political opportunism! You talk of chaos. Do you remember the chaos last year when you ran out of salt?' Snowballs came thick and fast from the Labour backbenches. After one particular vituperative outburst from John Spellar, Phil said: 'People will see you've got nothing to offer except a meaningless rant!'

Phil said that Labour seemed to want him to institute 'some kind of Moscow central-control'. Tories laughed but, actually, Russia does know more than most about snow.

Tom Watson, attack dog, started to shout. 'What we are asking for is leadership! People are sleeping on airport floors! They've been turfed off trains! They have been frozen in their cars! They are cold in their homes because they are not getting deliveries of domestic fuel. Where is the Prime Minister? He's the Invisible Cam!'

The Snowman hated that. 'I can tell you that people sleeping on airport floors are not helped by this kind of ridiculous rant. What they need is calm, measured, considered response. That is what we are doing. This is an extreme weather event. We will do better than his government did last year.'

Actually, Snowman Phil, I think people sleeping on airport floors probably enjoyed that ridiculous rant. ♥

22 December 2010
Boom-boom! Vince pushes all the wrong buttons

*Nick and Dave had wanted to renew their vows over mulled
wine and mince pies, but then Vince went and ruined it all*

What a car crash. The more I think about it the more furious Nick and Dave will be at what happened yesterday. Vince Cable let them make fools of themselves and it is this, as much as anything else, that will have infuriated the two men who found themselves playing the part of protective dads. Can they ever trust him again? I think we know the answer.

They had woken up (though not together; there are limits to coalition) to find that Vince, despite being a sixty-seven-year-old economist, had been a naughty boy. He'd been taped by a newspaper, bragging about how important he was. He'd called the coalition 'Maoists'. He'd claimed that he could press the 'nuclear button' to end the coalition if he wanted to.

Like so many parents, Dave and Nick decided that the best idea was to maintain a united front. They had already scheduled their first joint press conference since their garden wedding in May. It was at 2 p.m. and I think the original idea had been to renew their vows in public. They laid on mince pies and mulled wine.

Then the whole event was hijacked by Vince's remarks about nuclear buttons and Mao. They came up with a damage control policy that could be summed up as 'Vince, mince, wince'. They would defend him: Vince may have been a fool, but he was their fool. He'd been caught smoking by the bike shed but, at this point, no one realised he'd torched the thing.

Nick took the role of primary parent. 'Vince is embarrassed about what has happened. He's right to be.'

Dave chimed in: 'I agree with what Nick said.'

We had an hour of this. Nick explained away Vince's Maoist gibe as an 'off the cuff' way of saying the coalition had an ambitious agenda.

Dave chipped in: 'I'm not an expert on Maoism and I'm certainly not going to insist on being called the Great Helmsman! Be reassured!'

Nick and Dave provided personal testimonies. Dave told us that he worked well with Vince. They'd been to India together. 'We have a good and businesslike relationship. I think what he said was obviously wrong. He was apologetic in Cabinet. He has good reason to be apologetic. In a coalition, you do have private disagreements. If we all agreed, we'd be in the same party!' Then Dave added playfully: 'Do we find what happened in the paper today embarrassing? Yes! Is it a relief to find a Lib Dem who is so enthusiastic about nuclear weapons? Well, that is another subject altogether!' Nick laughed. 'Boom-boom!' he cried.

The Deputy Prime Minister tried to draw a line under it. 'Vince said he was embarrassed. I totally understand why he was. End of story.'

Except that, of course, it wasn't the end of the story. For as they exited that room, Dave's hand on Nick's shoulder, the news was breaking about Vince's other, far more explosive, remarks about 'declaring war' on the Murdoch empire.

Boom-boom indeed.

(P.S. Within hours of the Murdoch news emerging, Vince was allowed to stay on as Business Secretary but was stripped of all responsibility for media policy.) ❣

December 2010
A sex guide, a compass and other gifts

I dole out my Secret Santa presents to Dave and Nick, Ed and Ed. Of course George ended the year with a sneer...

The political year of 2010 was, for me, the gift that just kept on giving. Elections, coalitions, weddings and even fratricide – it's been non-stop. I am sure you will agree that it's only natural for me to want to give something back. So here, with festive jeer (sorry, cheer), are my Secret Santa presents.

- To Harriet Harman, some respect. She held the Labour Party together after Gordo but, more importantly, her 'Ginger Rodent' joke was tip-top. The new jokey Harriet is a revelation. I'd always assumed she'd had a sense of humour bypass at birth. I was wrong. You've come a long way, baby, as the feminists say.
- To Nick Clegg, some space. Poor Cleggers. It's been a fag of a year, up, down and then, alarmingly, hung in effigy. Do you remember when, at his first PMQs, he declared the Iraq War illegal? That was his finest hour.
- To Tony Blair, peace in the Middle East and, more importantly, a good sex-writing guide. 'I was an animal,' he wrote of a night of passion with Cherie. First she told us about her 'contraceptive equipment' and now this. Too much information on every level.
- To Dave, your own photographer and something for hair regrowth. Actually, he may already be using that stuff. Dave's disappearing bald spot is one of the under-reported stories of the year. Is it a weave? A tiny toupée? Stay tuned in 2011.
- To the Loving Couple (I speak of Dave and Nick, of course), a spa weekend. How else to smooth over those bumps and bruises brought on tuition fees, Vince and general madness?
- To Gordon Brown, a real compass. Last week Gordo said: 'I am not going to the House of Lords. Never. That's not who I am. That's not where I am.' Well, I have to ask, where IS he? Forget going to the Lords. Will he ever be coming to the Commons again?
- To Ed Miliband, some Balls. I know Ed thought it was good management not to give the job of Shadow Chancellor to the fiercely ambitious Other Ed. But when many other Labour frontbenchers fight like sissies (sorry, Harriet), Ed Balls is a hellcat who is wasted on Theresa May.
- To Vince Cable, a helmet. Ditch the Fedora, Vince. Armour up and prepare for the siege.

- To George Osborne, some joy. George, the hate figure that never
  happened, continues to excel in glowering and playing the cad.
  Take this week in the Commons, when he took a question from
  Chris Bryant, a fine parliamentarian who is best known, inevitably, for posing on a gay website. 'You take a particular delight',
  he said to George, 'in playing the role of Baron Hardup.' George
  frowned at this reference to Cinderella's father. Chris burbled on:
  'But can I just say in the nicest Christmassy way possible that all
  your austerity talk does provide real anxiety for my constituents.
  Can I please just encourage you, just sometimes, to play Prince
  Charming instead?' The Chancellor looked appalled. 'At least I'm
  not the pantomime dame,' he shot back. Chris looked stunned.
  'Withdraw!' cried a Labour backbencher at George. But the
  Chancellor just chuckled to himself. I've always seen George as a
  scorpion and I could almost see the venomous tail twitch.
- Finally, I would like to give Jacob Rees-Mogg a slim volume
  of poetry. The new MP for Somerset North East is becoming one of my favourites. The Mogg, as he is called, is like
  a character from another century as his lanky form reclines,
  languidly, watchfully, on the green benches. Now, it has long
  been my belief that there is not enough poetry spoken in the
  chamber. So imagine my delight when I learnt that the Mogg
  had recited 'God Speed the Plough' as part of a filibuster
  mounted against a Private Member's Bill about sustainable
  farming. 'I have fruits; I have flowers / The lark is my morning
  alarmer,' he intoned but barely had he godspeeded when he
  was interrupted by the Labour MP Joan Walley, who claimed
  to speak for thousands of people who did not want poetry in
  the chamber. 'In the run-up to the 800th anniversary celebra-
  tions of the Magna Carta,' she said, 'they want this place to be
  dealing with real issues about sustainable food.' Is she serious?
  Surely poetry is the food of love, as Mr Darcy might have said.
  Actually, I wonder if the Mogg knows him?

Chapter Six

Playing Happy Families

It was a grim midwinter – what with health reforms, tuition fees, and forest fires – and the economic news was as bad as the weather. Dave and Nick tried to keep smiling through it all, though at times those lips looked frozen. But Nick in particular had reason to be happy for he was heading towards the great Lib-Dem moment that was the Alternative Vote referendum. Other reasons to be cheerful included the Royal Wedding, not to mention Ed Miliband's nuptials. But it must be said that sometimes it felt as if Dave and Nick were just staggering together towards their first anniversary party, the location of which was a shock to us all. 💔

11 January 2011
If Ed Miliband had a vision for the future, it was beyond me

The first press conference of the new year was a painful affair, with Alan Johnson in the naughty chair

The new year for Ed Miliband began not with a bang but a stare. 'Happy new year to you,' he trilled to the fifty or so press who had assembled for his New Year, New Me press conference. But, as he said this, his giant, brown panda eyes were staring not at us but someone else hovering above and beyond us. What WAS he looking at? He spoke at us, but his eyes were elsewhere. It was most discombobulating, like seeing someone who had over-Botoxed so that only the mouth moved. I craned my head round. Was it a Teleprompter? A camera? A ghost? Or, better yet, his brother? I could see nothing, but Ed looked so alarmed – we are talking full myxomatosis mode – that I feared that he must be looking in a mirror. If so, I understand his concern.

It was an hilarious set-up. Ed was at the lectern, staring but not at us, while Alan Johnson, the Shadow Chancellor Who Knows Nothing, was sitting in a black leather chair next to him. It was like the opposite of *Mastermind* (Mini-mind?): how many basic economic questions can you get wrong? Every once in a while Ed would let Alan answer a question, standing by, watching him closely, as if he were a bug under a microscope.

'Are you saying it doesn't matter that your Shadow Chancellor doesn't know what VAT is applied to?' asked a hack.

'No,' countered Ed. 'Alan clearly does know these things.'

Alan, who clearly doesn't know these things, looked at us (finally, eye contact!), blushing. Ed announced: 'I would take his judgement over George Osborne's any day.' Alan squirmed. He was on the naughty chair. It can't last: Alan Johnson looked like a dead man sitting.

It is a dubious honour to report that Ed is getting better at the political art of not answering questions. Did he think that David Cameron was a liar? 'My mother taught me to never call anyone a liar, and so I'm not going to,' he chirped. 'I think they are practising a deceit about the past to justify a series of ideological judgements about the future.'

So, not lying, just deceiving. As opposed to Ed, who may just be making it up. When asked about his brother's alleged TV career, he said: 'David will be successful in anything that he does.' I laughed but Ed did not. Finally, he was asked to sum himself up. He told us that he was 'passionate' about Britain. He said this woodenly, without passion. He stared out beyond us. Was he getting messages from outer space? If so, I think we should be told. ❦

Polished and unbreakable, Ten-Carat Bob lived up to his name

The subject of bankers continued to provoke fury, but MPs couldn't dent this Diamond

Diamond is the hardest natural material in the world and I can attest that, after watching the eponymous Bob for two and a half hours yesterday, he is true to his name. Bob was unbreakable, a sheer cliff face of self-belief. Actually, there is a good chance that Bob is harder than diamonds: in future we may go to the jewellers and ask for a Ten-Carat Bob.

MPs on the Treasury Select Committee, chisels in hand, were driven by something close to fury. The new Barclays CEO repelled them easily with a pure Master of the Universe performance. For him, the banking crisis is so last year. 'There was a period of remorse and apology for banks – that period needs to be over,' he explained. 'The biggest issue is how do we put some of the blame game behind us?'

People say he is brash. No less an expert than Lord Mandelson has called Bob the 'unacceptable face of banking'. But yesterday Bob was not brash. He was precise and controlled. He arrived at the packed hearing room, arranged his papers just so and placed his pen on top at an exact angle. Only his smile, big and American, whiter than white, was flashy. He rarely deployed it.

'Listen,' said Bob, his flesh-coloured lips blending perfectly into his face. 'I understand there is a lot of debate in the area of bonuses. There is a lot of sensitivity. I am committed as Chief Executive to being responsible and to providing any restraint I can. I can assure this committee that bonuses are not taken lightly. We pay what is appropriate to pay.'

Everyone stared. Of course they did not take bonuses lightly;

millions of pounds make a heavy load. Bob's own reputed bonus for 2010, in which he seemed utterly disinterested, is £8 million.

'Do you understand how toxic this issue is in the real world?' asked Stewart Hosie, a Scot Nat, 'where people cannot get mortgages and they hear about £7 million or £8 million bonus pools?'

'We are sensitive,' said Bob. 'We are listening.' The banks had done a 'poor job' of explaining their 'compensation process'. Bonuses were part of an integrated system. He wanted to tell us how investment banks contributed to society.

John Mann, bulldog Labour MP, demanded: 'Why are you worth all the money that you are paid?' Bob, face like glass, ventured: 'My own remuneration, that is a decision that the board makes.'

John noted that Bob had said that he wanted to show 'any restraint he could'. 'If offered a bonus this year, will you agree to take no bonus?' he demanded.

Bob did not answer directly. He never does. Diamonds are Forever Vague, as Shirley Bassey almost sang. Bob explained that he had taken no bonus for the past two years. 'Today I have not been awarded a bonus,' he noted. 'The process has not taken place yet.'

Yes, said the Bulldog, but if offered one, would Bob reject it? 'I think the best answer I can give you is to go back to how the process works and if I was going to make a personal decision I'd make that decision with my family, as I did last year.'

See what I mean? Almost inhuman but, true to his name, brilliant. ❦

14 January 2011
Mr Invincible fires blanks at bankers

Vince Cable, nuclear warrior, came to the Commons, but would he be armed and dangerous?

I rushed to the Commons to see Vince, the nuclear warrior. It is his first appearance since he told an undercover reporter that he thinks the Government is Maoist and that he could bring it down because he has nuclear weapons. What a shame, then, to see him in civvies without even one ICBM in tow.

Tommy Watson, the Billy Bunter-ish Labour backbencher, couldn't resist having a bit of fun at the expense of the man who, in another life, joked that Gordon Brown had managed to go from Stalin to Mr Bean. Mr Watson noted: 'The House will have noticed in recent weeks your remarkable transformation from Chairman Mao to Mr Has-Been. Will you tell us how you are enjoying the long march of Government?'

Vince did not laugh. Indeed, his mouth formed a little moue of disdain. Since obtaining nuclear weapons, he has lost his sense of humour. After all, he is a soldier now. 'It is like fighting a war,' he said of Government. And now I could just see him thinking that here he was, Mr Invincible – it was no coincidence that the aircraft carrier has his name – having to endure this oversized pipsqueak in pinstripes who had dared to adapt his very own wonderful joke!

'That must be about the tenth repetition of that joke,' noted Invincible drily. 'It was nothing like as good as my original.' He sat down with a huff, scattering his mad array of papers even further. I suppose that when you are, like Russia, armed at all times, you need to have a bit of an ego. As Mao almost said: 'Let a thousand flowers boom!'

Actually, forget Mao and Stalin. In Westminster, Dr Cable's actual transformation has been from Mr Bean to Has-Been. At least he is not a Never Was. But there is no doubt that the Sage of Twickenham, the only one who spoke sense about the financial chaos, is no more. Instead, in the chamber was a man who seemed prickly and defensive. His hands shook, he mumbled, he dodged questions on banks and bonuses. He repeatedly looked up at the press gallery, for we too are the enemy.

He seemed a lonely figure, though, as Mao must have also

said, the long march was never going to be a picnic (unless, of course, you are an ant). It was noticeable that Vince received no support from any backbencher, with Tories and Labour united in a call for Vince to unleash his 'armoury' against the banks. Vince opened his mouth and a thousand flowery words bloomed – but no action.

MPs got increasingly frustrated. Finally, Gordon Banks, for Labour, exploded: 'We have just heard a lot of drivel from the Secretary of State!' Would Vince use his 'nuclear option' to stop bonuses? Or would he dance away? Vince accused him of 'tortured metaphors'. I had a vision, briefly, of a dancing metaphor in a Guantánamo jumpsuit. But it must be said that Vince, if not tortured, looked quite miserable. Still, as he should know, war is hell. 💔

20 January 2011
MPs play to gallery as Devil wears Thatcher

Everyone was agog when a Hollywood A-lister dropped in to watch our weekly pantomime

I was wondering why Ed Miliband and David Cameron seemed more nervous than usual at Prime Minister's Questions when I spotted, in the VIP seats, the pale and luminescent face of someone who looked exactly like Meryl Streep. I peered closer. The trademark tortoiseshell specs could not hide the fact that it was, actually, her, a Hollywood A-lister watching our weekly political panto.

I willed PMQs to live up to Meryl. She is our most famous observer since Brucie. Later, I learnt that Dave had 'facilitated' her visit as she is to play Mrs Thatcher in a movie called *The Iron Lady* (I had rather hoped it was to be a musical called Maggie Mia but sadly this is not the case).

So how to explain yesterday's PMQs to Meryl? Well, to coin one of her film titles, it's complicated. First I must apologise for some shameful overacting in the chamber. Yes, Mr Speaker, I mean you.

For the past few weeks, PMQs has been a flippant affair. This week it was far more serious. Ed began with a short, sharp question about hospital waiting times. Dave, lamely, said: 'We want waiting times to come down.' The jeers were overwhelming and, as he struggled on, Mr Speaker pounced. After all, Meryl was here and he wanted to shine.

'Order!' he cried, for it is his catchphrase. 'Last week a ten-year-old constituent of mine came to observe PMQs and asked me, "Why do so many people shout their heads off?"!' He paused before shouting: 'It is rude and should not happen.' Was it my imagination or did Mr Speaker, having delivered this little cameo, glance over to Meryl?

After this pause, Dave and Ed resumed tearing chunks out of each other. 'You are taking the "national" out of the National Health Service,' shouted Ed. 'Why are you so arrogant as to think you are right and all the people who say you are wrong are wrong?' At which Dave, neatly, shouted: 'First of all, you are wrong.' What followed was a great deal of smoke and fire, but the Devil does not wear Prada in the chamber (sorry, I had to get that in) but is in the detail, and yesterday Dave did a bad job of explaining why he is reorganising the NHS.

It all ended, for this is certainly not Hollywood, badly. Ed tore into Dave for breaking promises, at which point Dave threw down his briefing notes (I'm sure he hoped that Meryl noticed the measured yet powerful way he did this). 'The same old feeble pre-scripted lines,' Dave said with a perfectly pitched chuckle. 'I am sure they sound fantastic in the bathroom mirror!' So who won? Only Meryl, I'm afraid, who didn't leave the chamber until Norman Baker began to drone on about sustainable transport. I think it was the words 'community bus' that, finally, made her flee. ❦

22 January 2011
A reckoning of sorts as Blair voices his regret

*Finally, after years of blood, sweat and tears, Tony Blair says
the words that people have been waiting to hear*

Tony Blair was nearing the end of his marathon session
at the Chilcot Iraq Inquiry when, behind him, a woman
dressed in black began to cry, openly and silently. Her face,
etched in grief, crumpled. Mr Blair could not see her but I swear
he must have felt her. Suddenly the entire room seemed to swoon
with emotion.

'I wanted to say something,' said Mr Blair and his voice, previously so confident, agile, powerful, began to crack. His almost
preternaturally blue eyes blinked too quickly.

The audience was full of those who had lost family members
in Iraq. They had waited years for an apology, dreamt of it, prayed
for it, raged for it. Now it was nigh, it seemed a surprise. 'At
the conclusion of the last hearing, you asked whether I had any
regrets,' Mr Blair said, staring ahead at the committee, though
surely his words were for the sixty people behind him. 'I took it
as a question about the decision to go to war and I answered that
I took responsibility.'

The woman – later I was told it was Sarah Chapman, who lost
a brother in Iraq – was still crying.

If this was Hollywood, Mr Blair would have turned around
and faced them. But it isn't (even his acting talents appear to
have their limits) and so, instead, the audience in this strange
claustrophobic basement room at the Queen Elizabeth II conference centre in Westminster could only watch his back, clad in
an immaculate blue suit, with red and wary eyes. The disem-
bodied voice continued: 'That was taken that I had no regrets
about the loss of life, and that was never my meaning or my
intention.'

The whole place was a virtual flotation tank of emotion. 'Of course, I regret deeply and profoundly the loss of life, whether from our own Armed Forces, those of other nations...' No one heard the end. 'Too late!' cried someone. 'Too late!' echoed another.

Mr Blair's back did not move, there was not even a wrinkle of acknowledgement.

'Quiet please!' shushed Sir John Chilcot, who hates outbursts and has worked hard to avert them for the past fifteen months. Mr Blair, gathering himself, began to expand on lessons learnt. Two women in the audience stood up and turned, until they had their backs to him. They stayed there, silent witnesses, silent protesters, for a minute, before leaving early.

The last time Mr Blair had faced the committee was a year ago – the occasion of the famous non-apology. Then he had begun nervously and ended on a rampaging high, warning the world about Iran. This time he oozed confidence and righteousness throughout. We could see the word IRAN in big letters in one of his binders and, sure enough, there was a plea on that.

But it will only be the 'regret' that we remember. As he walked from the room, his eyes never flicking from the side exit, a voice crackled through the air. 'Your lies killed my son,' said Rose Gentle. 'Hope you can live with it.'

Then the audience left quietly, almost dazed. 'He'll never look us in the eye,' muttered Sarah Chapman. This may indeed be the case, but the scene in that room seemed to me like some sort of reckoning. Imperfect and messy, yes. Dysfunctional, certainly. But a reckoning, nonetheless. 💔

26 January 2011
There's no excuse like a snow excuse

It's cold, it's snowing and it's the wrong kind of weather on the line for the Chancellor

Memo to Dave and Co: the next time there is bad news, don't make it worse. As the appalling growth figures were announced yesterday, George Osborne loomed on to our screens, coatless, in front of some dead twigs in the No. 10 garden. Unusually for Downing Street, there were no actual rats scuttling by.

We haven't seen much of George lately. Indeed, I think my last sighting was that photograph of him skiing in Klosters in that lovely skull-and-crossbones-patterned snood. This time he had ditched the snood, but he was just as scary.

'The weather had a huge effect,' announced George. 'It was the coldest December in 100 years. People couldn't get to work.' (Though, of course, some could get to Klosters.) The man from the BBC noted that, if you stripped out the snow (which sounded painful), growth would still be flat. 'The weather clearly had a bad effect,' insisted George. 'Look, we've had bad weather. It's the worst December for 100 years.'

Surely, though, this was the worst case of blaming the weather in 100 years. As a commuter, I am an expert on excuses. I have heard it all: the wrong kind of snow, leaves, ice, hail. But now George had gone one further: the wrong kind of news was on the line, it must be the weather's fault. (Snow in December: who knew?) In three minutes, George blamed the weather eleven times. The other thing he kept saying was: 'We are not going to be blown off course by the bad weather.' Even though, actually, it was obvious to everyone that they just had been.

Vince Cable, allegedly in charge of growth, was due to hold a celebratory press conference yesterday morning. It was abruptly cancelled and blamed on the traffic (the worst traffic in 100 years). The press conference was rescheduled for 12.30 p.m. I got there on time, one of ten journalists in a room that could accommodate a hundred. It would never have happened in Lord Mandy's day. Vince was then fifteen minutes late (the wrong kind of news means delays all day).

My, but it was a grim affair. Vince has the air of a man who is walking the plank but still looking around to see if anybody has noticed that he is. Vince was alarmingly off-message on the weather: 'We had a bad quarter, lots of it weather-dependent, not all of it.' Not all of it? I do fear for Vince's future. Sometimes you don't need a weatherman, as Dylan once almost sang, to know which way the snow blows. 💔

27 January 2011
Magnificent Mogg is a gift to the rambling Ed

It was turning into a busy January, what with Ed Balls taking over from Alan Johnson as Shadow Chancellor and Dave's aide, former News of the World *editor Andy Coulson, resigning and slipping out of Downing Street*

The two Red Eds entered the Chamber, walking together in stride, rapt with interest in each other, talking away as if this were a first date. Which, of course, it was. They sat down, smirking. They must have thought, sitting there in their matching lavender ties, that this was their lucky day. The growth figures were appalling. The PM had lost his key aide Andy Coulson. And there were (real) rats in Downing Street. How could they lose?

Ed M began with his trademark sharp and short question, this one about what the cause was of the 'disappointing' growth figures. Dave cast aside his briefing book, which could mean only one thing: he had actually been briefed this time. He agreed the figures were disappointing. And he didn't blame the weather. He blamed the economy he'd inherited. The recovery was always going to be 'choppy' and 'difficult'. This answer, straightforward and honest, for a politician at least, threw the Eds completely. Ed Balls, who really must try to stop smirking at some point, smirked. Ed M floundered.

What is one of the worst crimes an Opposition leader can commit at PMQs? The answer is in the title. This time Ed got up and asked, well, nothing at all. Instead he invited the PM to 'confirm' that growth was flat, setting aside the weather.

Fingers NOT on buzzers!

Test paper over. Tea-break moment. Ed M looked quite goofy. Ed B smirked. Ed recovered only when he accused Dave of being arrogant. Dave looked up at that, for it is his weakest point, and answered by saying something patronising, then childish, then arrogant. Labour and Tory MPs, thrilled that the contest was back on their level, i.e. the gutter, shrieked with joy.

It was time for Ed's last 'question'. He noted that it was said that, without Essex Boy Andy Coulson next to him, Dave could not relate to ordinary people. 'You are out of touch with people's lives,' Ed ranted. I waited for a question but it never came. What was going on? Was this Prime Minister's Rambles? It was another gift to Dave, which he accepted with alacrity.

But then Ed got his very own gift, for the next person to be called was Jacob Rees-Mogg. The Mogg arose from his corner position, where he likes to languish like someone out of *Brideshead Revisited*, to huge Labour cheers. If there is ever anyone who personifies the words 'out of touch', it may be The Mogg.

His voice, which has an antique timbre of the very posh, boomed as if it were from another century: 'Is not the lesson from the noble Baroness Lady Thatcher that, when you have set an economic course, you should stick to it?' Labour MPs screamed, 'MORE!' Dave, abashed, agreed. The two Eds smirked.

I do hope they are grateful to the Magnificent Mogg who, in his own pithy way, made their points for them. So who won? It has to be Mr Mogg. ❧

1 February 2011
Bottoms up! Here's to the Lansley revolution

The Health Secretary tries to explain his top-down bottom-up revolution

Blood and guts, threats and screams of pain. In so many ways the Health debate was like a scene from A&E on a Saturday night. It was like *Casualty*, but with much more talk about bottoms.

I thought that Andrew Lansley, the Health Secretary, the technocrat's technocrat, might blow a gasket (a technical term understood by all A&E doctors). He didn't help himself because he never does. 'The purpose of this Bill can be expressed in one sentence...' he began. Labour MPs interrupted, shouting: 'It's a scandal.' Mr Lansley grimaced.

The thing about plotting a revolution is that it helps to be a revolutionary. Mr Lansley, phlegmatic and laborious, is anything but. He is about as inspiring as a toothbrush. He loves detail. The whole speech felt like small print. The language is all about pathways, empowerment – and bottoms.

'An NHS organised from the bottom up, not the top down,' said Mr Lansley. What does it mean? Can someone at the top order a bottom-up revolution? There is a rumour that all it means is that Mr Lansley is putting himself forward for Rear of the Year. He attacked Labour for their endless reorganisations (he is an irony-free zone). He can hardly wait to start giving away his power. (We'll see how that goes.)

Mr Lansley has been doing Health for seven years, and believes that no one understands it as he does. I thought he might hit a Labour MP who dared to ask about hospital closure. 'Time does not permit me to explore the extraordinary ignorance of that,' he said in a bottom-up, pain in the rear, sort of way.

John Healey, for Labour, treated the plan like a piece of gum on his shoe and pleaded with the Lib Dems, looking pathologically glum, to see it for what it was, partial privatisation: 'This is not your policy, but it is being done in your name.'

Behind Mr Healey sat a tremendously excitable David Miliband. What a joy to see him in the chamber. Some people's emotions show on their sleeves, Mr Miliband's are on his face. Cheeks out, lips popping, forehead scrunching. In a short, sharp, eloquent speech, he dismissed the Bill as a 'poison pill'. I do hope that the Milibanana returns to the front bench soon; he is much missed.

No debate on the NHS would be complete without a loud sneer from the Beast of Bolsover. 'Why on earth should the Health Service be changed?' cried Dennis Skinner, feet apart, ancient sports jacket flapping. 'All those miners in my constituency who were wanting those knees replaced, those hips replaced, they've all been done! That's what the people in Bolsover know.'

He sat down to cheers.

Mr Lansley looked disgusted. Clearly, bottom-up does not include Bolsover. ♥

2 February 2011
Weary Lordships suffer weird brand of democracy

The Lords were in a revolting mood over Nick Clegg's beloved AV referendum Bill

To the Lords, to see Day Sixteen of the epic filibuster battle being waged by Labour peers to thwart the Parliamentary Voting System and Constituencies Bill. It was, I must report, carnage. Indeed, it is impossible to describe without the words 'mad as a box of frogs'. Let's hope no one protesting in Egypt, willing to die for democracy, ever tunes in.

So Day Sixteen, Hour Eighty-Five, amendment 110ZZA and 110ZZB, and the debate was whether the Electoral Commission should be required to tell us what we are voting for on 5 May, i.e., explain the AV voting system. The proposition was that they should do this in an 'unbiased' and 'impartial' way and in plain English.

Impossible! That was the view of Lord Davies of Stamford, formerly known as Quentin with the Terrible Comb-Over. He used to be Defence Procurement Minister (enough said). Now he was telling us why he (and Hegel) were sure that the Electoral Commission could never attempt this. 'The anti-positivists, the traditional Hegel–Heidegger post-modernists, would say there is no thing as objective reality anyway,' he announced. As it happens, he proclaimed, the positivists also would advise the Electoral Commission that such a thing was not possible.

'It is asking human beings to do what no human being can do,' announced Lord Davies. 'I don't think any of us can produce an opinion which is genuinely unbiased. It think it is philosophically impossible and practically impossible.'

At this, Lord Anderson of Swansea popped up, confusing his nineteenth-century German philosophers. Had Lord Davies just been talking about Nietzsche's view of 110ZZA?

'Hegel!' cried Lord Davies.

'Then I wonder if one might follow the Marxist dialectical and have a thesis, an anti-thesis and a synthesis,' offered Lord Anderson, immediately coming up with a problem for this. 'No one actually favours the alternative vote,' he proclaimed.

A fellow Labour peer disagreed and shouted: 'Mr Clegg!'

Lord Anderson considered this. 'In God-like isolation he may well but I suspect that even Mr Clegg does in fact prefer other systems!' he said. 'What is clear is that the AV is a total orphan system.'

A Lib Dem got up wearily. 'Are you aware that the leader of your own party supports AV?' he asked. Lord Anderson admitted he had never spoken to Red Ed Miliband (unlike Marx, with whom he obviously has regular contact). But he still knew that, given a choice, Mr Clegg, Mr Cameron and Mr Miliband would prefer another voting system.

As this nonsense raged, Lord Strathclyde, the Tory Leader of the Lords, sat, like a mountain, impregnable. How can he stand it? I glanced over to see if the new Black Rod, Lieutenant General David Leakey, introduced only an hour earlier, his lace cuffs and jabot a wonder to behold, was in his place. He was not. Good man.

I knew I could not take much more.

Now Lord Foulkes explained that, whatever Hegel and Marx put together on AV for the voters, it would have to be made available in Punjabi, Polish and, most importantly, Welsh. And it all needed checking. Hadn't someone once said that, when translated, the Welsh were asked: 'Do you believe in God or would you prefer a daffodil?'

It seems incredible that there are not only more hours of this, but more days. Democracy has never been this weird. ❦

3 February 2011
Do I hear the cry of 'TIMBER'?

Labour lumberjacks were in full roar over the coalition plan to sell off the forests

TIMBER!' This was the cry that should have gone out across the land at about 5.15 p.m. Caroline Spelman, Secretary of State for Woodland Sales, did not crash when she sat down. She is far too genteel for that. Instead, she sort of fluttered on to the front bench, not a mighty oak felled but a sapling at rest.

Across the way, Labour lumberjacks were in full roar.

'Why would a community buy back a forest that they already own?' demanded one MP, axe in hand. 'It's like having your car stolen and then sold back to you.'

Caroline flapped a dainty wrist and looked earnestly, plaintively at the lumberjacks. She wittered, in her well modulated and well-heeled way, that this must be seen as an 'opportunity'. It was 'really exciting'. Behind her, Tories watched with what can only be called alarm. It got worse. 'I have children,' she shared. 'I know what a lifeline those woodlands are in the long summer holidays.'

Ms Spelman does not make it easy to take her seriously. She fights like a hairdresser or, even worse, a lady who lunches. It was as if she were doing battle with a cucumber sandwich in one well-manicured hand, her pinky finger extended. 'I am glad that I am not so cynical about society,' she scolded the lumberjacks. And then she had a little flounce.

In contrast, Mary Creagh, for Labour, proved that she's a lumberjack and she's OK. 'The countryside is on the move against this Tory-led Government's plan to privatise England's forests,' she cried. 'People are furious at the environmental vandalism.'

The chamber was packed and febrile. Ms Creagh is one to watch, sharp, clever and, that rarest of things in politics, human. It helped that, unlike poor Caroline, her backbenchers were rooting for her. (Sorry about the roots, but I hope yew have twigged that, fir sure, this sketch could be so full of puns that it would be barking mad.) Actually, there was much pun-fun among the lumberjacks. 'The Liberal Democrats on this issue can't see the woods for the trees,' cried a Labour backbencher as the Commons cheered, for we all knew that someone would have to say this.

'He's stealing all my lines,' moaned Ms Creagh, who then began to wonder why the forest-loving Danny Alexander wasn't in the chamber. (You may remember, he is a ginger rodent and they do live in the woods.) This enraged the Tory minister Jim Paice, who shouted for so long that his microphone had to be turned off. The Deputy Speaker screeched: 'Sit down! Minister, you will sit down,' as if he were a Labrador.

The Lib Dems, tree-huggers all, kept their axes, but not their anxieties, concealed. They are fearful of what could happen to public access. As yet another Lib Dem issued a warning on this, a Labour backbencher shouted: 'He's branching out.' To which, you can only say, fir sure. ❦

4 February 2011
MPs giddy at the thought of Whitehall's wine cellar

*Sir George Young shows a bit of bottle as Leader of the House
at Business Questions*

Some MPs are taking the Age of Austerity personally. Take Tom Watson, the Labour troublemaker who looks as if he has enjoyed the good things in life, much to the distress of his long-suffering, Al Capone striped suits. Yesterday he arose during Business Questions to announce that he had a 'vintage' query.

Sir George Young, the Leader of the House, smiled. He knew what was coming. For MPs, the days of wine and roses may be over, but not, for Mr Watson, the ways of whine and rosé. He is on a personal mission to make the Government sell its cellar. 'The Information Commissioner has forced the Foreign Office to give me a stock list of the ministerial wine cellar,' boomed Mr Watson. 'There's a Chateau Latour 1962 in there valued at £3,600!'

Oooohhhhh! MPs let out a little cry of surprise and longing. For this fact, on a day in which the Independent Parliamentary Standards Authority (Ipsa) had rejected one MP's 50p claim for a bottle of milk, seemed fantastical. (Other bottles in the cellar include a Chateau Petrus 1978 worth £2,500. And, ludicrously, the Chateau Palmer 1975, £120 plus, was described as a claret 'rich and excellent with some austerity'.) Mr Watson, who knows when he's on to a winner, teased: 'Can you tell me which minister deserves to drink it?' Sir George ducked his head as MPs giggled. You've heard of gallows humour. This was austerity hilarity.

Yesterday the only possible candidate for such a prize was Sir George himself, widely praised for showing a bit of bottle with his restrained but deadly attack on the hated Ipsa expenses regime. Now Sir George produced his own amazing fact. 'I have made some enquiries and you will be pleased to hear that consumption of wine has fallen 30 per cent since the coalition took over.'

Can this be true? Although this brought calls for more sober Government, if anything everyone seemed a bit giddy yesterday, if not tipsy. This included Hilary Benn, the Shadow Leader who is a secret star of the Labour front bench, who revealed that he had been reading Sir George's blog. Sir George grimaced as Mr Benn trumpeted: 'Musing on hard times he wrote, "I predict that *The Times*' list for the most popular girls' names of the year may include a new one: Austerity".'

But, Mr Benn predicted, unpopular boys names this year would include Dave, George and Nick. 'If you are looking for alternatives can I suggest Complacency and Incompetency and, as for the Deputy Prime Minister, that's an easy one: Duplicity. What's in a name? A lot!'

Sir George mouthed the word 'naughty' at Mr Benn. Sure enough, the Speaker popped up. 'I think I will take the last observation as a joke,' he announced, 'but in any other context the use of the word "duplicity" would not be appropriate.'

Sir George suggested that perhaps Prudence should make a comeback. The chamber seemed not so much live and unplugged yesterday as just a little bit uncorked. ❣

15 February 2011
The Big Relaunch takes place in a very small room

It's all a bit of a joke as the Big Society has yet another relaunch

If you don't know what the Big Society is, then you are reading the right column. Only yesterday morning, I too had no idea what the Big Society was. I was plagued by questions. Not, sadly, how do you make the world a better place, but questions such as why isn't it called the Large Society or, even, the XXXL

Society (thus potentially attracting lager drinkers as well)? But then I went to the Big Relaunch and discovered all the answers.

First, Big Society, small room.

Yesterday it was standing room only and it made us feel cosy, if not a little nauseous. Dave was in the middle, stripped down to his white shirt (which, as all Dave-watchers know, means he is trying to get closer to the people). He roamed around a little circular bar table, wired for sound with his microphone pack on his belt.

Big Society, huge personality.

Yesterday, at 9.15 a.m., John Bird, the founder of *The Big Issue*, suddenly took over and shouted: 'Knock, knock!'

How exciting, I thought, an ice-breaker game.

John shouted: 'Mayonnaise!'

Stunned silence, followed by John singing: 'Mayn-eyes have seen the glory of the coming of the Lord…!'

Oh dear. That's the thing about a crammed room. It's hard to leave. Then Mr Bird told a joke about a man who goes into a shop and asks where the camouflage jackets are. The shopkeeper answers: 'They're good, aren't they?'

Oh dear. We were all grateful when the Prime Minister arrived. He told us that, at breakfast, his daughter Nancy had said: 'What are you doing today, Daddy? I suppose it's another one of your boring speeches.' Dave looked a little sad, though, it must be said, Nancy was right.

Dave defined the Big Society for us. It's vague, but it's not. It's not one thing but lots of things. It's about us having power. It's not a cover for cuts. It's not going to make him popular. He's passionate about it anyway. The one word that summed up the Big Society was 'responsibility'.

What did it mean? Dave took questions. He was told that the Scouts have a 50,000 waiting list because there are too few Brown Owls because of all the criminal bureau checks. Dave agreed that was terrible and revealed that he had run a Sunday School crèche 'very badly' and 'very occasionally'.

The key tool of the Big Society is transparency. Dave's forcing councils to reveal all so we can be empowered to run our local failing pub. (Yes, I know it sounds strange. I am only the messenger.) Dave can't tell councils what to do: 'This is a democracy. It is not a dictatorship.' He sounded wistful.

One of the Big Society people there told us that there is a 'global marketplace for sharing'. She wants to 'harness the power of sharing'. After all, many people didn't even know their neighbours. 'Obviously I know mine,' chortled Dave. 'It's George Osborne!' This got a laugh, I know not why.

Someone told Dave that she was 'confused dot com' about the Big Society. I do hope that you, dear reader, are no longer confused dot com. We now know that the Big Society is: small rooms, knock-knock jokes, big ideas and harnessing the power of sharing. Well, it's a start. Remember, you read it here first. 💔

16 February 2011
Desperately in search of glamour

The 'No to AV' launch was unlike anything I had ever been to before. Yes, that bad.

We had been enticed to the 'No to AV' launch with the promise of a 'special guest'. I immediately thought of the Prime Minister. The pro-AV camp had already scored the double coup of Colin Firth (a king) and Helena Bonham Carter (a queen). The 'No' campaign needed some glamour. In lieu of an actual prince, surely Dave would have to step in.

The event was held in the London Film Museum with, yes, a red carpet. My hopes raised. In the actual room, I looked around for someone 'special' but saw a random collection of people, famous only to their own families. Then I saw that the cameras were trained on a moustache, as large and fuzzy as a giant inky caterpillar. It was Lord Winston of baby fame.

Was he the celeb? I felt let down, though, actually, that moustache could win an award for best supporting facial hair. But where were the other heavy hitters? Even Lord Prescott, who is political royalty, was absent. As the event began, I looked around the room. John Pienaar was the most famous person there.

The idea, as became clear, was to hold an anti-politician political launch. It's a novel plan, like the Oscars without actors or the Brits without musicians. And, as the event unfolded, it became clear why no one has ever done it before.

The panel was made up of an ex-MP, Jane Kennedy, Lord Winston and A. Nother (he never told us his name). Carole Walker, of the BBC, the second-most-famous person there, asked Lord Winston how he felt about being an anti-politician politician. 'I am a member of the House of Lords,' he said. 'I am not a politician.'

Argh. The whole event seemed to be submerged, as opaque as the grey and grim waters of the Thames that flowed outside the window. No one answered any questions directly. Finally, one journalist exploded about the anti-politics politics: 'If it quacks it's a duck, and you quack.'

The quacking got louder. Someone noted that the 'Yes to AV' campaign had glitz and glamour but that the 'No' campaign had, well, Lord Winston. What did he have to say to that? 'I can't really answer that. I think they are lovely people. Not that I know them,' he burbled. 'I would love to talk to Colin Firth. I don't know if I would be able to persuade him.'

Jane trilled: 'They may have the beauty but we have the brains!' Lord Winston didn't like that. 'I think you'll find that Colin and Helena are both very intelligent people.'

At which point Jane murmured: 'I'm digging myself a hole.'

And how. Let's just all forget the whole thing ever happened. ♥

18 February 2011
So the lady was for burning

The Environment Secretary issues a tree-a-culpa on forests

So the lady was for turning after all. As Maggie T almost said: Yew turn if you want to. Yesterday Caroline Spelman did just that on forests. The Twittersphere is calling it a tree-a-culpa, a word that demands a definition of 'epic grovel'.

'I would first like to say that I take full responsibility for this situation,' said Ms Spelman, her voice flute-like and small. Everyone had got the 'wrong impression' about her policy on forests, so she was axing it and setting up a new board (sorry, but she is). She ended simply: 'I am sorry. We got this one wrong.'

She wilted on to the front bench. There, with her in her hour of need, was George Osborne. Yes, that bad. If I were Caroline, I would know it was over. When the Dark Lord – the man who gave you the chainsaw and urged you to use it – comes to show his support, the clock is ticking.

Mary Creagh, for Labour, was more than a little bit chippy. Her response included the execrable line: 'Today the air is filled with the sound of chickens coming home to roost.' Ghastly. A Tory cackled: 'Bwack bwack bwack bwack.'

Ms Spelman wittered away, as she does in her lady-who-lunches way. But then, struck by her own magnanimity, she noted: 'As regards humility, perhaps ultimately that is the difference between you and me.' The Tories cheered. Was she really bragging about her own humility?

Labour MPs sympathised with her, saying that the PM was just as much to blame. 'Is it not deplorable,' declared Sir Gerald Kaufman, 'that you have been made to stand in the corner with the dunce's cap?' Ms Spelman, humility expert, bristled: 'It is only humiliating if you are afraid to say sorry. One of the things is that we teach our children to be honest. It is not a question of humiliation, it is my choice.'

Sir Peter Bottomley popped up to announce that he'd once said he was sorry in the House. Ms Spelman twittered back that he was a living example of how you can apologise and continue to do valuable service. 'I think it is a very good example why humility is a good quality in a politician,' she fluttered.

At which point, a heckler shouted at her: 'If I say so myself…'

This brought laughter, though not from Ms Spelman, who is missing a sense of humour as well as of irony.

Ms Spelman, controversially, now came out in favour of honesty. 'I can assure you that honesty is always the best policy. That is indeed what I always try to teach my children.'

I looked at her. Was she even real? We should have known, but a yew-turn is just too sappy for words. 💔

1 March 2011
Dave tries to play three conflicting roles

As Libya exploded – and Britain's attempt to evacuate its citizens turned to farce – everyone demanded an apology as the Prime Minister turned the 'unwritten' page of history

David Cameron couldn't quite decide who he was yesterday. Was he a world statesman in control of the hand of history? Was he an air traffic controller with special expertise in how not to charter an aeroplane to Libya? Or was he a politician who loves democracy, but hates being held to account in the Commons? In the end, he decided to be all three. It was quite impressive in an impressively confusing way.

Indeed, I may give Dave an Oscar for even trying to play three conflicting roles at the same time. First we had Dave in world leader mode. Britain, which last week had trouble getting an evacuation flight to leave Gatwick (admittedly a country unto itself at times) was now penetrating Libya by air, sea and land. Nothing was too big. No-fly zone? Good idea. Arming the Opposition? Good idea. Middle East peace? Obviously. Suddenly, in this Arab Spring, the air was filled with promise. 'This is a moment when history turns a page,' proclaimed Dave. 'The next page is not yet written.'

It sounded grand, big, important. How irritating then that MPs weren't on the same unwritten page but kept going on about last week's page about not being able to get a plane. A look of disdain flicked across Dave's face when Ed Miliband said Britons had felt let down by 'chaos and incompetence'. 'I am surprised you haven't taken the opportunity to apologise,' said Ed, his tone relatively mild. At this, George Osborne whispered something to Dave. (By the way, Nick Clegg, so forgetful these days, was again nowhere to be seen.) The PM retorted to Ed: 'Perhaps if apologies are in order you should think about one – the appalling dodgy dealing with Libya under the last government.' Ed's eyes, already orbiting Earth, headed into infinity.

Dave wasn't giving an inch. He did not accept that Cobra should have met earlier. He had been 'impressed' by the Foreign Office response last week. He did not accept that there was anything wrong with the timing of his leading an arms-trading delegation to the Middle East last week. The problem with planes was all to do with the intricacies of chartering, nothing else.

David Winnick, the Labour maverick, pointed out that Britain took part in an arms fair in Libya last November. 'Frankly, Prime Minister, isn't it time this country, whichever Government is in office, stopped selling arms to murdering b******s who terrorise their own people?' Dave hardly skipped a beat: 'The point I would make is we do have some of the toughest arm control legislation anywhere in the world.' That wasn't quite the question though. Sometimes it's easier to lead the world than the Commons.

2 March 2011
Run the country? Are you clegging?

Nick Clegg tries to explain how it was that he was on holiday
last week instead of running the country

What a relief to see Nick Clegg in the Commons. It seemed unlikely he would forget his monthly question time but don't forget (his new catchphrase) that last week he forgot he was running the country. He needs to get a mnemonic device and put it on expenses. Or, failing that, perhaps just write in his diary: 'Dave away. Feed the cat. Run the country.'

He had a tough time. As they say on the slopes, where we all knew Nick would be if he could, Labour MPs were taking the piste. 'Switzerland!' they shouted at him. It was most definitely a slippery slope and he was sliding down it.

He tried to brave it out, brow furrowing faster than a field in springtime as he told us about his constitutional reforms. He came, as if straight from a Lib-Dem 'group hug', with a phalanx of supporters. I was, as always, quite surprised to remember that Chris Huhne is in the Government.

A Labour MP began by teasing him, almost gently. Why had he left the country when Dave had been away too? Mr Clegg stumbled over his words: 'In the end I spent, I think, just short of two days, uh working days, away and as soon as it was necessary, uh, obvious that I was needed here, I returned.'

For a man who'd been on holiday, he seemed a bit tense. What, I wondered idly, a word that sprang effortlessly to mind, was a 'working day' for Mr Clegg, who closes his red box at 3 p.m.? Harriet Harman tried, as she does, to tease, claiming that in addition to forgetting he was running the country, he has also forgotten every pledge he made. 'There is a new word now,' she said. 'If you want to say someone has been the victim of a total sell-out, you say, they've been clegged! Are you proud of that?' Mr Clegg spluttered. 'What an extraordinarily laboured question.' I tried to imagine what Harriet would mean as a verb. Had Nick just been harrieted? He was barking on about the deficit and how there was no money, even for new words.

John Mann, Labour bulldog, eyeballed the metrosexual Mr Clegg. 'The first Deputy Prime Minister in British history to fail to turn up to work when the Prime Minister is abroad for a week,' growled Mr Mann. 'I think I am wanting to ask: what's the point of Nick Clegg?'

The answer came as laughter filled the chamber. 'Uhhhh…' said Mr Clegg. 'Another much-rehearsed question.' More laughter. I felt sorry for him now. Mr Clegg puffed with faux exasperation. 'When a Chief Executive goes on a business trip, it still means he is the Chief Executive,' he shouted. 'When the manager of a football club goes on an away-game, they are still manager.'

So there you have it. I tried to imagine what football team David Cameron was managing on his 'away-game' to sell arms to the Middle East. Was Team Cabinet even in the Premier League? I think Harriet is wrong. For starters, clegg cannot be a verb (too active). Instead, to be a clegg is to be a person who makes himself into a laughing stock. That's how it seemed yesterday. It was unforgettable, even if you are Mr Clegg. ♥

8 March 2011
A Vague attempt to set up a no-flies-on-us zone

A top secret SAS and MI6 mission to meet the Libyan rebels ended in farce when, after a night-time helicopter drop, they were captured by the self-same rebels. The Brits didn't help matters by claiming they were unarmed and only looking for a hotel. The Foreign Secretary had a James Bond moment as he tries to explain what happened

Iknew that the Foreign Secretary was about to arrive when I heard the deafening whirr of a helicopter over Parliament. His mission, as I discovered from top secret sources (Twitter), was to penetrate the Commons and establish a credible position on Libya. Or, as the spies would call it, 'finding a hotel'.

For this, the Foreign Secretary had taken on a new identity. 'The name's Vague, William Vague,' he whispered to himself as he rushed to take up his position to begin the task of covering himself in verbal camouflage. He wished, just for a moment, for a bit of glamour. James Bond, 007, dazzled at the craps table while he, Vague, 000, had to endure having the same kicked out of him by politicians who didn't even have numbers.

His arch-enemy, Wee Dougie Alexander, didn't look even remotely menacing. He called Vague a 'serial' bungler and then, emboldened by this rare show of boldness, Wee Dougie moved on to mockery: 'The British public are entitled to wonder whether, if some new neighbours moved into the Foreign Secretary's street, he would introduce himself by ringing the doorbell or instead choose to climb over the fence in the middle of the night.'

William Vague smiled the smile of a man who had to grin and bear it for his country. Wee Dougie was being silly. William Vague 000 would do neither. He would arrive, instead, by chopper with nightvision goggles and a map in invisible ink.

The attacks came thick and fast. Everyone was cautioning him about a no-fly zone. Vague was vague. On this day it was his job to establish a 'no flies on us' zone. It was a struggle.

Sir Ming Campbell, the Lib Dem who may not know that his codename was Vase, said he regretted what he was about to say. 'Isn't it clear this mission was ill-conceived, poorly planned and embarrassingly executed? What are you doing to restore the reputation of the UK?' Vague threw more camouflage into the air. The UK was leading the world in diplomacy. As for Libya, the Opposition there said they would 'welcome' more contact.

Ben Bradshaw, hair standing up like a cockatoo, asked: 'If the object of this mission was to make contact with the leaders of Free Libya, why didn't they just go straight into Benghazi as scores of international journalists have?' Vague replied, teeth gritted: 'Whenever we deploy diplomats into a dangerous situation, we provide a level of protection based on the professional and military advice.'

He was being as bland as blancmange. But some attacks were beyond ridiculous. There was even one Tory MP who accused him of sending a ship (HMS *Cumberland*) named after a pork sausage to a Muslim country. Honestly. The final insult came when a Labour MP accused him of 'overdosing' on James Bond. At this, Vague thought of what Bond would be doing at that moment, a blonde at his side, playing craps. Surely Vague's was the harder mission. ♥

9 March 2011
Happy ending for Snow White

It's a fairytale ending for 'dwarfgate' with the Speaker, finally, happy indeed

Breaking news. I come straight from Health Questions where, much to everyone's shock, Simon Burns, the minister in constant need of anger management, has ended his feud with the Speaker. Snow White will be pleased. Snow is known, unlike one of her famous seven little men, to have been Unhappy about the entire saga.

It all began, once upon a time as they say, when Mr Burns was ticked off by the Speaker for not facing forward when addressing the chamber last June. At this Mr Burns, more firecracker than slow fuse, began to live up to his name. His face got redder and redder until, twitching with anger, jumping round the bench as if he had been hijacked by Mexican jumping beans, he began to mutter loudly, calling Mr Bercow a 'stupid sanctimonious dwarf'.

Mr Bercow ignored the outburst. Others did not. The Walking with Giants Foundation objected and Mr Burns apologised, but not to Mr Bercow. The Speaker, who admits to being vertically challenged, is believed to be 5ft 6in. But I do not think that even makes him the shortest man in the Commons. (By the way, the man with the shortest name is Tim Yeo and no one abuses him.)

The feud simmered on. Mr Speaker is a man whom many Tories love to hate. They resent that he used to be right wing but became left wing, though now, of course, as Speaker he is supposed to be no wing (do keep up at the back!). Plus, there is the issue of his (very tall) wife Sally, who was last seen in a newspaper wearing only a bedsheet and talking about sex. Snow would not approve of that either.

But I digress. The plot took an unexpected twist a few months ago when the Prime Minister, of all people, repeated a joke told by the minister in which he backs into Mr Bercow's car. 'I'm not Happy,' the Speaker said. 'Well, which one are you anyway?' came back the reply. Cue uproarious laughter.

Yesterday, at Health Questions, Mr Burns was being his usual pugnacious self. Labour MPs, on the warpath over the unpopular NHS reforms, were needling him very badly. For example, here is John Mann: 'When will you listen to the country and get your sticky mitts off the Health Service and stop meddling?' Mr Burns, flexing his mitts, flailed away. Then a Labour MP asked Mr Burns a question that had nothing to do with the subject being discussed. 'Mr Speaker!' objected Mr Burns. But Mr Bercow did not rule the question out of order and, instead, advised Mr Burns that the Labour MP wanted to meet him.

I feared an explosion. 'Mr Speaker!' exclaimed Mr Burns. 'You are a wise owl to be able to interpret what honourable members opposite are thinking but may not be saying!' At this, an owl sound – which I can only translate as 'twoooot' – could be heard. And Mr Bercow was, unmistakeably, happy. 'Wise owl is the kindest description you have ever offered of me. I'm going to take it that you mean it!' he said, to much laughter. 'It's the best I'll get!' At which point, a Labour MP shouted: 'It's a hoot.'

It's also a happy ending but then, don't forget, in fairy tales, as opposed to politics, everything ends happily ever after. ❣

11 March 2011
Pooh-Bah Patten suffers interference on telly habits

Chris Patten, candidate for BBC Chairman, explains to MPs why he loves programmes on tractors

To see Lord Patten of Barnes in action was to see a man who was, emphatically, not of the people. He was wonderfully grand, a talking Taj Mahal. When he ran Hong Kong, he was called Fat Pang but now, surely, we must upgrade him to Grand Pooh-Bah Pang?

My only question, after he appeared for two hours before MPs, was not whether he was big enough for the BBC but whether the BBC was too small for him. Surely what he needs is not a corporation but a small but immensely erudite country to run.

He was gloriously out of touch. The Tory MP John Whittingdale began by asking what TV he watched. Well, he said, the night before he'd watched an 'extremely good' programme on BBC Four on wheat production. He'd then switched to *MasterChef*. He said this with a flourish, as if it were wildly hip and groovy. 'I went from BBC Four to BBC One with no stopping point.'

He doesn't watch breakfast television. 'I listen to the *Today* programme, as most people in this room do.'

Mr Whittingdale interrupted: 'But not most people in the country.'

By way of an answer, Lord Patten said that he had watched *Strictly Come Dancing*. His voice was tinged with pride.

He loved Radio 4. He mentioned Melvyn Bragg on string theory as a particular joy. He woke up to Radio 4 and went to bed with it. 'Interesting life,' he noted (he is saved from total Pooh-Bahness by a sense of humour as dry as the Sahara).

He said he was also guilty – now raising his hands in an arrest pose – of listening to Radio 3. But what about 6 Music? Pause. 'Honest injun,' he said (something I haven't heard for decades), 'No.' I suspect he had no idea what it was.

How about Radio 1? 'Only when trying to get to Radio 3 or 4!' When was the last time he'd watched *EastEnders*? Pause. 'Um. I should think longer ago than I last had a McDonald's.'

I think that means never. The Labour MP David Cairns noted that what little TV Lord Pooh-Bah did watch was hardly seen by anyone else (by the way, just in case you want to catch it, that wheat programme was called *Mud, Sweat and Tractors: The Story of Agriculture*).

'The fact is that I watch the sort of television programme which you would expect somebody with my background to watch. I'm sixty-six, I'm white, I'm relatively well educated,' he noted. (Fact: he is the Chancellor of the University of Oxford.)

But most people are watching something else, persisted Mr Cairns.

'I'm not going to pretend that I'm suddenly going to morph into a sort of sub-Reithian enthusiastic for programmes which it would be perhaps difficult to place in the Temple of Arts and Muses which is over the door of Broadcasting House,' he said.

Mr Cairns was remorseless: 'I get the sense that your idea of going downmarket is to watch BBC Two!' This got a laugh. 'Last night I watched in fascination *MasterChef*, which is on BBC One!' It was wonderful. I really think he needs his own TV programme, *Masterclass with Pooh-Bah*. Go on, BBC, you know it makes sense. ❦

14 March 2011
Nick sets Alarm Clock Britain for wake-up call

The leader of the Lib Dems tries to explain to his party at their spring conference in Sheffield what makes him tick-tock

Briiinnnggg! Nick Clegg yesterday reached out to something that he calls Alarm Clock Britain. It seemed a strange thing to do. I regret to say that, unlike almost everyone else in the country on a Sunday, he did not hit the snooze button.

It was a grey and rainy day in Sheffield. Inside City Hall, Nick was bestriding the stage in his best David Cameron walkabout impression. He seemed utterly at home. He was here to woo his party back. Forget the snooze button, this was the schmooze button.

He knew there had been 'some criticism', which is one way of putting it, but he told us about one delegate who had welcomed him back, saying: 'I thought we'd lost you when you walked through that door of No. 10.' Nick glowed. I could see how much he loved saying the words 'No. 10'. Now he added, superfluously: 'I want to reassure you, David Cameron hasn't kidnapped me. Although I gather some people were planning to this weekend.' That would be the students. Nick looked immensely happy at the idea of being important enough to be kidnapped.

'My life may have changed a fair bit since the last election,' he said. 'But I haven't changed one bit!' Then he looked down, ruefully, at his new round little tummy. No, not pregnancy (even for a Lib Dem that would be hard). This was a power tummy from power breakfasts, lunches and dinners. 'Maybe,' he noted, 'I should get a personal trainer, like David and Samantha, but I have 5,000 protesters to chase me through the streets of Sheffield!' He loved his tummy and he loved being important enough to chase. The packed hall – briinggg! – was waking up now and loving him back. They may hate the policies, but it was clear that they loved everything to do with power, even the tummy.

Nick told them that the Lib Dems would never lose their soul. Whose side were they on? 'We're on the side of people I call Alarm Clock Britain.' What does it mean? It was people who want to 'get up and get on'.

People who had to work (what world does he live in?). People who are only one pay cheque from their overdraft. I could go on (he did) but I think you get the idea.

'These are the people liberals have always fought for,' he announced. Lloyd George had fought for them in the People's Budget. Keynes had fought for them. And so had Beveridge.

'They may not have called it Alarm Clock Britain,' said Nick (and there would be a reason for that). 'But they had the same people in mind.' The people in the hall were the 'true radicals' of British politics. 'We are liberals,' he insisted (what happened to the democrats?). 'We are governing from the middle, for the middle.'

I could not help but look at his new tummy. Can you govern from and for the spreading middle? I don't see why not. Surely the message of yesterday is that, if you're Nick Clegg, you can get away with almost anything. ❦

15 March 2011
Leadership with two Eds and no Nick

We came to hear Ed and Ed, but then we ended up hearing a great deal about why Ed (the Red one) won't share a platform on AV with Nick

The Ed 'n' Ed show was surprisingly fun. It's strange how double acts do and don't work. I have painful memories of Ed Miliband's press conference with Alan Johnson, his first choice for Shadow Chancellor. It was stilted, formal and embarrassing. But Ed Balls, his erstwhile enemy, turned out to be a good straight man.

'I have two questions for Ed,' said a hack. 'Which one?' asked Ed Milibanana. 'Ed Balls,' came the cruel reply. Red Ed, eyes twinkling, didn't seem to mind. I don't know why, but they just complement each other. Red Ed seemed miles more relaxed while the Other Ed seemed much less of an econo-bore. It's a marriage made in, well, hell probably, but it works.

Actually, Red Ed was asked about his own alleged wedding to partner Justine, the existence of which, like UFOs, enjoys periodic sightings in the press. Would his brother David be his best man? 'The one thing that I can tell you, categorically, is Gordon is not going to be organising my stag do, for reasons that may be obvious,' announced Red. I tried to imagine a stag do organised by Gordon – everyone in suits, growling, throwing mobile phones. Fun.

I can also categorically tell you something else. Red Ed hates Nick Clegg. That was the other revelation. 'What's the problem with Nick Clegg?' he asked rhetorically. 'Well, where do you start?'

OK. Well, let's start with the fact that, today, Ed Miliband was supposed to be launching the 'Yes to AV' campaign with Charles Kennedy and Caroline Lucas, the Green MP. Then, suddenly, the launch was cancelled. Why? 'This question should be directed to Nick Clegg's office,' said Red Ed. 'He didn't want us, as I understand it, to share a platform together – myself, Charles Kennedy and Caroline Lucas. He felt he had to be there as well. I'm sorry about that. I hope the event will be rearranged.'

But not with Nick Clegg? 'I will share a platform with anybody who will help us win,' said Ed. So not Nick? 'The best thing that Nick Clegg can do, to be frank if he wants a "yes" vote in the referendum, is lie low for a bit.'

Lie low? Nick Clegg, the man who loves Alarm Clock Britain, doesn't do lie-ins or even lie-lows. So what, exactly, was wrong with Nick again? Red Ed said that he was a man who talked about new politics but was an exemplar of the old politics. He was a man of broken promises. But did that mean Ed wouldn't share...?

'No!' cried Ed. 'I'm not going to share a platform with Nick Clegg. I don't think it will help win the referendum!'

Yikes. So there you have it. Nick Clegg – prima donna, promise-breaker, egomaniac. I think that's Yes for AV, No to Nick. The Other Ed seemed to agree. Suddenly they appeared to share many opinions. 'I agree with Ed,' said Ed. 'I agree with Ed,' said Ed. For now, at least, two Eds are better than one. ♥

18 March 2011
First save British bacon, then crack the egg problem

Pigs fly, of course, as MPs tuck into a debate on food

The Great British Breakfast is in danger. If you are reading this over bacon and eggs, consider the fact that what is on your plate is also on the Government's. For, apparently, there is a pig farming crisis. Ministers are also talking tough on eggs. But on the plus side, I did manage to find out which came first, the chicken or the egg.

But very first, actually, came pigs. Normally in politics, pigs fly. Now even that may be too expensive. The first pig question was asked by an MP with the eggy name of Dr Daniel Poulter. British farmers are losing £20 per pig while retailers make £100 profit. What was the Government going to do? Jim Paice, the Minister of State and almost the definition of lacklustre, murmured that he was meeting the British Pig Executive about this. I had a vision of a board of porkers in suits. Mr Paice didn't seem to have any actual plan other than hope. 'I'm sure prices will recover at some stage,' he said pathetically.

The Tory MP Richard Bacon arose to what can only be called oinks of laughter. 'Do you think Tesco customers will be surprised if they understood the disgusting animal welfare practices which are supported by Tesco and others by importing meat produced under poor animal welfare conditions?' he demanded. They should go to Morrisons, which has a policy of 100 per cent British meat!

But Mr Paice, plodding and cautious, is not a rasher (sorry) man. He didn't want to get involved in 'internecine' wars. But he was 'really keen' on country-of-origin labelling.

Claire Perry, the new Tory MP for Devizes, is one of those ultra-efficient, take-no-prisoners-type women. Whenever I look at her, the words 'spit-spot' come to mind. She told us that less than 1 per cent of the bacon served to the Armed Forces was British. 'We should put our money where our mouth is,' Ms Perry said, 'and encourage the public sector to buy our meat.'

Mr Paice said that he was working with the British Pig Executive and the Ministry of Defence on exactly this. New rules would soon require all meat to conform to 'British standards'. But, in this case, there were 'specific challenges' to do with the fact that bacon had to be frozen. 'They've done trials using sow bacon,' he noted, 'but we are still working on the challenge.'

We went straight from bacon to eggs. From next year, in the European Union, battery cages will be banned. Some EU countries wanted to delay the rule. We are fighting that. Certainly in Britain, from January 2012, all eggs will have to come from chickens who live in 'enriched' cages. (Doesn't it sound opulent? As if there are gold taps in the en suite.)

By this time everyone was a bit, dare I say it, peckish. The session was over but we had learnt one vital thing: in Britain, the enriched caged chicken comes before the enriched caged egg. And that, the politicians promise, is not a porkie pie. ♥

19 March 2011
Heir to Blair has, in these matters, learnt from him

Eight years to the day since the Iraq War debate, the Prime Minister addresses the Commons on the eve of the bombing of Libya

t was the moment when David Cameron arrived on the world stage, but there was no 'ta-da' or prideful flourish. Indeed, there was no drama – which was, of course, in itself a bit dramatic. In its place was a steadfast determination of purpose over what we, and the UN, had to do over Libya. 'I absolutely believe that this is the right thing to say and to do,' he said.

It was, in every way, a vindication for the Prime Minister, but he wore it lightly. Less than three weeks ago he had stood at the same despatch box, just back from his chaotic tour of the Middle East, looking a bit of an amateur. All of that had changed. He seemed a different man.

The praise, from the Tories, was overwhelming, a Niagara Falls of approval. James Arbuthnot, usually so gloom-laden, said that the Prime Minister had shown a 'breathtaking degree of courage'. Sir Malcolm Rifkind enthused over his 'superb leadership'. Bernard Jenkin pronounced it a 'brilliant success'.

There was no preening. Nor did Mr Cameron mention the war – as in the Iraq vote eight years ago to the day – but you could see it hovering in the background, informing his actions. His Attorney-General was right next to him. He explained that the Cabinet had met and discussed the legal advice. He may be heir to Blair but, in these matters, he had learnt from him, too.

Like Blair he was at his best when addressing those with doubts, which, yesterday, came only from Labour. Jeremy Corbyn, a veteran peacenik, said that civilians were under attack in other countries such as Bahrain, Yemen, Saudi Arabia. Would we intervene there too? 'Just because you can't do the right thing everywhere doesn't mean you can't do the right thing somewhere,' said Mr Cameron to a Tory rumble of support.

David Winnick, the veteran Labour sceptic, said he believed that in Britain at large there was 'great anxiety' that we would be dragged, through escalation, into our third war in nine years. Mr Cameron noted that the resolution specifically ruled out occupation. The world, he said, was with us. If we did not act now, then when? 'There is always a case which goes something like: don't start down this path because it may involve you taking so many difficult steps. But there is a stronger argument, which is to do nothing and to witness the slaughter of civilians when it is so clearly not in your own national interest means it is better to act than to remain passive.'

The questioning went on for more than an hour. Mr Cameron's voice never rose, or fell, was never shrill or resentful. He didn't mention Labour's past. The future, he acknowledged, was unsure. 'In many ways the easy decisions have been made,' he said, adding: 'There will be difficult days ahead. These things never go entirely according to plan.'

This may be the understatement of the year. But still, whatever lies ahead, Mr Cameron began well. 💔

22 March 2011
Leaders hear doubts from the poor infantry

With the multi-force bombing of Libya underway, MPs hear that Libya is 'not Iraq' but there are still plenty of doubts

Dennis Skinner, the Beast of Bolsover, his voice rasping, cut to the chase as he stood to question the Prime Minister. 'It's easy to get into a war, it's much harder to end it.' How, he wanted to know, would we all know when the Libyan war was over?

The Prime Minister grabbed the moment. 'This is different to Iraq,' he said. 'This is not going into a country, knocking over its Government and then owning and being responsible for everything that happens subsequently. This is about protecting people and giving Libyans a chance to shape their own destiny.'

That this was not Iraq was the übertheme of yesterday. For the spectre of that war, sanctioned eight years ago to the week, did not hover so much as haunt this, the most important debate of the Parliament. It was a riveting occasion.

The politicians did not let themselves down. This is one Hansard that I will keep. For once the leaders, eloquent and passionate, really were all in this together. Ed nodded while Dave spoke. Dave nodded with Ed. And Nick Clegg, whose party was the only one to oppose Iraq, nodded with everyone.

Mr Miliband gave, easily, his best speech. He noted that the debate was conducted in the shadow of history of past conflicts but also, for him, his family's past. 'Two Jewish parents whose lives were changed forever by the darkness of the Holocaust yet who found security in Britain.'

His brother David watched from the farthest back bench as Ed continued: 'In my maiden speech I said I would reflect the humanity and solidarity shown to my family more than sixty years ago. These are the kinds of things we say in maiden speeches, but if they are to be meaningful we need to follow them through in deeds, not just words. That is why I will be voting for this.'

If the leaders were united, the poor bloody infantry had more doubts. 'There is nothing glorious in war, nothing romantic,' warned Kris Hopkins, a former soldier who is now a Tory MP.

Bob Ainsworth, the former Defence Secretary, spoke in a voice laden with the experience of wars gone wrong. 'I am a late and very reluctant supporter of this operation,' he said heavily. 'It is relatively easy to support things on day one and relatively difficult to support them on month three.'

Perhaps the best speech came from Tory Rory Stewart, the former soldier and diplomat, who noted how easy it was to become captivated by fear. 'This is very, very dangerous. It is very dangerous because we must again and again get out of that kind of language and get into a language which is humble, which accepts our limitations.'

The chamber was rapt. They are going to war, but not with their eyes wide shut. ❦

24 March 2011
The Chancellor gets oily with us

The Chancellor helps us live the dream with a Budget full of 'zzzzzzzz's'

If you think about it, George Osborne, with his black hair, slick suit and braggadocio swagger, does seem a bit like an oil man from days gone by. They were brash and confident, men of vision. Many were also conmen, but let's brush over that. Yesterday George, faced with having to sell a Budget for (lesser) growth, decided to seek his salvation in oil.

His was a vision of a land that flowed not with overpriced milk and honey but with cheaper petrol and feverish enterprise. We've had the Iron Chancellor in Gordon Brown (now an official missing person in the chamber). Then, there was Alistair Darling, so boring he could only really aspire to be the Ironing Chancellor. Now, we have the Oil Chancellor. No, not oily, though, it must be admitted, he does bear a resemblance to Olive Oyl.

The oily bit did not come until the end of the hour-long speech that taxed his milquetoast vocal cords to the utmost. I counted the coughs to stave off the tedium but Ken Clarke, the Justice Secretary, actually nodded off. Later Ken's office issued a Sleepgate denial, saying that he was stitched up like a kipper (I paraphrase). But I have seen pictures: he was a kipper.

The good news is that it's all going to be great. The bad news is that we don't know when. But, at some point, growth will be up, inflation down and our country will be a giant enterprise zone full of happy non-doms, tax non-evaders and Big Society charity givers. There will be no planning laws and fewer cigarettes. 'That is our vision for growth,' he said. Certainly I could see that Ken, zzzzzzing away, was living the dream. Ed Miliband, later, mocked, but one politician's vision is another's hallucination.

Then, finally, just as Ken entered the REM sleep stage, George mentioned the words we'd all been waiting for. The moment he said 'fuel duty', the Tories went berserk. George said that in six months the cost of filling up a Ford Focus had gone up £10. I wondered how he knew this: perhaps he had asked his chauffeur.

George now took us for a ride on the fuel duty escalator, which, he told us, had seven stages. (Why not, I wondered, just take the lift?)But George was deep into escalator detail now, saying that the fourth stage, due next week, would add 5p to something. Then George jumped off the escalator into the North Sea. He cancelled the 5p. He introduced something called the fair fuel stabiliser. He told us that the stabiliser would stop the escalator for now but, if the price of oil went down, the down escalator would go up again. It was confusing. I didn't blame Ken for sleeping.

'And one more thing!' he cried, just like the Great Gordo used to. 'I am cutting fuel duty by one penny per litre!' Tory MPs, already pumped up, went petrol-tastic.

George, his voice faltering so much that I wanted to give him a little Zimmer frame for it, finished by saying: 'We have put fuel into the tank of the British economy.'

Has he? I thought it was just a Ford Focus. It all seemed very slick, as in oil. Just ask Ken. ♥

25 March 2011
In harmony, it's the fabulous Ditto Brothers

Dave and Nick take their winning show on the road to Nottingham where they agree about just about everything

The idea, as I understood it, was for Nick and Dave to go to Nottingham to launch Enterprise Zone Britain and to hold one of their 'live and unplugged' events aimed at meeting real people. But, from the very beginning, it felt very unreal.

The Boots 'campus' may be just outside Nottingham, but it felt like Toytown. We gathered at somewhere called D80 and were bussed, quite unnecessarily, just up the road to a giant tin can called the Stores Service Centre. We weren't allowed to see Nick and Dave arrive. We waited in a cavernous hall where, under huge pipes and in front a giant conveyor belt, 200 chairs had been set up, surrounded by stacks of nappies and Boots ads.

The Boots people in the chairs didn't seem all that real either – i.e., white, besuited, and very, very polite. They clapped like mad when Dave and Nick bounded in and perched on their Val Doonican chairs. 'Don't worry – we won't sing!' chortled Dave. I don't see why not. They are in perfect harmony these days, linked by an invisible hymnsheet. They often repeat each other, word for word. So Nick would tell us about his dream of helping Alarm Clock Britain. Then Dave told us that his dream was to make the world a fairer place for people who wake up in the morning – briiing! – and go to work. It was, actually, very Val Doonican.

The Ditto Brothers left, after a final warble about how life would be better by the 2015 election, to more applause, striding past the nappies. 'If we keep doing this we won't find anything to bloody disagree on in the bloody TV debates,' Nick told Dave, his microphone still on. So not so unplugged after all, then. It wasn't so much bigot-gate, as in Gordon Brown's little mike experience during the election, as spigot-gate.

I tried to talk to Nick and Dave afterwards but was banned. Thus I was reduced to standing in the car park watching as Nick and Dave walked out of the tin can. The Prime Minister gave everyone a thumbs-up – it's the definitive Dave economic crisis gesture – and jumped into the back seat of a beautiful gleaming Jaguar. Nick, though, kept on walking towards what can only be called a somewhat distressed Audi (scratch down the side), saved slightly from ignominy by the fact that he was chauffeured. As he went by, Nick gave us a little royal-type wave. As I said, quite surreal. ♥

29 March 2011
Speed networking with the men from Mars

*I was there to watch Start Up Britain start up (at least I think
it was up)*

went to the launch of Start Up Britain which did not, of course, start up on time. I examined the launch poster, which looked a bit like a Union Jack billowing like a duvet. This made sense because I am sure that Start Up Britain and Alarm Clock Britain are connected, possibly by a duvet. (When will there be Duvet Day Britain? Surely that is the question the nation wants answered.)

Start Up Britain was for entrepreneurs, hundreds of whom had gathered to 'speed-network' and eat a fabulous lunch at Microsoft in London. Dave was there, as was George. Vince was too, but no one cared: he didn't even get a speech.

Our Prime Minister was on 'Dazzling Dave' form. He was preceded by two men who were, for the likes of me, from Mars. The first one, Oli (with an i, naturellement) Barrett, was pathologically upbeat, his blindingly white smile flashing constantly. Oli loves to speed-network. 'My motto is, if you can't beat them, join them up,' he said, flash, flash, flash (it was like Morse code but for incredibly happy people).

Dave was in the front row. I was worried that the teeth strobe might hurt his eyes. But that was the least of it, for then another entrepreneur, Michael Hayman, popped up and said to Dave: 'We want to morph you with Martin Luther King!'

What would a Dave/MLK morph be like? I tried to imagine the 'I have a dream' speech as 'I have a start-up'. No, don't think so. Now Michael was showing us a picture of Martin Luther King at the Lincoln Memorial before millions of people. 'Start Up Britain is about something that Martin Luther King said: "The fierce urgency of Now",' said Michael. 'This needs to be done NOW. If recovery looks like anything, it looks like Start Up.'

Dave bounded up. The MLK morph operation had failed. He was 100 per cent Dave. 'Entrepreneurs have a very special place in my heart, not least because I go to bed with an entrepreneur every night of my life,' he said to (teeth-blinding) laughter. 'Before *The Sun* gets too excited, I wake up with the same entrepreneur!'

Samantha is, of course, that entrepreneur. Dave told us the Sam Story. After she left Bristol Poly, she wanted to start a business. 'So she just started going to shops and asking if she could do up their shop windows, and it ended up with doing up the shop window of the business she then went to work for and became a co-owner of,' he said, making it sound as if it wasn't that hard to transform Smythson into a wildly successful luxury brand. (Again, I tried to imagine 'I Have a Handbag', but it felt wrong.)

Now Dave had an MLK moment. 'We need to set Britain free!' he said. 'There are millions of success stories that haven't been written. We need to seize this moment!' Or, alternatively, do as I did and seize one of the lovely fruit kebabs laid out for lunch though, I fully recognise, 'Seize the Kebab' isn't the kind of thing Martin Luther King would say. ❦

31 March 2011
Is the honeymoon finally over for Dave?

If so, it seems to have just started for Ed Miliband and Ed Balls but, for Dave, it is all very irritating indeed

Who is the most annoying person in British politics? Forget the issues of Libya, tuition fees and police cuts. At PMQs, the only question that mattered was that rather annoying one. But, this being Britain today, the event began with breaking wedding news.

Dave noted that Red Ed was to wed (Wed Ed?) his partner Justine. Ed said he may ask Dave's advice on his stag do and Dave beamed back: 'When I was leader of the Opposition, I would have done anything for a honeymoon! You probably feel the same.'

Dave and Nick may still act like they are on honeymoon but, for the wider world, the honeymoon is so over. The Prime Minister will be pleased that this is the last PMQs until after Easter. Yesterday Ed beat him on the issues (tuition fees and police cuts) until finally Dave, clearly annoyed, fell back on his old stand-by, the personal attack. 'Has anyone seen a more ridiculous spectacle than you marching against the cuts that your Government caused?' he chortled. 'I know Martin Luther King said he had a dream – I think it is time you woke up!' Now Dave let the insults fly. This was Flashman at his finest (which is also, of course, at his worst). His answers got more and more blithe, not to say glib.

Labour was barracking, with Ed Balls on particularly irritating form. Ed sat almost across from the Prime Minister, heckling him about how he hadn't being briefed, which must have been all the more annoying for being, manifestly, true. Suddenly the PM stopped, in mid-answer about enterprise zones in Stoke, and snapped. 'I wish that the Shadow Chancellor would occasionally shut up and listen!' 'YEAAAHHHHH!' cried Tory MPs.

Ed Balls was thrilled. His mouth, always open, like a frog catching flies, snapping shut with satisfaction. 'Am I alone in finding the Shadow Chancellor the most annoying person in modern politics?' cried the PM. Ed B, who loves a bit of am-dram, poured a glass of water and offered it to the PM. 'No!' barked Dave, looking over at Ed Miliband: 'I have a feeling that the Leader of the Opposition will one day agree with me!'

This may be so, but not yet. The two Eds are still on their own honeymoon (so many weddings, so many honeymoons!). So who is the most annoying person in British politics? Ed Balls so wants it to be him but, I have to say, it's a very crowded field. ❦

1 April 2011
We're a joke in Mexico, but Vince
doesn't get the poncho line

Reader warning: this sketch may seem like an April Fools' spoof but I can assure you it actually happened

So this is what it has come to. The moment anyone mentions the words 'Nick Clegg', people start to laugh. Except, of course, Vince, who never laughs these days. Yesterday Kevin Brennan, for Labour, asked if the Business Secretary had read the reports of Nick Clegg's visit to Mexico.

'He was humiliated first by a Mexican student, who said that he could no longer afford to come to study in Britain,' said Señor Brennan, 'and then by the Mexican President, who said that British students should go to study in Mexico instead.'

Mr Brennan flicked his imaginary poncho. 'Are you in any way embarrassed by the fact that your policy on tuition fees has become a laughing stock across the world?'

Vince, face like a burrito, peered at the poncho. 'Well, I wasn't in Mexico,' he announced. 'I was in another country, Wales, discussing the issue there.' People stared. Was he serious? He was. 'The simple truth is,' continued Vince, 'as I'm sure we communicated to the Mexican authorities, Mexican students are welcome to come to the country. There is no cap on the limit of overseas students.'

This answer managed to miss all points at the same time. It was as if Vince, blindfolded, were trying to hit a piñata but had, somehow, hit himself instead. We'd had other misses too. Earlier a Labour MP noted that the University of Hull wanted to charge £9,000. How would this encourage more youngsters to go to university? This is the answer Vince gave. 'The introduction of graduate contributions at the level we have will ensure that universities are indeed properly funded.' Whiffle, whiffle. Was

Vince working off some kind of tape? Had his voice box been
stolen too?

Simon Hughes exists now only to remind the Lib Dems
of who they once were. He arose and asked if Vince was still
reminding universities that it was 'unreasonable' for them to
charge such high fees. Vince heaped praise on Simon and
then emitted another non-answer, saying that no one needed
to charge more than £7,500 and, with efficiencies, that could
be £6,000.

It was, actually, embarrassing, like an exercise in denial. It
must be said the future looks uncertain for the man who is still
the Big Enchilada – for now. ♥

5 April 2011
Health reforms hit by a viral rap infection

The Health Secretary explains why he needs to take a break

Andrew Lansley began by telling us what a big success his
NHS reforms are. His 'bottom-up' reorganisation is a total
triumph. All over the country, people are becoming path-
finders and joining health and wellbeing boards.

It's all going incredibly well, so brilliantly that, well...
He's having a pause. No, it's not a lie-down. It's certainly not
a resignation. It's a 'natural break', like when you have a Kit
Kat, or hit the pause button on the TV remote control to
make a cup of tea. That's what Mr Lansley is doing. He's been
told by the Prime Minister to make the biggest cup of tea in
the history of the NHS. And that's tea as in 'T' as in triumph,
by the way.

I don't want to make it sound like he thought he was right
about everything, but he thought he was right about everything.

There's no change in that, just a pause as he considers how right he is. And anyone who disagrees is just plain wrong.

Poor deluded John Healey, for Labour, claimed that, actually, the NHS reforms had brought 'confusion, chaos and incompetence'. Mr Healey did praise Mr Lansley for one thing. 'I have to hand it to the Health Secretary – it takes a special talent to unite opposition from Norman Tebbit to MC NxtGen.'

At the mention of MC NxtGen, there were titters. The rapper's critique of Mr Lansley's reforms has gone 'viral', as they say in the NHS, which is like a virus but worse:

'Health Minister, I mean sinister,
You know the public will finish yer,
Is your brain really that miniature?'

Yesterday the Commons' version of MC got to his feet and swayed. 'Why don't you admit that the policy is unravelling before the eyes of the British public?' sneered the Beast of Bolsover (BB Skinner). 'Instead of waiting for a "natural break", and then a reshuffle, and then a resignation, do the honourable thing now and resign!' Mr Lansley thought this a bad rap. He told BB that, up and down the country, everyone is going bottoms-up and full of wellbeing.

Now another Labour rapper had a go: 'Wouldn't the normal process be to put the brain into gear to avoid putting the foot into the mouth?' At this Mr Lansley, who has never doubted the size of his brain, scoffed.

Yet another Labour virus told him that his nickname was 'Broken Arrow' – 'doesn't work and can't be fired'. Mr Lansley looked sad at the silliness of this criticism. He told the virus that viruses are wrong and that he is the cure (I paraphrase).

There was a wonderful moment when Mr Lansley lapsed into reverie: 'Maybe I am sometimes very close to all of this, because I am very close to the NHS. I spend my time thinking about this. I spend my time with people in the service.'

Lucky NHS. I am sure you can see how right that is. ♥

6 April 2011
Is that the Deputy Prime Minister or Wayne Rooney?

Nick Clegg seems to be in a Rooney-esque temper as he explains his mission

I am worried that Nick Clegg is finding his role as great social reformer too stressful. No one ever said that being the New Gladstone was going to be easy, but Nick seems way too close to the edge. Indeed, as I watched him in the Commons, face contorted, voice crackling with rage, he reminded me of that great advert for social mobility – footballer Wayne Rooney, whose own angry outburst, caught on camera, has earned him a ban.

'Calm down,' cried Labour MPs, hands outstretched. This only upset him more. 'No! No!' he shouted, face of fury, as he decried the deficit and how it would burden our country.

He was shouting at Harriet, which I think we can all understand. She'd wound him up by claiming that he wasn't the New Gladstone. She said that when Nick was on a mission, the opposite seemed to happen. He wanted to end tuition fees, they trebled. He was against higher VAT, it rose. He supported the educational maintenance allowance, it was abolished. 'If you care about something, the very last person you want on your side is the Deputy Prime Minister,' she insisted.

Ouch. Nick gave in to Deficit Rage. 'Your leader,' he shouted, 'recently went to Hyde Park and emulated Martin Luther King.' At this he threw out both arms, just like MLK would have (for MLK was also a great social reformer). 'I never heard Martin Luther King say: I have a dream, we need cuts but a little more slowly and a little bit less than the other lot!'

Was Nick going to explode? His face was a firecracker. Forget social mobility. Nick's campaign for facial mobility is already a huge success. He tried to stay calm but ended up contorted with frustration and rage. Why couldn't Labour MPs acknowledge that his policies were helping the poor? Nick, as we should have known, also has a dream. 'It is true that most people don't sit around talking about trans-generational social mobility,' he said, voice tinged with sadness, 'but at the heart of this strategy is a common instinct.' Parents just wanted the best for their children.

Labour got personal. They had heard that Nick's own father had got him an internship at a Finnish bank in that awkward period between Westminster School and Cambridge. (Not so much a gap year as a social mobility gap year.) Was it true? 'Yes,' cried Nick. 'I did, as I suppose many others...' He was drowned out by shouts from MPs without Finnish connections. 'Well, OK. That's very good for you if you didn't.'

Nick then accused a Labour MP of calling him a liar from a sedentary position (this, by the way, is trans-generational socially mobile talk for what you and I would call 'sitting'). This caused a huge hoo-ha.

When another Labour MP refused to acknowledge that he was helping poor students, he exploded again. 'You shake your head,' shouted Nick. 'This is an example of evidence-based policy! I know that you don't like it! You probably wouldn't acknowledge it if it hit you in the head!' Poor Nick. Totally misunderstood. If he doesn't watch it he could end up, like Rooney, with a ban. ♥

27 April 2011
Sir Peter brings MPs up to speed
with Punic Wars despatch

*The eighty-one year old Father of the House reminds us of wars
gone by*

Of all the armchair generals in the Commons – and there is a small battalion – the grandest armchair of all is occupied by the majestical form of Sir Peter Tapsell. At eighty-one,

he is our version of Father Time or, in this case, General Time
Gone By.

I swear that I could hear a faint trumpet fanfare as he arose,
as round and grand as Humpty Dumpty, pre-fall, in a three-piece
suit, his mahogany tan set off by a white pocket handkerchief.
'May I suggest that it may be over-optimistic to assume that the
civil war in Libya will cease when Colonel Gaddafi departs the
scene because, as you know, Tripolitania and Cyrenaica have been
estranged dating back to the Punic Wars...' I quite liked that 'as
you know'. So did William Hague, for he did, of course, know.
It felt like a quiz question gone out of control (how I wished for
a 'fingers on buzzers' moment so that all MPs could tell us those
infamous Punic War dates).

Sir Peter paused, possibly for a reverie on his service in those
wars '...which is why Ernest Bevin in 1946 wanted to restore
Mussolini's single Libya to their two historic entities.'

The chamber was rapt, eyes agog, lips twitching upward.
'Moreover,' continued Sir Peter, for that is how he talks, his
words marching slowly, a lexicon on parade, as he explained to
the Foreign Secretary that the only possible lesson of the Punic
Wars was that partition was the way ahead.

Mr Hague inclined his head in tribute. 'I absolutely take your
point about the Punic Wars and the historical division between
Tripolitania and Cyrenaica,' he said. But what was right in previous centuries, or indeed millennia, was not right for now. There
would be no partition.

Sir Peter rocked back, medals clanking, looking pleased to
have raised the issue, oblivious to the titterers in the House who
probably think that BC means Before Cameron.

Up jumped General Bob Ainsworth, moustache twitching
like mad. 'Fear is growing that we are doing enough to keep this
operation going, but not enough to bring it to a successful conclusion,' he said, urging that we make more of an effort to bring it
'swiftly' to an end. (I think this may be code that we should get
rid of Gaddafi any way we can.) Scarily, the moustachioed call-

to-arms was supported by the unlikely duo of rebel command-
ers Bill Cash and Sir Malcolm Rifkind, both of whom want to
arm the rebels. Sir Malcolm said that he welcomed the military
instructors but more was needed. 'These are not instructors,' said
Mr Hague primly. 'It is a military liaison team.'

I looked over at Sir Peter. Is this what they said in the Punic
Wars? No boots (or, perhaps, sandals) on the ground? Don't send
instructors, only a liaison team? In the name of Tripolitania, we
should be told. ❦

28 April 2011
Moment Dave decided that he was a Winner

*Dave, distracted by what to wear to the Royal Wedding, not to
mention NHS reform, has a 'Calm Down' moment*

Dave, dear, calm down. It's only PMQs. But, actually, if
you want to blame someone for your outburst, I've got
a list for you. There's been the distraction of the Wedding
(calm down, dear, it's only a morning suit). You could blame Ed
Miliband because you always do. Or Ed Balls for shouting at you.
Or how about Andrew Lansley, for having to answer questions
about his top-down, bottom-up NHS hash-up?

It's my theory that Ed Milibanana is the culprit. He planted
the seed a few minutes earlier. He'd asked Dave why 98.7 per cent
of nurses disagreed with the NHS shake-up. (Don't you feel sorry
for that 1.3 of a nurse who doesn't agree?) 'Inevitably,' said the
PM, sounding weary and, just for a moment, deflated, 'when you
make changes in public services, it is a challenge taking people
with you.'

Ed shook his head, mock sadness in his Labrador eyes: 'Dearie
me, that wasn't a very good answer, was it?' Dearie me, but when
is the last time you heard anyone who didn't own an antimacassar

say 'dearie me'? I am not sure that anyone ever says this who is not in *Midsomer Murders*.

It is my theory – for there always is a theory in Midsomer – that this 'dearie me' was the subliminal trigger for what happened next. Dave had been boasting that the reforms were supported by the former Labour MP Howard Stoate. 'He is no longer an MP because he lost the election,' noted Dave.

Angela Eagle, the feisty Shadow Chief Secretary, screeched: 'He stood down!' Dave looked at her and, for unknown reasons that would require years of therapy to uncover, decided to channel Michael Winner and his car insurance commercial. 'Calm down, dear,' he said. 'Calm down. Calm down.'

Tory MPs crowed with laughter. 'Listen to the doctor!' cried Dave, which, actually, is rather creepy when you see it written down. Dave read out a Dr Stoate quote to a scene of Hogarthian mayhem, until the noise defeated him.

'I said calm down! Calm down, dear,' he chortled. Yes, Dave, I think we've got it by now: the collective noun for this many dears has to be a herd of insults.

Dave began to mix up his Inner Winner with his other alter ego, Flashman. It was a dangerous derring-do (dearie-do?) territory. Dave glowered at Ed Balls, the Shadow Chancellor, who was gesturing towards Angela Eagle and, confusingly, his wife, Yvette, also on the front bench. For one mad moment, a duel loomed.

Dave challenged Ed: 'I will say it to you if you like.' Ludicrous. The Speaker tried to impose order, but had almost no impact. Ed Balls was shouting: 'Apologise!' Flashman dismissed this. 'I am not going to apologise,' he said. 'You do need to calm down.'

But no one was calm. The antimacassars were in a flap, saying Dave was sexist. The doilies were rioting, saying that he was patronising. 'I think the Prime Minister has finished!' bellowed the Speaker. I do hope not. After all, it was only a joke. 💔

29 April 2011
Nuptial delight sends politicians all of a Twitter

Love was in the air, though I don't know what Shakespeare
would have had to say about it

Whatever the opposite of a perfect storm is, it happened yesterday at Culture, Media and Sport questions in the Commons. Love was in the air, Bank Holidays were on the way and everyone seemed a bit a-Twitter if not actually twitterpated. It really did feel as if the Bank Holiday(s) had begun early and, since the Culture Department is in charge of such things, maybe it had.

The Secretary of State, Jeremy Hunt, long, lean and languid, could not stop smiling. He had the look of a man in possession of a Royal Wedding invitation which, of course, he was. Indeed, there was a suggestion yesterday that he might tweet throughout the ceremony, a suggestion that only made his smile wider.

'As Culture Secretary,' he announced, suddenly rather stilted, 'I would like to read a couple of lines from the nation's greatest playwright.' At this MPs looked vexed, if not a little panicked. Was this a trick? Was the answer Alan Bennett? It is so rare that there is any actual culture at Culture Questions.

'These come from Sonnet 136 by Shakespeare,' said Mr Hunt who then read out, perhaps a little self-consciously:

'Make but my name thy love, and love that still
And then thou lovest me, for my name is "Will".'

At the word 'Will', he nodded his head in emphasis just in case MPs didn't get it. Then he sat down to stunned amazement. 'I'm not sure I can follow that quite so elegantly,' said Dr Julian Huppert, a Liberal Democrat, who proved himself right.

The Culture Minister Ed Vaizey could easily be a Shakespearean character, jolly and round and way too carefree for his own good. Now, in answering a question about local radio from Duncan Hames, he narrowed his eyes as he realised that he had a potential bridegroom in his sights. Mr Hames is engaged to fellow Lib-Dem MP, Jo Swinson (it is said that he popped the question on Twitter). Even now Jo was looking at Duncan with puppy eyes.

For no apparent reason, Mr Vaizey now congratulated Mr Hames on his forthcoming wedding. Then Ed admitted that he wasn't sure if the nuptials had happened already. 'I am not on top of them enough to know whether they have now occurred,' announced Mr Vaizey to laughter. Shakespeare would have approved.

It really did feel like a Bank Holiday (can you have a pre-BH?). But Amber Rudd, a Tory MP who does not take any prisoners, was already worried about future Bank Holidays. She said that a hundred Morris dancers, Green Men and Bogies had come up from Hastings to make sure that the May BH stayed in May. The minister who had met the Bogies assured her that he was neutral. As you would be.

If confirmation was needed that Westminster had gone loopy, Kevin Brennan (Labour) raised the subject of Twitter, which, at Westminster, is practically an obsession. 'Would it be technically possible to install a screen in the chamber so MPs could follow a live Twitter feed during the course of our debates and therefore be able to see what people are saying about us, including our own colleagues?' MPs loved this and immediately started tweeting about it. If Shakespeare were alive, would he be twitter-pated too? It's the kind of thing you think about on a pre-BH holiday. 💔

30 April 2011
Everybody back to Sam and Dave's

There was nothing normal about the Royal Wedding street party at Number 10

t felt more like a film set than a real event but, on this day, perhaps that was normal. Downing Street, usually the coldest of streets, felt a much warmer place yesterday, decked out in homemade bunting and wreathed in smiles. Clues that it wasn't your normal street party included the five-piece brass band, the ice-cream cart and a giant screen overlooking all.

Then there were the guests. The Prime Minister and his wife Samantha didn't arrive until 3.59 p.m., straight from Buckingham Palace, he still in morning dress, she still missing that hat. They arrived just after Babs Windsor, who is apparently the street party czar for London.

I have to say, though, that the stars of the show were the cupcakes, made by Sam Cam, who didn't wear a hat for that either. She made them – chocolate, complete with edible icing pictures of Will and Kate and Union Jacks shaped into hearts – with two of her guests, Alina and Fynn Kiewell, ages nine and six, who had raised £2,020 for Save the Children in a swim-a-thon. This was their reward and they were having a blast.

Dave is wonderful at these events, for he has the gift of making the totally unreal seem quite normal. He sauntered among the ninety guests, all invited by charities and served by Downing Street staff, most dressed up in red, white and blue. He drank lemonade from a Union Jack cup, signed autographs, and even accomplished a few high-fives. Samantha chatted away, completely at home (but then, of course, she was).

Eventually Dave came over to the press pen (also festooned with bunting) , eyes sparkling, morning suit a little tight around the middle. 'It has been an amazing day, the whole country has had something to celebrate.' It was, he said, 'like a fairy tale'.

A journalist noted that this was the new generation of royals. Dave nodded.

'It's the day we've seen the new team.'

Had his wife consulted him on her outfit? 'What do you think?' he guffawed.

His lasting memory of the day? 'There is something about singing 'Jerusalem' in Westminster Abbey with the whole orchestra behind you, and you feel the roof is going to lift up and that there is no greater country and no greater place to be.' And then he was off, to find a Union Jack cupcake. ❣

7 May 2011
Nick stays out for the AV count

Everyone who was no one was at the ExCel centre for the AV referendum count

You could almost see people thinking, as they roamed around in a cavernous 'nerve centre' of the AV count: whose idea was this anyway? And, as if in answer, there stood the quintessential Lib Dem, Simon Hughes, in his summer beige suit, mouth constantly moving, emitting a stream of equally beige words.

Who needs Nick when you've got Simon? It says everything that, for at least an hour, as the count began, Simon Hughes was the most interesting man in this room at the egregiously misnamed ExCel centre, a giant tincan in the badlands of East London.

As Simon finished one pre-record, only to be grabbed by a TV guy, I scrambled behind him. 'Simon!' I cried. 'You are the biggest celeb in the room.' He smiled, a man totally happy for that moment: 'As opposed to an elephant!'

Actually there was room for an elephant or two – make it a herd – in the room. The Great AV Vote Count didn't begin until 4 p.m. for reasons that no one could really understand. Maybe everyone wanted a siesta. At least it gave Chris Huhne time to announce the result on TV before the count even began. He loves the attention so much. I asked someone if Nick was coming and they raised one eyebrow. Say no more.

A stage was set up in the corner for 'announcements'. On the opposite side were three platforms for the TV broadcasters and their spaghetti soup of cables. In between was a yawning expanse of carpet which, gradually, began to fill. Every result, for hours, was No. Broxbourne, early on, was incredible (4,988 Yes, 19,386 No). Danny Alexander was our new elephant in the room (don't knock it, it's a step up from ginger rodent).

Lord Reid swept in. 'The people have spoken,' he said, terse and scornful of a referendum hatched in a 'backroom deal'. He attacked the insults and whingeing of the Lib Dems. I realised, as I listened to the bile, that I have missed the former Home Secretary very much.

It soon became clear that the people had not just spoken, they had shouted, catcalled, boomed, screamed, cried, jumped up and down and kicked the door down. As Amy Winehouse once sang in her song 'Rehab': 'No, no, no…' 💔

11 May 2011
Man with two brains left with no leg to stand on

David Willetts made no sense as he tried to explain his policy of 'off-quota' places at university

I bring you mind-bending news. David Willetts needs a third brain. Mr Willetts, the Minister for Higher Education, is called 'Two-Brains' because he is so clever but yesterday neither brain seemed able to explain the words coming out of his mouth, proving two brains are not always better than one.

First, Brain One told the Commons that this plan to allow 'off-quota' places was not new at all. It was ancient history, old news, yawnsville. Both he and the Secretary of State, Vince Cable – curiously absent, and so No-Brains – had mooted it. Was this true? Mr Willetts had been dragged to the Commons to answer an urgent question – by definition, not ancient history. Brain One asked Brain Two to explain. Nada.

Brain Two announced that, actually, rich students couldn't buy places. Instead, charities and businesses would do that. Mr Willetts couldn't say how because he now realised he didn't have enough brains for the day. (I paraphrase.)

John Denham, for Labour, was relentless and scathing. Mr Willetts had let us believe that he wanted wealthy families to buy places. Now the Minister had changed his tune. 'Where are these charities that want to pay £70,000 per student? Who are the employers who want to pay for the second best?' Mr Willetts couldn't say.

Was this, Mr Denham wondered, a climb-down? If so, was it the 'fastest U-turn' ever? Mr Willetts pretended he hadn't heard. Brains, as everyone knows, can't drive.

Mr Willetts was having a terrible day and Labour piled on the questions. Were universities to be like easyJet boarding? Weren't public schools actually charities? Why couldn't they buy places? Wouldn't this just mean more 'thick rich people' at uni?

The only people who looked more miserable than Mr Willetts were the Lib Dems. Labour was having a party. Heckler-in-chief Chris Ruane shouted in a bizarre posh accent: 'There may be many on the Tory benches who think this is an absolutely spiffing idea to allow Mummy and Daddy to purchase privilege through this toffs' quota. Should this be extended to allow Mummy and Daddy to purchase a parliamentary seat?' Mr Willetts looked disgusted.

David Watts, from the farthest Labour back bench, piped up. 'Can you explain what's to stop a rich businessman with a son buying him a place at university?' Many words came out but no answer. It was, quite simply, a no-brainer. ❤

12 May 2011
Flash, bang, wallop: Dave loses the plot

*As David Cameron struggles to control his inner Flashman, I
pose as his PMQ adviser and give him some dignified advice*

Memo to Dave from your PMQ trainer: Where to start? As
you know, we have been working to get you to ditch your
tendency to behave like Flashman, the dastardly swash-
buckling cad of George Macdonald Fraser's series. I know that
you love Flash but, as I explained, even tiny flashes of Flash allow
Labour to paint you as a posh, arrogant public schoolboy.

So, to recap. The goal was dignity. As you may remember, I
got you to sing it out like Tammy Wynette: D-I-G-N-I-T-Y.
No more gratuitous insults, no more meaningless attacks. We
knew that Ed M would try to make you lose your cool. I wasn't
surprised at all when he led on the NHS and claimed waiting
times were getting longer. You were right to insist they weren't,
and to demand he apologise.

Ed may be a plodder but he's also a prodder. He never lets
up. It was predictable that he would say your listening exercise
on NHS reforms was a sham. I was listening to your entirely
reasonable reply (good gag about Shadow Health Secretary John
Healey, by the way) when, suddenly, I heard you say: 'When I
look at this, it all reminds me of Labour thirty years ago. They
had a leader with the ratings of Michael Foot and he was being
undermined by someone called Healey, as well!' Flash! Yes, I
know your backbenchers loved it. As I explained before, they
love Flashman. Don't pander to it. Remember, not dastardly,
D-I-G-N-I-T-Y.

Ed now reached for his soundbite. 'We read in the papers
about a PMQs makeover. Well, I have to say that it did not last
very long because Flashman is back. The thing is, Flashman does
not answer the questions...'

And you were off! You were preening, turning this way and that at the despatch box, your hair apparently sprayed into a permanent quiff. 'I have to accept that some of the recent cultural references – Michael Winner, Benny Hill – are all a little bit out of date...' you said to Ed. 'But I must say that when I look at you, who told us the fight-back would start in Scotland before going down to a massive defeat [in the election], it rather reminds me of Eddie the Eagle!' For goodness sake, Eddie the Eagle? Where do you get this stuff? Do you have some secret database of retro naff characters? Please stop before you get to *Mork & Mindy* or *The Dukes of Hazzard* (Yee-haw). Stop the Eighties madness.

Of course Eddie – OK, so the Eagle gibe was kind of funny – came back with a pre-cooked 'Calm down, dear'. I think we've had enough of that now. But just when I thought it was over and I began to relax, I heard you react to Eddie's taunt about not being able to trust the Tories. 'There is only one party you can trust on the NHS,' you shouted, 'and it is the one that I lead!' Flash! Flash! Dave, you are in a coalition. Flashman may always be out for himself, but you have Nick and the Lib Dems. Yes, I know, you hated that movie *Brokeback Mountain*. Live with it. ♥

13 May 2011
A year on and the fuzziness lingers

Dave and Nick invite us to their first anniversary party – in a dirtpile

What a difference a year makes. Last May it was 'The Wedding' in the sun-dappled Rose Garden at No. 10. This year it was 'The Handball Event' in the giant lunar-like dirtpile that is the Olympic site in East London. It was heaven – for JCBs.

Whose idea was it to come to Diggerland for their first anniversary? As we were bussed there, an Olympic guy pointed at what looked like another pile of dirt. 'That's a sewer!' he noted. The whole thing felt a bit like North Korea, with flags and billboards exhorting us to do good things. 'Be safe, be healthy, be considerate, be proud,' waved the flags. Outside the Handball Arena, there were six little flags that waved 'Complete' at us. By law, everyone had to wear that awful Olympics logo on their lapel.

The Handball Arena – 'Complete!' – was fabulous with 7,000 multi-coloured seats. It was like being in the middle of a bowl of Smarties. Apparently, they do this because then it won't look so empty on TV if the seats aren't all occupied. No one seemed to know a thing about handball: it was soccer with hands, someone said, and it was huge in Iceland.

Nick and Dave were there to talk about youth unemployment. About 120 business leaders and apprentices had been bussed in (see what I mean about North Korea?). Nick and Dave arrived, various ministers in tow, a bit late, a bit rushed. 'I don't know anything about handball!' trilled Dave. 'Mind you, I'm a politician, so that won't stop me talking about it.'

Nick gazed at him through tired, bloodshot eyes. Both gave short speeches on how to tackle the scourge of unemployment and took questions from the apprentices. It was all very well-meaning but the whole event felt stage-managed and false.

This was highlighted when the media asked about David Laws and the one-year anniversary – topics unrelated to handball. Lucy Manning, from ITV, noted: 'A year ago we were in the warm and fuzzy atmosphere of the Downing Street garden.'

Nick stubbed the toe of his shoe into the floor. 'Fuzzy?' he asked, looking almost bashful. 'What does that mean? Fuzzy?'

It was noted that, in the Rose Garden, there had been much joshing about how, when asked during the election what his favourite joke was, Dave had answered 'Nick Clegg'. And now, Dave was asked, a year on, wasn't it true that Nick Clegg had actually become a joke?

Nothing fuzzy about that question. Dave warbled on about how he felt the same about the coalition. He and Nick had 'robust discussion, even arguments, in private'. 'And,' he said, 'we've obviously got used to each other's jokes in the last year!'

Nick smiled at him and chuckled: 'They change – not!' Dave smiled at him and chuckled back.

It was a moment of warmth and, well, fuzziness. Then Nick, furrowing his brow, began: 'On David, for a start, David is a close friend of mine and a good colleague…'

At this the Prime Minister interrupted: 'That's David Laws?'

Nick laughed. 'Yes! And that's a new joke!'

They still have the old chemistry, that's for sure. One year on and, despite it all, they are still as fuzzy as a caterpillar. ♥

Chapter Seven

Marriage is Hard Work

Dave and Nick's first anniversary was over and it seemed as if the parliamentary session was limping towards the summer recess. There were a series of amusing scandalettes, the most notable involving Chris Huhne's driving licence. Ed Miliband's performance was a cause for much concern in Labour as he bounced along the bottom of every ratings graph. Even Dave, the perennial Mr Sunshine, was looking a bit overcast amid the gathering storms of health reform and sentencing policy. And Nick? Well, Nick was a laughingstock. And then, suddenly, bang! The hacking scandal erupted. Ed Miliband led the way on his white charger. Dave was most definitely not on the front foot (possibly because of the ball and chain marked 'Andy Coulson' that he was dragging along). Suddenly the Lib Dems, always outspoken on this, didn't look so foolish after all. The whole thing peaked with a Hollywood-esque appearance by the Murdochs themselves before a select committee. For once, it wasn't an anti-climax – though it wasn't their fault that Wonder Wendi stole the show. 💔

17 May 2011
The obscure art of the fog of war

After much dawdling, the Government was more or less forced to enshrine the 'Military Covenant' in law. But what exactly was it?

I have heard of the fog of war and now I have experienced the fog of the Military Covenant. What was it? Where was it? In the Commons Liam Fox, the Defence Secretary, talked mostly about what it wasn't. It wasn't a list of rights, but more of an idea, a principle, really, that our military personnel should 'not be disadvantaged'. Can you enshrine a negative? Apparently so.

Then he was accused of another negative. 'The Government is doing the right thing for the wrong reason!' cried Jim Murphy, for Labour. Dr Fox had been faced with the prospect of defeat on his Armed Forces Bill if he hadn't enshrined whatever it was that he was enshrining. This, then, wasn't so much a victory as a hastily organised retreat parading as victory.

Dr Fox ignored this. He may be leading a retreat on a double negative but he was going to take credit for whatever it was he was doing. After all, this was the most popular thing he'd ever done and he was going to enjoy every foggy moment of it.

Dr Fox, famously feisty, was in a bouncy mood. One of his team, the Veterans Minister, Andrew Robathan, was accused of doing a 'double U-turn' on the Covenant. 'I'm not sure what a double U-turn looks like,' said Dr Fox to some laughter, though, obviously, a double-U can only be a W.

The armchair generals in the Commons had many questions. Shouldn't the Military Covenant guarantee soldiers the right to proper equipment? Dr Fox became shrouded in fog again – I was beginning to wonder if he had a secret supply of dry ice somewhere – as he told us how the Military Covenant was to do with the community, but equipment was to do with the Government.

Bob Ainsworth, who is so much better in Opposition than he ever was as Defence Secretary, declared it a victory for the British Legion. 'It is their campaign, more than anything else, that forced this most welcome retreat,' he said, moustache quivering.

Dr Fox, beaming, insisted he wants a 'maximising of transparency'. What WAS he talking about? Several Tory MPs were worried about whether enshrining anything in law would give more power to the biggest enemy of all: Europe. Were there enough safeguards to stop the lawyers bringing endless court cases?

Dr Fox decided to share a 'joke': 'I have a sister who is a doctor and a sister who is a lawyer,' he said. 'My father used to say we had the best of both worlds: the licence to kill and the licence to steal, but I have never taken such caricatures as being necessarily the honest truth!' Everyone laughed. Finally, something they understood! But then Dr Fox, once again, disappeared once more into the mist. ❦

18 May 2011
Chris Huhne tries not to get the point(s)

A very British non-scandal: as Chris Huhne's estranged wife claimed that he asked her to take his speeding points, Labour MPs tried to drive him crazy

Smug. Superior. Lecturing. Patronising. That was Chris Huhne when he came to the Commons to tell us about his fourth carbon budget triumph. As I looked at this man, infuriating in a hogging-the-centre-lane sort of way, belligerently insistent of his rightness in all things, I could see that his estranged wife Vicky Pryce may have a point.

Ah yes, points. With Mr Huhne embroiled in the Great M11 Speed Zone Scandal, Labour MPs took joy in asking pointed questions with the word 'points' in them. Indeed, they may be giving each other points for such points.

At various points (sorry), Stephen Pound, the court jester of the Labour benches, would bellow at Mr Huhne: 'How many points was that?'

Mr Huhne, face set, colourless lips in a grim line, ignored that and any other references to his wife's claim that he had asked her to accept speeding penalty points incurred on the M11 after he had flown to Stansted in March 2003.

Oh, the mundanity of it all! As I watched Labour MPs delight in all references to transport – even the word 'accelerate' brought joy – I thought how very British it all was. There's Dominique Strauss-Kahn in New York with his Air France first-class cabin and a $3,000 hotel suite. Here we have the Lib Dems, Ryanair and a 30mph speeding zone on the M11. If this scandal were a car, it would be a Ford Fiesta.

Labour's Barry Gardiner has made a non-career of trying to be interesting. Sure enough, yesterday he noted: 'I think it is good that you have established that you, and not the Business Secretary, are in the driving seat, at least on this one!' This brought guffaws. Another Labour MP asked Mr Huhne if he would be able to devote his 'full attention' to green issues over the coming days. 'I can indeed,' said Mr Huhne.

He droned on. Soon Labour MPs were reduced to random shouts of: 'What about Stansted?'

Finally Geraint Davies got to the point (sorry) by asking if Mr Huhne thought lowering the speed limit would help the carbon targets. 'Or do you think the speeding limit for cars should be raised, like the Transport Secretary and, presumably, your wife?'

Mr Huhne, deadpan, said this wasn't his responsibility. 'It is well above my pay grade.'

It was a relief for everyone when Mr Huhne left the chamber, just as a Labour MP was setting out a ten-minute rule Bill called Dangerous Driving (Maximum Sentence). You couldn't make it up. ❤

20 May 2011
The Government sends in the clowns

It was a three-ring circus when the Government explained why it wouldn't ban wild animals

Step up, step up and come with me to the circus that was the Commons yesterday, to see an incredible act of human madness, a political death-defying stunt in which the Government tried to explain why it won't ban the use of wild animals in circuses.

'Send in the clowns!' cried Dennis Skinner.

But he was already there. The Defra minister Jim Paice already has that tell-tale bald pate fringed with hair which, just for the day, he should have dyed orange. Certainly his cheeks, if not his nose, by rights should have been fire-engine red.

'A total ban might well be seen as disproportionate action under the European Union Services Directive and under our own Human Rights Act,' he droned to screams of derision. I swear I could see his shoes grow longer and his trousers get baggier.

He was standing in for Caroline Spelman, chief clown of the Environment, Food and Rural Affairs. She was the one who brought us the great forest sell-off. I have to say that coulrophobics should steer well clear of that department. After yesterday, she owes Mr Paice big-time (or should that be big-top-time?).

It was incredible to see a Tory minister hiding behind Europe quite so shamelessly. He explained that circus owners may – note that 'may' – take action against Austria. This, plus our very own human rights law, has the lawyers quaking.

Mary Creagh, for Labour, was scathing: 'The Defra big top is spinning out of control on these legal cases that don't exist and hiding behind human rights legislation.'

A Tory shouted at her: 'Pathetic!' She hit right back: 'It's this department that is pathetic!' And it was. To watch Mr Paice yesterday was to see a man shooting himself in the foot as well as out of a cannon without a safety net.

Sir Gerald Kaufman, whose extraordinary outfits are an inspiration to clowns everywhere, was incredulous: 'You talk about human rights but what about animal rights! What we want is action by you and not subordination to lawyers.'

Mr Paice mithered on about EU law and the importance of

lawyers. 'This is just not good enough!' cried the Lib Dem Bob Russell, who branded Defra as the Department for Error, Failure and Rotten Administration.

Mr Paice said that thirty-nine wild animals were now in circuses in Britain. But, he noted, after a recent press attention, there were no elephants. 'The last one, Nellie, which we saw being very badly treated, is now in a home,' he reported. Well, her name wasn't Nellie and not many homes comprise thirteen acres. Please, somebody, free Mr Paice from this cruel fate. ♥

24 May 2011
Now we know, but who will tell people living in igloos?

The Government announces it will set up a super-important super-committee on superinjuctions

MPs had gathered to discuss superinjunctions with a level of pomposity that rivalled the ash plume from Grímsvötn (I do wish that there was a superinjunction out against this Icelandic volcano, for it is fearsomely hard to spell). Dominic Grieve, the Attorney-General, as dry and desiccated as south east England in May, was spouting words such as 'comity' and 'heretofore'. He announced, with immense gravity, the setting up of a super-committee to look at superinjunctions: it would take a super-long time and would be super, super-important.

Tory John Whittingdale observed that the law was in danger of looking 'an ass'. 'You would virtually have to be living in an igloo not to know the identity of at least one Premier League footballer who has obtained an injunction,' he noted, neatly managing to insult igloo-dwellers, who probably know the name better than most, and, of course, donkeys. (Asses of the world, unite, and get a superinjunction against this traducement!) MPs lined up to condemn those who used parliamentary privilege to breach superinjunctions. It was 'usurping' the power of the courts, it was interfering in the separation of powers, it was a slur on Magna Carta, not to mention powdered wigs.

Out of the corner of my eye I saw the Lib-Dem MP John Hemming. Was he standing up? For Mr Hemming has used parliamentary privilege before to name and shame those behind superinjuctions. Would he do it again? 'With about 75,000 people having named Ryan Giggs on Twitter,' he said, thus informing igloo-dwellers across the world, 'it is obviously impracticable to imprison them all.'

There was a sharp intake of breath and I think that some MPs did want, at that moment, to arrest him. Yes, 75,000 was too many to jail but surely one would be OK? After all, he was guilty, not least of being a Lib-Dem. Still, I am sure igloo-dwellers will be happy to know that Mr Hemming is no longer hawing. 💔

25 May 2011
Yellow Baskets squirm as Tories indulge in more Clegg-baiting

Nick Clegg, now universally known as Poor Nick, needs protection from the Tories

It is quite amazing that we have banned bear-baiting but not Clegg-baiting. Yesterday was the first outing for Nick Clegg's new extended Question Time, now forty minutes long, giving an extra ten minutes for this cruel blood sport. The Tories haven't had so much fun since foxhunting was banned. Plus, it was the first Question Time for Poor Nick (he is changing his name by deed poll, I understand) since the disastrous AV referendum. The bad news for him is that the Tories hate Lords reform even more.

David Winnick, the seventy-seven-year-old Labour MP who

is beginning to resemble the Ancient Mariner, succumbed to the trend of saying something shocking in the Commons. 'At a recent meeting last week of Tory MPs,' noted Mr Winnick, 'it was reported that one Conservative described the Liberal Democrats as "yellow" and then the second word beginning with "b" then "a" and ending in "s". Were you as shocked as I was by such behaviour?'

The crowd bayed but the Speaker, suddenly chivalrous, threw his small but dense body between the question and Mr Clegg. Behind him, the Tories stifled smiles. The Lib Dems just stared ahead, trying to figure out the riddle – Yellow Baskets? Yellow Barbecues? Was it a cryptic clue, like a crossword?

Mr Clegg and Lords reform has an unfortunate effect on Tories, turning even mild-mannered ones like Andrew Turner, from the Isle of Wight, into peevish contrarians. 'Shouldn't you drop this unpopular policy, which does not resonate with the majority of the public, and concentrate instead on finding a solution to the West Lothian question?' 'HUZZAH!' cried the Commons (or something like that).

Such was the hue and cry that Jacob Rees-Mogg, who always seems to be visiting from the nineteenth century, took off his top hat and unwound his lanky Abe Lincoln frame from his languid pose. He noted that Mr Clegg's plan to use proportional representation to elect the Lords would mean the Yellow Baskets would always hold the balance of power. 'Are you intending to make being Deputy Prime Minister a job for life?' he inquired.

Mr Clegg was in his extra time now. Next up was the permanently baity Edward Leigh, who begged him to 'ditch' these proposals. After all the country was in crisis (he didn't mention which one) and Lords reform would just result in gridlock. Did I see Nick making 'time out' signs? The Tories could barely contain their glee. How they love to hate the Yellow Bs. ♥

26 May 2011
A very special relationship with Mr President

Nick and Dave, Tony and Gordon, Tom Hanks and the man sometimes known as Forrest Gump were all on hand for the Obama moment

The man has stardust on his shoulders and even the wooden angels, carved into the magnificent roof trusses of Westminster Hall, could see that. This hall is so big that at first it made Barack Obama, the most powerful man in the world, look small as he stood, thin as a pencil, before us. But there was nothing small about his message, rousing and global, full of warmth and poetry and, amazingly, jokes.

The President was a bit late, as you are after a heavy day of meetings and barbecuing at No. 10. He and Dave (wearing ties) had flipped burgers. Michelle and Sam had served salads. I didn't see anyone actually chewing. Burgers, ping-pong and Libya: this is the new definition of a special relationship.

Security required that we'd all been in the hall for ages, the media crammed into a back corner, agog as we watched the action in the VIP seats. The front row contained Gordon Brown, Tony Blair, Sir John Major, Nick and Dave. Nick talked non-stop to Tony (over Sir John). I cannot remember the last time I even saw the Lesser-Spotted Gordo. Across the platform, on the American side of the platform, was Tom Hanks. I wonder if Ed Miliband, sometimes compared with Forrest Gump, thought 'snap' as he looked over and saw the real, so to speak, Mr Gump.

Finally, the eight state trumpeters, dressed as playing cards, standing before the kaleidoscopic glory that is the memorial stained-glass window, sounded the fanfare and the President hove into view – with Mr Speaker seemingly clamped to his shoulder.

This was his moment (I speak of Johnny Bercow). The atmosphere in the hall, which you might expect to be solemn, had been light, almost giddy. Earlier, someone dressed in a penguin outfit had explained to us that Mr Bercow would be making a 'brief' welcome speech and the hall had rocked to laughter. Mr Bercow and the word 'brief' are not well acquainted. But he did it well, invoking Abraham Lincoln which, I think, is almost required by law when introducing this President.

Then Mr Obama was before us, his casual elegance immediately recognisable. He told us the past three speakers here had been the Pope, the Queen and Nelson Mandela. 'Which is either a very high bar,' he noted, 'or the beginning of a very funny joke.' It was a very funny joke about a very funny joke.

There has rarely been so much talk about relationships outside of a Relate marriage therapy room. Ours was special, indeed extra-special, indispensable – if a little rocky to start. First there was that 'small scrape about tea and taxes'. Then there was a snag when the White House was set on fire during the War of 1812. But since then it's been, well, you fill in the S-word. His voice went up and down like a lullaby. The hundreds of peers and MPs, with notable exceptions like a drowsy Ken Clarke, gave Mr Obama their greatest compliment, rapt attention. It was such a grand occasion that even Lord Mandelson seemed an ordinary member of the audience. Outside the VIPs, there was no seating plan that I could see.

There were copious references to Churchill which, again, I believe is a legal requirement for any American president giving a speech here. After a standing ovation, he embarked on what was, more or less, a hug-a-thon. This ancient hall has seen many trials and tribulations. It can be a cold and unforgiving place, but yesterday was full of warmth. It really was quite the S-word occasion. ❦

8 June 2011
Pause button? Lansley was on fast-forward

The frenetic Health Secretary says that his 'listening exercise' is over. Some wondered if it every really began

Andrew Lansley is not one of life's pausers. He is a relentless, focused, eyes-forward type of guy. This is a man who probably doesn't even know how to hit the pause button on his TV control, much less on his NHS reforms. Indeed, what he seems to have done is simply to redefine the word pause.

Dictionaries, beware. The word pause used to signify a break in activity. But yesterday Mr Lansley made it clear that, for him, a pause was no such thing. Indeed, he has used it as an excuse for frenetic behaviour.

Yesterday, he told the Commons that The Pause was over (just about suppressing a 'yippee!') and that the two months had been crammed with 250 events.

But there was another new definition too. BL (Before Lansley), a pause meant that whatever was happening on the ground – as in real people doing real things (always a difficult concept in politics) – stopped for a bit.

But, a Labour MP noted that, in his patch of the world during The Pause, the reforms had been steaming ahead. 'Hasn't this been an absolute farce?'

Mr Lansley's shock of white hair vibrated with outrage. No, no, no. It wasn't a farce, it was what he'd always intended. Ever since he announced The Pause on April 4, he'd been clear that this Pause was about 'listening' but was nothing to do with what was happening on the ground. He wasn't going to stop any NHS staff implementing his reforms. 'They are engaging in those positive changes and we aren't stopping them!' he cried.

Actually, I suspect that Mr Lansley has another definition entirely for pause, which is: 'Keep your paws off my reforms.' He was on bullish form yesterday. John Healey, for Labour, has a good name for a Shadow Health Secretary, but is most unconvincing. The Lib Dems love The Pause so much that they are still on it, possibly lying in hammocks, sipping long, cool drinks, dreaming of how important they are. Only four Lib Dems even showed up yesterday.

But the Tories were there in droves and backing Mr Lansley to the hilt. Take this from one named Karl McCartney, who got up to give a sermon in favour of competition and accused the Lib Dems of being 'flip-flopping' coalition partners. Little Duncan Hames, a Lib Dem who seems almost desperate to please, squeaked that he, for one, wasn't wearing 'sandals or flip-flops'. We shall see. For Mr Lansley, the hell that has been The Pause is over. He looks like a man released. 💔

9 June 2011
Just a minute! What is this repetition, deviation…?

Even by Ed Miliband's standards, hardly very high, this was an abysmal performance

There was only one word to describe Ed Miliband at PMQs and it is 'Mayday'. Dearie me, as Ed would say. I looked at his front bench – a row of grey men, most second-rate – and felt they should be running for the lifeboats but had decided they couldn't be bothered. Waving, not drowning? They wish.

Some call him Milibland but yesterday he was just Milibad, and what's strange is that he had everything going for him. The Government is in mid-U-turn (you know, that bit where you are smack in the middle of the road) on its sentencing policy. There sat Ken Clarke, red of face, bold of belly, as subdued as his brown-suede Hushies. Just down from him was Chris Huhne, frantically nodding, a man himself in search of a lifeboat. And then there was the hulk that is Andrew Lansley...

You get my drift. It was all there, on a plate for Ed. He began with a short, sharp question: 'We read in the newspapers that the Prime Minister has torn up the Justice Secretary's policy on sentencing. Have you?' That was the high point.

Dave tore up that question and Ed asked it again. ('Just a minute,' I thought, 'do I hear someone saying "repetition"?'). Sadiq Khan, the hopeless Shadow Justice Secretary, kept muttering next to him. If he is coaching Ed, that would explain a lot.

Ed abandoned his topic in mid-flow – so abruptly that it felt rude – and turned to the health reforms. (Just a minute, surely this was 'deviation'?) 'I am not surprised that you want to move on because on the first subject you were found guilty,' crowed Dave.

Ed was in trouble now, awkward as he turned this way and that at the despatch box, as if he didn't know where to go. It was like watching someone trying to walk under water: slow, wavering, feet never quite landing properly. He repeated not just words but entire phrases. He called Dave 'shameless' (Dave preened) and embarked on a tortuous question on waiting times. There was so much hesitation that I felt that this may be a specially extended *Just a Minute* (as in Just Thirty Very Painful Minutes).

Dave probably should have left Ed alone to sink. But that is not Dave's way, for Flashman dies hard. 'The best that can be said about this performance is that – quite rightly – you were not thinking about politics on your honeymoon,' noted Dave, ducking his head in appreciation of his own little joke.

But Just-Wed Ed, intent on following his own dislocated script, was not capable of a riposte. Instead, he embarked on a cumbersome, not to say galumphing, series of insults. Dave demolished him in reply. Just a minute, surely it should be Dave in trouble? But instead it's Mayday for Milibad. They don't call it the cruel sea for nothing. 💔

17 June 2011
After knives in the back, what can go prong now?

Ed Balls revealed Plan B (for Balls). It's all about forks, prongs and, yes, taramasalata

I think we all know what Plan B is now. It's Plan Balls. No, not plain, plan. As Ed revealed his idea that one way to kick-start growth in the economy would be to cut VAT, I could hear George Osborne sneering all the way from the Treasury. But then, he would, wouldn't he?

The Opposition is, slowly and not very surely, taking form. It is extraordinary that, for the first year of this coalition, there has been a Labour economic policy void. Part of this is because Gordon Brown has disappeared. Alan Johnson's only economic speech was so lightweight that it should have been delivered in a balloon. Since Ed got the job in January, he has been on a short leash – until yesterday.

The bulldog of Labour politics is back. It wasn't a speech but a lecture at the LSE which, of course, since its links with Libya were revealed, knows a thing or two itself about damaged reputations. It was 'keynote' – a word that should be banned. And it was timed for the morning after George Osborne's appearance at the Mansion House dinner. The speech was called 'The Fork in the Road'. So no food, only cutlery, for Labour, which seemed perfect for a party that is capable of knifing itself in the back so often.

'Don't worry,' he began. 'This is not a lecture on economic theory.' Wasn't it? Admittedly, he never once said 'neo-classical endogenous growth theory', but there was still a lot of talk about macro-fiscal credibility. It was all about why Mr Balls was right. It's all related to the ERM. When the road forked on ERM, we took the wrong prong. He couldn't stop talking about the ERM, which felt just a bit retro. It was like an Eighties/Nineties party, though instead of Duran Duran we had Norman (Lamont) and Nigel (Lawson).

Ed is convinced that, on the deficit, George, too, has taken the wrong prong. Basically, and I paraphrase, but only a bit, he claims that we are on the same prong as the Greeks – the taramasalata prong, if you will. George O denies this, but Ed insists it is true. There is no macro-fiscal credibility in taramasalata. We must return to the fork in the road.

He didn't reveal Plan Balls – the VAT cut – until almost the end of his fifty-minute speech. By then, we were all in need of a little oxygen. He accused the Chancellor of putting politics before economics. Shocking, I'm sure you will agree. ❦

22 June 2011
Ken twists and turns with a suede-shoe shuffle

The Justice Secretary is forced to abandon his plan to cut sentences for those accused of rape

Tough on Ken, tough on the causes of Ken. That was the Commons yesterday, but Mr Clarke simply doesn't seem to care. His face, as rumpled as his trousers, which he was constantly hoicking up, creased in joviality when he heard the toughest Ken question of all.

'Are you on probation?' demanded the Labour MP Stephen McCabe. 'And do you anticipate time added on or early release?' Ken fell forward on to the despatch box, stomach hitting first, elbows propping him up. 'I've been on probation for the last few decades!' His chuckle was low and soft and sounded, in cartoon terms, like 'yuck yuck yuck'. 'Sooner or later I'll get the hang of it, but I'm working on it!' The rest of those words were lost forever as they collided, slipped and slid out of his mouth.

He added: 'The Prime Minister and I and the Cabinet have developed these policies together.' This brought cries of hilarity. 'Yes, we have,' he insisted, his voice going falsetto now. Labour frontbenchers made rather rude-looking gestures intended to be Pinocchio's nose growing.

Earlier in the day the Prime Minister had, extraordinarily, called a press conference to pre-announce Ken's announcement. That's how much he trusts the Justice Secretary. And, as I watched Ken perform what can only be called his stand-up comedy shtick, I could see why. Dave may hug hoodies, but if he's hugging Ken, it's only to keep him close.

The Tories remain more or less furious with Ken. Edward Leigh, always close to explosion, castigated Ken for saying he was going to introduce drug-free wings in jails. 'The public believe all parts of jail are drug-free, and to them this sums up the irretrievably soft attitude to the entire prison system!' Ken embraced this. 'I share your amazement!' he cried. 'The fact is that drugs are very widely available in prisons.'

The Tories looked disgusted, while all the Lib Dems nodded madly. The coalition was hanging together by a thread. Bill Cash denounced 'wishy-washy liberals'. A Lib Dem stood up and pleaded guilty to wishy-washiness. Other Tories urged Ken to be more right-wing, to throw away human rights, to imprison at will.

Ken turned this way and that, doing his trademark suede-shoe shuffle. He was accused of multiple U-turns. 'I've done many U-turns in my time and they should be done with purpose and panache,' he trilled. 'But I actually don't think that this is a U-turn at all!' This brought more guffaws from Labour but, for the Tories, this is no laughing matter. Probation? I think that they'd rather lock him up. 💔

24 June 2011
The whips fail to tame the political circus

If I had to pick the most ludicrous debate of the year, it would be this strange event in which the Government tried to squash the mouse that roared

Wild times in the political jungle. Whips. Chains. Cages. The Government tried everything to tame its back-benchers over a motion to ban wild animals in circuses. No. 10 may be able to control lions and tigers, but not Tory MP Mark Pritchard.

Mr Pritchard wanted a ban. No. 10 did not. Yesterday Mr Pritchard was the mouse – some would say rat – that roared. 'On Monday I was offered reward and incentive,' he revealed. 'If I didn't call for a ban, I was offered a job.'

But Mr Pritchard would not be bribed. 'It was ratcheted up last night where I was threatened. I had a call from the Prime Minister's office directly and was told that unless I withdraw this motion, that the Prime Minister himself said he would look upon it very dimly indeed.'

Ahhhhhh, cried the Commons, riveted by such a public career suicide. I have to say, it was just like a movie.

'Well, I have a message for the whips and the Prime Minister of our country,' Mr Pritchard declared (where was the swelling soundtrack?). 'I may just be a little council-house lad from a very poor background, but that background gives me a backbone ['Yeah!' shouted the crowd]. It gives me a thick skin ['YEAH!' again], and I am not going to be kowtowed by the whips or even the Prime Minister on an issue I feel passionately about. We need a generation of politicians with a bit of spine, not jelly. I will not be bullied by any other whips!'

The whips were flying round the chamber like bats out of hell. The hapless minister, Jim Paice, whose balding pate and horseshoe of hair is alarmingly clownlike, perused his papers with obsessive interest. Now he was the one in the cage: forced to defend a policy which said that, basically, we would not enact a ban because of a potential legal case in Vienna.

There was a bizarre speech by a Tory named Andrew Rosindell, who insisted wild animals in circuses are not wild at all. 'I am fed up with animals being used as a political football,' he cried (now, that would be cruel). He said 'tenth-generation circus tigers' should not be 'wrenched' away from their home.

So, Mr Rosindell was asked, would he say that third-generation slaves in America had felt less enslaved? 'I am sorry that the debate is being dragged to such a level,' despaired Mr Rosindell.

His was a lonely voice (actually, the word used by a Labour MP was 'idiotic') as MPs jostled to castigate the Government.

Like all animal stories, there were some 'ahhhh' moments, such as when the Tory MP Bob Stewart told us: 'I found a bear in a cage – in no-man's land in Bosnia. He was entirely miserable. Wouldn't even be coaxed out of his cage by honey. We managed to ethnically cleanse that bear out of Bosnia!' Wow. Bribes, threats, Europe, slavery and now bear ethnic cleansing. Mr Paice hadn't looked up from his papers once.

The Commons was revolting, the animals were out of the cages. I don't think anyone was really surprised when Mr Pritchard announced that the Government had given up trying to control the debate and had decided to allow a free vote. In the end, the motion was nodded through – cue *Born Free* music – without a vote. For once, the Government was whipped. ♥

29 June 2011
Aggression? It's just not Michael's bag

Thwack! As the teachers' strike loomed, Michael Gove was on feisty form

I think I know who bought Margaret Thatcher's iconic killer handbag at that charity auction for £25,000. It was Education Secretary Michael Gove. Yes, I know the black Asprey doesn't accessorise well with his suit, but he was certainly wielding it with force – bash, bash, bash – in the Commons yesterday.

Mr Gove had been dragged to the House to explain what

was going on with tomorrow's teachers' strikes. Labour's Andy Burnham – he of the bedroom eyes – accused Mr Gove of being 'high-handed' and wanting to return to the battles of the 1980s.

At this a Tory shouted: 'RUBBISH!' But Mr Gove kept his voice on an even keel, each word distinct, as if clipped from a newspaper. His manner was über-über polite and utterly passive-aggressive. He critiqued Mr Burnham's speech as 'irresponsible'. Whack (also, for consistency's sake, he pursed his lips). It was 'inappropriate' – the great sin in the world of über-über polite – to 'ratchet up the rhetoric'.

Whack. Andy took up a defensive position with his arms. Mr Gove did his own ratcheting.

Andy had been 'pandering' to the unions. Mr Gove said 'of course' he was keeping the law under review. The 'of course' was really ominous.

Why, asked the Labour bruiser Tom Watson, didn't Mr Gove leave the chamber and try to avert the strike? 'It's not too late,' he said.

Mr Gove waved the black Asprey.

'The question for Labour MPs is what are you doing to keep our schools open? Are you doing everything possible to encourage unions to lower the temperature?'

David Winnick, the ancient but respected warhorse, got out his own old ragtag of a handbag (was it macraméd?). Many teachers felt that the Government had declared 'war' on them. 'They are sick and tired of a Cabinet made up of a good number of multimillionaires taking an attitude so hostile.'

Mr Gove's voice grew ever more clipped – we're talking bowling greens. 'I hope you will reflect on your rhetoric and recognise that it is not helpful to your own community.'

Finally the Beast: class war, classroom war, it's all the same to the Skinner-o-saurus. 'This smug, arrogant Government has revelled in the part that it's played in this dispute,' Dennis Skinner growled. Mr Gove said that he respected Mr Skinner's passion, then bashed him too. Baroness T will be proud.

5 July 2011
Sombre issues, over there and over here

The war in Afghanistan was a running theme in Parliament
with sharp anxiety about how we are treating those who fight
– and those who die

The spectre of Afghanistan hung over the Commons yesterday, heavy as the air before a thunderstorm. The sombre mood was set by Liam Fox who confirmed that a soldier was missing, the next of kin had been notified and a search was under way. He didn't want to say more, speculation was not helpful.

But throughout Defence Questions, as it dealt with the daily business of war (and it does seem mostly about deals sometimes), came flashes of anxiety, as sharp as lightning, about what is going on there as well as how we are treating the fallen here.

Dr Fox answered all questions about training up Afghan police and soldiers with an optimism that, being so very, very determined, gave room for doubt. Yes, he said, having recently been to Afghanistan he had 'great hope' of progress. 'Things that may seem small to us, such as literacy training, have phenom-enally increased their capability,' he said.

It felt like clutching at straws. Then he was asked to give an indication of how successful we've been, to say how many chil-dren are in school in Helmand. Dr Fox did not, unusually, know the figure. 'What is very clear is we have taken to Afghanistan a large amount of military equipment, a large amount of money but perhaps the most important thing we've taken is hope,' he said, 'hope for a generation that actually may be able to be educated, that may have some economic capabilities.'

Labour's Jim Murphy sought assurance that decisions about troop numbers in Afghanistan would not be made for political reasons. Dr Fox's answer was terse, saying these decisions were only made after politicians and the military sat down. It was clear that, whatever happens, we are sticking to the withdrawal timetable.

More lightning as MPs criticised the new cortège route from RAF Brize Norton in Oxfordshire, which has been described as leaving by the 'back door' and avoiding nearby towns. This was in stark contrast with what has been happening at RAF Lyneham (which is due to close) where the cortèges have gone straight through the town of Wootton Bassett with crowds lining the streets. In March, in honour of this, the town was given the title of 'Royal'.

Defence Minister Andrew Robathan, very prickly, said the new route was respectful and solemn, going down a 'very digni-fied' avenue of limes to a gate that was being refurbished and called the Britannia Gate.

Paul Flynn, for Labour, was scathing: 'You miss the point.' Why was the new route mostly rural, making it hard to replicate the scenes in Royal Wootton Bassett? 'Shouldn't the people of Brize Norton and surrounding area have the right to express the grief of the nation in order that we are all reminded of the true cost of war?'

Mr Robathan said the cortege could not go through the nearby garrison town of Carterton because the streets were 'very narrow' and had speed bumps. It wasn't convincing: Mr Flynn wasn't the only one looking disgusted. 💔

6 July 2011
Mañana Nick adds procrastination to his portfolio

Nick loves to talk about constitutional reform but he wouldn't want to actually do anything

It's official: Nick Clegg is suffering from his very own syndrome. I believe dictionaries are introducing a new word – Cleggophobia: the fear of anything actually happening.

As I watched him procrastinate and fulminate simultaneously at Deputy Prime Minister's Questions, it struck me that Mr Clegg has finally found something that he is truly brilliant at. Admittedly, he is quite good at nodding at the PM. And there's his other new talent for travelling to Brazil, the land of carnival (Business Class, with a night at the Copacabana Palace: remember, we're all in this together). But I believe that only now has he found his true forte: doing nothing well.

It seems there are two trays on his desk: one marked 'long grass', another marked 'even longer grass'. He is, in golfing terms, a man who is never allowed on the fairway. This suits him just fine. The Tories like it too, for they hate Lords reform.

A Tory said that she admired his 'ambition' to hold elections to the Upper House by 2015, before adding that surely he was a silly billy (I paraphrase). 'Ambition is clearly intended as faint praise,' burbled Mr Clegg, 'and I will take it in that spirit!'

Penny Mordaunt, one of the new Tories with great hair, said that the 'elegance' of our unwritten constitution allowed it to adapt to meet a pressing need. But change for change's sake in the Lords might be seen as constitutional vandalism. What did he think? Mr Clegg babbled so expertly that I understand that brooks are going to organise a masterclass with him: 'Well, I don't think it's a new need. In that sense it's not a pressing need. It's an enduring need!' Ah yes, an enduring need. That means nothing has ever happened and never, ever will.

There was another moment when an MP – a Lib Dem no less – suggested he might want to 'make haste' on Lords reform. 'What we aspire to do is to create a reform that, whilst evolutionary in its implementation, wouldn't be overnight...' murmured Mr Clegg, soothing himself as he spoke.

Alan Reid, another dastardly Lib Dem, noted that talks with Commonwealth governments to reform the rules for succession to the Crown seemed to be dragging on. 'What are you doing to ensure these come to a speedy end?' he wondered.

Panic stations! Nick babbled about the need for consultations.

'That is not a very rapid process,' he announced, relief flooding (sorry, brooks) over him.

Eleanor Laing, a Tory who is permanently irritated at someone, said this sounded like an excuse for inaction. As Mr Clegg began to explain why it was exactly that, a Labour MP heckled him and Nick snapped: 'You say, "Do something about it"! You can't just do something about it! No! I accept totally that it seems a little anachronistic that there are rules of succession in place which appear to discriminate against women and that clearly should be looked at...'

The crowd was baying. Mr Clegg was caught between a belief and a hard place. 'But!' he cried, 'it affects other governments as well. It would be wrong to act with haste!' Was that a cold sweat on his upper lip? I tell you, Cleggophobia is no joke. ♥

7 July 2011
Ed's volcanic endeavour erupts

After a year of blows and lows, Ed Miliband suddenly found his voice on the explosive subject of phone hacking and the News of the World

Ed Miliband is a natural geek and when I think of him I often cannot help but hear the words 'science experiment'. Thus it was yesterday, when he faced his biggest test to date. For Dave it was also tricky. Indeed, the PM, having just come back from Afghanistan, must have wished that he had stayed in the relative safety of Kabul.

Everything was in Ed's favour but, with a man whose nickname is Milibanana, that means nothing. Ed often tries to construct the political equivalent of a volcano for the science fair but, being made of papier-mâché, it never erupts. This time he had almost too much material at hand: phone hacking, police corruption, his former aide Andy Coulson, the impending BSkyB decision. This was either going to be Vesuvius or just very, very confusing.

He began with a promising rumble, voice low, tone serious. The country was appalled. How could the *News of the World* have hacked into the phone of murdered teenager Milly Dowler? Would the PM hold a public inquiry? The Prime Minister answered directly that, yes, he would.

This is almost a first and so you know how serious it was. Ed, sounding like the elder brother now, not a role that comes naturally for obvious reasons, was 'encouraged' by his response. His voice, still low, oozed reason: he listed a series of suggestions for the inquiry. Dave nodded.

Could Dave hear that rumble? Maybe not. The PM began to worry out loud that he didn't want to rush an inquiry. Ed, suddenly his consigliere, advised that it was important to do something now. 'Just because we cannot do everything it does not mean we cannot do anything,' he soothed.

Then, voice so even that it wouldn't have moved a spirit level, Ed switched topics to BSkyB. Surely the PM should delay the decision. The PM, voice rising, did not agree. Then, suddenly, Ed roared: 'I am afraid that that answer was out of touch with millions of people up and down this country!' Magically and, frankly, amazingly, Ed's volcano was sparking into life. As Dave spluttered, Ed tsk-tsked: 'This is not the time for technicalities or low blows.'

It all sounded rather, well, prime ministerial. Dave must have known there was more to come in the form of his former communications chief Andy Coulson, always controversial, as he was also a former editor of *News of the World*. 'With the biggest press scandal in modern times getting worse by the day, I am afraid that you haven't shown the necessary leadership,' sighed Ed. 'If the public are to have confidence in you, you've got to do the thing that is most difficult and accept that you made a catastrophic judgement by bringing Andy Coulson…'

The name was met by Labour screams. Lava spewed. Heat rose. Ed shouted: '...into the heart of the Downing Street machine!' Dave hated this. But Ed had built the perfect volcano – let's call it Mount Coulson – and there wasn't much he could do. ♥

12 July 2011
Feeding frenzy in the monkey house

Ed Miliband gets hacked off when he has to deal with the monkey and not the organ grinder

Ed Miliband, who is loving riding his white charger around Westminster, wanted David Cameron in the Commons for a mano-a-mano showdown over BSkyB and phone hacking. Instead, he got languid, elegant Jeremy Hunt, a Culture Secretary who is, er, cultured but has all the concentrated raw power of a straw in the wind.

'The Prime Minister was wrong not to come to the House!' roared Ed, who is savouring his moment with a furious right-eousness that feels almost biblical. Dave was 'running scared'. Actually, at that moment, the PM was running on empty as he re-re-re-relaunched his vision of the Big Society with yet another speech about the wonders of sharing. Westminster, swirling with rumour, awash with testosterone and excitement, on the edge of hysteria, found this bizarre.

Labour was savage, red in tooth and claw. 'WHERE IS HE?' they roared at Mr Hunt, who steadied himself by holding on to the despatch box with both hands. I feared he would blow away.

'I'm surprised we have the monkey at the despatch box and not the organ grinder,' sneered Labour's Alan Johnson, he of the apple cheeks, abandoning his nice-guy image.

'YEAHHHHH!' screamed the Labour monkeys.

Tory MPs shrieked back as Mr Johnson demanded Mr Hunt tell the House what exactly the Prime Minister had been told about his former communications chief Andy Coulson and when he had been told it.

Mr Hunt looked, eponymously, hunted. 'I do take being called a monkey very seriously,' he announced. 'In my wife's country they used to eat them.' His wife is Chinese, but this still seemed a spectacularly odd thing to say. No one knew how to react to that. Then he added, wavering this way and that, as he does: 'In respect to what the Prime Minister did or did not know, he will answer for himself.' This brought the monkey house down.

It was an electrifying session. MPs know what it feels like to be the national hate figure and they are turning the tables with a vengeance that makes the heart pound. The Murdoch press (which includes *The Times*, of course) was castigated on all sides, as was News International and its executives and certain police-men. Labour shrieked about Dave and Andy, the Tories screamed right back about why Labour did nothing for years. The BSkyB bid, supposedly the reason for the statement, at times seemed almost lost in the turbulence.

I knew we were in new territory when Mr Hunt praised Labour attack dog Tommy Watson for his 'tenacious' campaign. But the last word, as so often, goes to Dennis Skinner, who has made a career out of hating the press. 'Isn't it time, based upon the British public's reaction, that we send this non-taxpaying Murdoch back from whence he came...?' he shouted, finger stabbing at the straw man, '...and for the final humiliation get the Secretary of State for Energy to drive him to the airport!' Ha! Everyone laughed – even Mr Hunt's thin lips twitched – at the idea of Chris 'Speed Points' Huhne acting as chauf-feur. 'I'm not sure I can follow that,' wavered Mr Hunt. And he couldn't. ❧

13 July 2011
The day Clouseau became Keystone

The Home Affairs Select Committee summoned the top cops to ask them questions about phone hacking. The result was farcical

I t was, simply, incredible to see Britain's top cops try to explain themselves when it came to the phone-hacking debacle. These are the men who are, or were, in charge of counter-terrorism in our country, and they don't even seem to know if their own mobile phones had been hacked.

First up was Yates of the Yard*, John to his friends. In 2009 he took an entire day to dismiss the idea that the 11,000 pages of evidence about hacking might hold anything new. Yesterday he appeared defensive, withdrawn, unhelpful, superior. A tabloid hack might call him 'tight-lipped', but that does not do justice to the tension there (can you be 'tight-faced'?).

'Do you think your phone was hacked?' asked Keith Vaz, the rotund head of the Home Affairs Select Committee, who sees himself as some sort of Watergate-style interrogator (I am sure he is already thinking about who will play him in the film).

Mr Yates said that he had suspected it had been years ago, but he couldn't prove it. He didn't know about anything more recent. Mr Vaz, who adores drama and believes that life is, if not a stage, then there to be stage-managed, provided Mr Yates with a list of known hacking victims from *The Guardian*'s website.

'Is that the first time you have seen the list?' asked Mr Vaz.

Mr Yates nodded, leafing through. Gordon Brown's name was on there. So were other police officers. 'As is my own,' said Mr Yates in an almost robotic voice.

The Labour MP Steve McCabe noted mildly: 'You just don't sound like the dogged determined sleuth that we would expect.'

The robot hardly reacted. I didn't think that it could get worse – and then the man who used to be his boss, Andy Hayman, arrived before us. Tall, cocky and way too relaxed, he took a job as a columnist with News International (*The Times*, as you ask) two months after retiring.

Was it true that, while in overall charge of the original phone-hacking inquiry in 2006 he had accepted hospitality (as in dinner) from the company? 'Yeah!' he cried, entirely happily.

Was his own phone hacked? 'I haven't a clue!' he cried. Well, his name was on the list. 'If I am, so be it!' he cried. 'I've got nothing to hide at all! The shopping list will be there! And the golf tee-off time!'

It was a car crash. Mr Hayman said that, as a boy, he had wanted to be a journalist. He never thought about how it looked. But he had never done anything improper. Of course he couldn't influence anyone! No line had been crossed!

'All of this sounds more like Clouseau rather than Columbo,' noted Mr Vaz drily. Other MPs weren't so nice. Wouldn't the public just see Mr Hayman not as a top cop but as a 'dodgy geezer'? Dodgy geezer? It's perfect casting: I think he will have to play himself in the movie. Forget Clouseau. Think Keystone. If it weren't so scary, it would be funny. 💔

*To no one's surprise, Yates of the Yard had resigned within a week.

14 July 2011
The scary return of Dr Evil

Gordon Brown's spectacular rant was supposed to be about phone hacking but, actually, it was on another subject closer to (his) home

I have seen the wrath of Brown and it is frightening. The former Prime Minister stood up in the chamber last night and let rip with a roar of pain and fury that said more about him than anything else. It took my breath away. It was both brilliant and as close to bonkers as I have ever seen.

The hero of the speech was Gordon Brown. He explained how, when he became Prime Minister in 2007, he had known nothing of the evil that was News International. His goal was 'to unite the country, not divide it'. He was a healer at heart.

He stood awkwardly, hemmed in by the benches, for it was only the second time that he had spoken in the chamber since the election. The voice was booming and bold, its bass notes and cadences so familiar that they fit perfectly into a memory groove. In the gallery, Lord Mandelson, for it was he, watched, face inscrutable. Labour MPs looked like they'd seen a ghost (or a poltergeist). Tories who tried to intervene were ignored.

Our Hero of Unity explained that he was never, ever cosy with News International. How could he be when he had been called Dr Evil on the front of *The Sun*? And when, in 2009, allegations of phone hacking resurfaced Our Hero decided that it was time to set up a judicial inquiry. But the Forces of Stagnation – the Civil Service, the select committee and others – had stopped him.

'You were the Prime Minister!' screamed Tory MPs.

Our Hero ignored these voices, for they knew not of what they spoke.

Not only were the Forces of Stagnation against him but soon he noticed that, after 2009, the Tory policies were the same as the News International policies. It was an Axis of Evil. And, Mr Brown asked, why wasn't the current Prime Minister in the chamber for this debate? (This, coming from the mouth of the Lesser-Spotted Gordo, took particular chutzpah, I think.)

The Tories (idiots!) were shrieking but Our Hero would not give way. The Speaker was reduced to bawling like a cow giving birth: 'Order! Order! Order!' Mr Speaker screamed that this debate on BSkyB – calling for something that had already happened, which is bonkers in itself – was supposed to be in the spirit of a 'new tone' and a 'new mood'. It sounded the opposite to me.

Mr Brown poured scorn on the police and on the 'media criminal nexus' that was News International. The organisation had gone from gutter to sewer and, tragically, 'let the rats out'. I noted that Our Hero was now battling plagues on many fronts: rats, the police, the Civil Service and, of course, the Tories.

Suddenly, Mr Brown interrupted himself and gave way to the Toriest Tory of them all, Jacob Rees-Mogg, who asked: 'I wonder, with his very high moral tone, whether you will tell us something about Messrs Whelan and McBride?' (I fear this sketch needs an organogram: this refers to Brown's occasionally thuggish ex-spinners Charlie Whelan and Damian 'McPoison' McBride.)

Mr Brown treated this with contempt. Another Tory asked why Mr Brown had not told us the details of the slumber party his wife had given for Mr Murdoch's daughter and the News International CEO Rebekah Brooks (or, because of her flaming red tresses, Medusa, for purposes of organogram). Mr Brown looked disgusted at such trivia. Here he was, giving a historic speech and these dimwits wanted to talk about slumber parties? How crazy was that? He sat down to Labour cheers, a man happy that we now knew the truth – about him. ♥

15 July 2011
It's 1666 and all that as MPs await RSVPs

Parliament was desperate to flex its muscles over Hackgate but, comically, it was having trouble finding them (if they even existed)

Ding! It was Round Two of the Commons versus the Murdochs. MPs were beside themselves as they tried to figure out what powers they have to make the Murdoch Two attend the Culture, Media and Sport Committee hearing on Tuesday. News International CEO Rebekah Brooks*, who must be called flame-haired by law, was coming, but she was British.

How could they force Rupert and his son James (Americans) to come too?

I have seen herds of cats with more sense of direction than MPs on this day. They began, as usual, in total ignorance. What, asked Hilary Benn for Labour, could be done? As he understood it, the Deputy Serjeant-at-Arms (sans tights) was, even as he spoke, delivering a summons to Rupert and James. What next if the Two refused?

Sir George Young, the Leader of the House, is way too tall for the despatch box. He compensates by forcing one leg straight back. This makes him look like a very posh giraffe in mid-graze. Yesterday he was a giraffe with a notebook. He read out a procedure that made a maze look straightforward.

First, the select committee had to decide that a contempt had been committed. Then it was up to Mr Speaker (at this, Little Johnny Bercow puffed himself up) to decide if it was indeed contempt, and to refer it to the Committee on Standards and Privileges. (Are you asleep yet?)

So what was the punishment? 'One includes you, Mr Speaker [puff puff], admonishing somebody who appears at the bar of the House!' I tried to imagine the Murdoch Two in the chamber, flanked by men in tights, confronted by men in wigs, getting a ticking off from Little Johnny in his wonderfully ornate *Alice in Wonderland* chair, flanked by his trainbearer (who, sadly, no longer has a train). It's not exactly Wormwood Scrubs.

Sir George was smiling at the Speaker now. 'It's a responsibility that I know you will discharge with aplomb!' Mr Speaker giggled, his feet bouncing on his green leather footrest.

I suddenly got that feeling that I sometimes have when watching the Commons, that I am not sure what century this is. Sir George announced that the last time anyone was fined for contempt was 1666. Ah yes, the seventeenth century: I thought so.

As Sir George spoke, the Labour MP and Hackgate campaigner Chris Bryant was heckling. 'Wrong!' he muttered. 'Wrong!' Mr Bryant is a fearsome parliamentary trainspotter:

this is a man who reads *Erskine May* for fun. This was an urgent matter, he noted, for the House was to begin its summer recess on Tuesday (19 July to 4 September is, I am sure you will agree, a very short break indeed). Did Sir George realise that on Monday he could instruct the Serjeant-at-Arms (with or without tights) to bring in the Murdoch Two?

'YEAH!' cried MPs.

One Labour MP shouted: 'Come on, George, be a man!' Sir George looked appalled. I can only imagine that there was huge relief when the Murdoch Two decided to come, thus avoiding a repeat of 1666 and all that. 💔

* Rebekah Brooks resigned the day after this debate.

19 July 2011
The Ice Queen cometh

Theresa May's statement on policing and Hackgate was an icy blast of fury

Theresa May, Ice Queen, is so far the unexpected success of this Government. Yesterday, after a stonking statement on the police, in which she gave no quarter, the mutters in the press gallery were, 'Theresa for Prime Minister?' Who would have thought it?

Ms May came to the Commons, the icy calm in the eye of the firestorm, and presented Labour with a sheet of glass. Labour MPs, despite a desperate call for crampons, failed to make any progress at all. Her only real problem was that weird guy George who sat next to her, giving advice, though she didn't need it, and looking distinctly malevolent.

Ed Miliband was there, as he always is now. Are there two of him? He, or his cardboard cutout, is hard to avoid. Dave was in

Africa, a continent that he only goes to during a major crisis at home. Last time it was floods, this time Hackgate. He should know that the words 'I'm going to Rwanda' can only spell doom for him.

Ms May was in snakeskin shoes and no-nonsense mode. She came to praise Sir Paul Stephenson (newly resigned) and Yates of the (Knackers) Yard. She did not criticise them directly, setting up inquiries but keeping any questions she had to herself. Labour hated this.

Yvette Cooper, clutching an icepick, crampons visible, hacked away at the frozen wall. If the Met had shown bad judgement in employing the former *News of the World* journalist Neil Wallis, then so had the PM over Andy Coulson. 'People will think it is one rule for the police and one rule for the Prime Minister.'

Ms May, working on a Cruella de Vil impersonation, curled a blood-red lip. She pointed out that the police, not No. 10, had been investigating the NoW. She was derisive of the idea that she was both doing nothing and also doing Labour's bidding. 'That sort of politics is the "have your cake and eat it" sort of opportunism of Opposition politics, to which I know both she and the Shadow Chancellor belong.'

Yikes! Or should I say 'Yates!'? Ed Balls (or Yvette's husband, as he was at this point) looked outraged, though that icicle sticking out of his forehead is not a good look.

Labour kept demanding various resignations (there is hardly a need to be specific these days) while Ice Queen kept pointing out that Labour did nothing about hacking questions for years.

My favourite moment came when Madeleine Moon arose from the Labour backbenches. 'The stench arising from the rotting drains underneath this chamber seems to be an apt background to the debate today,' noted Ms Moon, who is, by the way, an expert on bats in Westminster.

'Obviously the drains haven't been cleaned out for years – but this Government is doing it!' retorted Cruella, words freezing in mid-air. 💔

A bit small for a hate figure, but the jowly old guy was the star

There was already drama enough when Rupert and James Murdoch came to testify and then, suddenly, Wendi jumped up to defend her man

I t was the first time that I have seen Rupert Murdoch in the flesh but can I just start this sketch by saying – Wendi Deng! Slap, bang, wallop! Forget Wonder Woman, this was Wonder Wendi to the rescue the moment that her man came under attack.

The historic session was almost over when it happened. I say historic, though what I may mean is hypnotic. James Murdoch, motormouth, talked incessantly, his flat American accent seeming to render almost all words meaningless. 'I share your frustration,' he kept saying to MPs, though I doubted it as they struggled to follow even one of his sentences to its end.

Rupert, though, spoke in short, dare I say tabloid, sentences in raw-boned Australian, punctuated with pauses so long and unexpected that you felt that, like a ha-ha, you might fall into them. 'I would just like to say one sentence,' he announced at the start. 'This is the most humble day of my life.' I am told that, in the overspill room, this got a laugh. In the real room, it seemed from the heart, if a bit Hollywood.

My first thought on seeing them walk in was that Rupert was quite small to be such a big hate figure. It was a cramped room, holding only fifteen press and thirty members of the public. Now four people stood up with signs that said 'The people vs. Murdoch'. They were told to leave, which they did, as silently as they had protested.

We then got on with the serious tedium. Very occasionally, like a rare butterfly, a new fact flitted into the room, surprising everyone. Some MPs – Jim Sheridan, Alan Keen, Thérèse Coffey

– seemed from another planet. Others, like Tom Watson, are starring in their own movie and have little room for us.

And yet, in this room of egos, there was no doubt who was the star, the old jowly guy, sitting slightly slumped, eyes often closed. When someone noted how often Prime Ministers kept asking him to No. 10, he shot back, quick-draw: 'I wish they'd leave me alone!' Everyone laughed and, again, it seemed true.

Wendi sat directly behind her husband, long hair hanging down, fussing over him, rubbing his back. When Rupert spoke, he often banged his hands on the table until, at times, I felt a bongo rhythm developing. Wendi reached out to stop him. James, eyes wide behind rimless spectacles, also tried to intervene. 'My son is telling me not to gesticulate,' noted Rupert, suddenly the octogenarian being watched by the protective son.

They seemed to be in their own cocoon. Rupert does a good line in homespun straightforward tycoonery. 'There is no excuse for breaking the law at any time,' he announced, reminiscing about his father, a great campaigning journalist. James is less impetuous, more managerial, setting great store by internal processes and committees. MPs, faced with these two, in sync with each other, seemed stymied.

I was sitting in the front row, just behind the Murdochs, at the far left.

At almost 5 p.m., more than two hours in, a man stumbled up from behind, plastic bag swinging. He took out a white paper plate with foam on it and, as the whole thing went into slow motion, he smeared the foam on Rupert. Wendi launched herself like an Exocet as the guy said, 'You are a greedy billionaire.'

Wendi, papers in hand, hit the protester in the face. She fell to the ground but scrambled back up. It was chaos but Rupert just sat there, silent, blobs of pine-smelling foam on his nose. 'I got him!' Wendi crowed, rarin' to go.

A policeman, also with foam on his face, watched. Rupert still said nothing. Wendi used bottled water to clean the foam off. James, angry, wanted to know how the guy had got past security. 'This is a circus,' he fumed. 'Honestly, this is a circus.'

We were all being ushered out of the room. A colleague reports that James demanded an adjournment. But it was Rupert, jacket off, defoamed, who had the last word. 'It's fine. Let's carry on,' he said, looking quite unfazed by that, or, frankly, anything else that day. ♥

21 July 2011
Too much Dave is bad for your health

Parliament had to be extended for a day so that Dave could rush back from Africa to tell us, well, about Dave, really

I think we now know why Dave cut short his Africa trip. He felt that we weren't getting enough Dave with our daily Hackgate. So yesterday was a Dave marathon. He warbled his way through a two-and-a-half-hour Commons statement, answering 136 questions, then opened a Hackgate debate. It was impossible not to conclude, as we staggered out, that there was such a thing as too much Dave.

But not, I suspect, for Dave. It was a performance of pent-up frustration that began, and I do not welcome this innovation, with what may be the first political pre-apology. 'If it turns out I have been lied to,' he cried, referring to promises given to him by his former aide and ex-*News of the World* editor Andy Coulson, 'that would be a moment for a profound apology. And, in that event, I can tell you I will not fall short!'

Ed Milibanana, who is suffering from Hackgate fatigue, did not demand a real apology. At least this makes a change from calling for a resignation (any will do). The PM, when it came to Andy Coulson, had been caught in a 'tragic conflict of loyalty'. He had 'built a wall of silence'. We were in cliché overload.

Dave was scathing. 'What I would say is, stop hunting feeble conspiracy theories and start rising to the levels of events.' He attacked Ed for petty party political point-scoring before embarking on what can only be called an orgy of the same.

Dave lavished praise on Dave for being so transparent and for not, like Gordon Brown's wife, holding a slumber party for Rebekah Brooks ('I've never seen her in pyjamas!'). 'We now know who was, if you like, the Slumber Party,' shouted Dave, obviously enjoying himself, 'and it was the party opposite!'

The smugness was overwhelming. My favourite moment came as Dave was wallowing in self-praise, about how he was the kind of man who never ran away from anything and took responsibility for every decision that he had ever made. Suddenly he stopped and looked over at his tormentor, Ed Balls, the Shadow Chancellor. Ed had just heckled Dave that Labour had never hired Mr Coulson. 'Look!' shouted Dave. 'You hired Damian McBride! You hired Alastair Campbell, who falsified documents in Government!' At this potentially slanderous statement Ed Milibanana's face was a picture. His panda eyes widened, his mouth forming a 'hoop of horror' (as they say in *Heat* magazine). But Dave loved this even more.

Amid the outrage, Dave leant across the despatch box and cried: 'GOTCHA!' Oh, please. Everyone claims that Hackgate is about the victims, but yesterday it was totally tabloid. How I yearned for Wendi Deng to rise up and administer a smart slap. ♥

Chapter 8

Trouble and Strife

It was a summer of discontent. The hacking scandal rumbled on and then, out of what felt like nowhere, came the riots which were so bad that the Prime Minister was forced to return early from his Italian holiday. The weather was appalling and the Eurozone crisis lurched from deadline to deadline. As September dawned, the TUC ramped up the strike threats. All of this meant that the political conference season felt even more of a bubble than usual. The Lib Dems were in Birmingham where Tim Farron took it upon himself to pre-announce the divorce of the coalition. Red Ed was in Liverpool where he told us he wasn't Tony Blair and Dave and Co were in Manchester where, as the world economy tanked, it felt even more surreal than usual to be enclosed in a blacked-out hall, listening to speeches about things that, probably, would never happen. ♥

9 August 2011
It's a riot and Calamity Clegg strikes again

The first top politician to respond to the riots was Nick Clegg. What was not clear, however, was if anyone really wanted him there

By the time that Nick Clegg got to the badlands of Tottenham yesterday, that particular bit of London wasn't burning so much as having a barbie. The only aroma that I could detect on this fresh spring-like day was that of barbecuing ribs. Overhead, a helicopter purred. On the ground, it felt a bit like a holiday.

Sorry, shouldn't have mentioned the holiday. As Nick sees it, he wasn't so much on holiday as working from Spain. He was in 'constant contact' with Dave, George, Vince, Chris, William (I just hope he's got them all on Friends and Family). Now he was back, and determined to be our first 'leader' to visit the badlands.

Except that Tottenham, by the time he got there, was more just the sadlands. The High Road, where the now famous burnt-out CarpetRight was located, had been cordoned off for more than a day. Nick's team told me that I wasn't allowed to observe him meeting victims and community leaders on police advice. I don't know why because, by then, Nick was in what was probably the safest street in Britain, a police-sterile zone.

My only chance to see Nick in the flesh was a question-and-answer with LBC Radio in Southwark, southeast London. About seventy people were there, a thin crowd, which meant they were stacking the chairs before it started. Maybe people wouldn't care if Nick were still on holiday (or working from abroad, as we must now call it).

Sirens wailed near by but the only calamity heading our way was named Clegg. If you were as accident-prone as the Deputy Prime Minister, would you try to enter a room from a balcony? And yet here was Nick, coming in from the outside, like Milk Tray man with a schoolboy haircut.

'Here's the Deputy Prime Minister,' cried the LBC host, Iain Dale. But as Nick came, a gust of wind blew over his four 9ft-high 'Meet Nick Clegg' banners.

Nick laughed: 'It's radio, isn't it?'

It was the perfect entrance for Calamity. He told us about his visit to Tottenham but the audience was more upset about the bankers. Why weren't the banks lending to small businesses? Why wasn't Nick making them do it?

'You say that we are all in this together,' noted one man. 'Prove it.'

Nick launched into another soliloquy, disarming his critics through a combination of charm and tedium. But, just as Nick told us about the importance of the high street, I heard a terrible racket.

'Speaking to businesses…' began Nick, though I lost the rest because of a noise which sounded like ducks.

'What is that?' asked Nick.

'Ducks,' noted Iain Dale.

'In here?' asked Nick.

No, out there, where all the bad things are. So I was there when Nick went quackers during the London riots. It could only happen to him. 💔

10 August 2011
Boris and the bristling crowd

The day after the nightmare before saw the Broom Army take to the streets. Boris, jet-lagged, met them at the bottom of Lavender Hill

Boris headed towards the mob, hundreds strong, at Clapham Junction. It was 2.50 p.m. The mob waved their multi-coloured brooms in the air as they, confusingly, cheered and jeered the Mayor of London who was, more or less, just off the plane from Vancouver. 'Vancouver,' exclaimed one chap from the strictly middle-class Broom Army. 'That fits. There was a riot there this summer – over a hockey game.'

The scene felt like it was in a movie. The mayor, white blond hair flopping in its Dulux dog way, bumbled down a cordoned-off Lavender Hill, past firefighters dousing what used to be a party shop. His smallish media mob – featuring fuzzy microphones, aides, cameras and hangers-on – headed towards the much bigger broom mob, waiting to start cleaning the street. It wasn't exactly West Side Story but it was, well, pretty strange actually.

'Where's your broom? Where's your broom?' they shouted at Boris. Suddenly, magically, a new broom was thrust into Boris's right hand. He brandished it like a trophy.

Moments earlier, up the hill, Boris had received a pasting from angry business owners about the lack of police. Behind him the Home Secretary, Theresa May, white-faced, slunk off. Now it was just him, heading towards the brooms. If there was to be a fight, at least it was going to be a clean one.

'Thank you to everybody who came out today to volunteer to clear up the mess,' cried Boris, his broom bobbing like a majorette's baton. 'You are the true spirit of this city.' The jeers turned into cheers. 'I want to say personally how deeply sorry I am and how much I regret the damage...'

The brooms shouted back: 'Where were the police?'

Boris ploughed on: 'To the rioters and thugs, it's time we heard a little bit less about the sociological justifications about what is, in my view, nothing less than wanton criminality.'

The brooms didn't like that. 'Boooooooo,' they shouted, followed quickly by other brooms going: 'Shhhhhhhh.'

Boris looked shattered. 'I ask anybody who has the faintest vestige of sympathy with these people to ask yourself what is the point in times of economic difficulty in destroying businesses that are the lifeblood of our community? What is the sense?'

Boris turned round and, rather rudely, talked into the fuzzy microphones. The Broom Army chanted: 'We want to clean. We want to clean.' Some warbled the Wombles song. Boris trudged back up the hill, away from this madding (if clean) crowd.💔

12 August 2011
Angry mob defies unity plea to hurl clichés

Dave recalled Parliament to rail against the rioters while the Lib Dems wittered

David Cameron and Ed Miliband began the public disorder debate with an appeal for calm in the chamber. MPs would stand 'shoulder to shoulder' or, in the case of women, shoulder-pad to shoulder-pad, with each other. It lasted thirty minutes.

The public disorder debate disorder wasn't a riot as much as a defy-it (for Labour) and a deny-it (for the Tories). The Lib Dems just sat there, wringing their hands and worrying about how to analyse the phenomenon that is social media. I am not criticising because wittering is not against the law.

The others fought with words, some used with clear criminal intent. Surely the word 'surge' should never be used, as Dave did, like this: 'We want to surge capacity.' Also, in future defy-its, we should ban the word 'robust' being used with 'policing'. We need a zero tolerance approach to word crime.

The Tories wanted to bring in the Army, let police use rubber bullets and water cannon, control Twitter and bring forward the marriage tax break. Labour MPs insisted that cutting budgets will result in less robust (argh) policing. They want more CCTV, an inquiry, fewer cuts and more youth services. The Lib Dems just want to witter.

Sir Peter Tapsell, the human rotunda, is so grand that he is Grade I-listed. The 81-year-old Tory speaks with a slight lisp that makes an 'r' sound like a 'w'. Sir Peter wants the police to arrest more 'hoods'. 'Do you remember that in 1971, at the peak of the opposition to the Vietnam (which he pronounced Vee-ate-nam] war, the US Government brought 16,000 troops into Washington? They wounded up the wioters, they arrested them, and they put 40,000 of them into the DC stadium.'

Someone exclaimed: 'Wow!' Sir Peter demanded: 'Do you have any plans to make the Wembley Stadium available for similar use?' Dave did not. Earlier he said those at the thrillingly named Cobra meeting was considering what the Army might do in future riots. 'For instance some simple gardening tasks,' he said. I imagined soldiers armed with trugs and hoes before I realised that Dave must have said 'guarding'.

Tory David T. C. Davies, who is also a special constable, cried: 'When you say we will be robust [argh], can you assure us that we will support the police if they have to strike people with batons or kettle them in?' Dave agreed that the police must be 'robust'. I give up. What does it mean? 💔

14 September 2011
Ed's friends tell him he's rubbish

Ed Miliband tried to make friends at the TUC Congress – but it all went wrong

Red Ed began his first speech as Labour leader to the brothers and sisters of the TUC with this greeting. 'Friends,' he said, quickly, tentatively, hopefully.

Friends? Hundreds of trade unionists watched him warily. What did Ed think this was – Central Perk? Did he think that somehow Joey, Ross, Chandler, Rachel, Monica and Phoebe had, inexplicably, infiltrated the TUC? If so, this episode of *Friends* was The One Where Ed Tries to Stand Up to the Brothers. The setting was surreal: a basement at the TUC in London, their usual seaside trip being off for cost reasons. It was 9.30 a.m. To put us in a calm mood, a string quartet played Mozart (I am not making this up).

Red Ed was wearing a purple tie (The One Where Ed Wears a Purple Tie) and an air of desperate sincerity. He had needed these people to kill his brother, and they pick up almost all of Labour's bills. But he was there to signal that he was his own man, not theirs. Thus 'friends', not 'comrades' or, even, the ghastly Sainsbury-esque 'colleagues'.

Ed began by saying how much they had in common. He told them how much he had admired the Sodexo dinner ladies that he had met in Richmond last year. 'Let us applaud them for what they achieved,' he exhorted. But no one applauded.

Then he tried the 'what doesn't kill us makes us stronger' argument. They would not, he noted, always agree. But theirs was a relationship that wasn't about 'romance or nostalgia' but 'respect and shared values'. 'We know what unites us is greater than what divides us,' he announced, again to silence.

Ed embarked, without romance, on the subject of pensions. He 'fully understood' why workers were angry. 'But while negotiations were going on, I do believe it was a mistake for strikes to happen,' he said to heckles and rumbles.

'Shame!' cried the 'friends' at Ed. He didn't seem to mind (The One Where Ed Gets Heckled) though he went on to tell them that they were 'agents for change', which seemed just a bit patronising.

The show should have ended there with perfect *Friends* sitcom timing (Central Perk, here we come). But then Ed pushed his luck with a Q&A session. Ed was asked if he would rescind the new pension indexation. He shook his head. 'I don't want to become Nick Clegg, someone who told you a promise before the election and breaks it afterward,' he explained to general disgust.

'Shame!' they cried at him over his stand on strikes.

'Rubbish!' they shouted as he backed academies.

This made Ed become even more earnest, huge panda eyes heading into orbit, spaghetti arms reaching out. So, friends, there you have it: The One Where Ed's Friends Told Him He's Rubbish. It will be a classic.♥

20 September 2011
No smiles allowed for Vince

The Lib Dems met in Birmingham where they delighted in castigating the Tories and patting themselves on the back. But then Vince told them some hard truths

ince Cable is taking the cuts so seriously that he has insti-
tuted a personal austerity programme. First to go was his
smile. What's the point of stretching your lips across your
teeth when we are in the economic equivalent of war? His lips
are sealed on this.

He's also cutting optimism back to the bone. 'Let me say that
when my staff saw my draft of this speech, they said, 'We can
see the grey skies but where are the sunny uplands?' Vince's lips
pressed together. 'I am sorry. I can only tell it as I see it.'

Vince Cable, grey-sky thinker. No cloud has a silver lining
because silver is just grey with sparkles in it. And sparkles are
another victim of his austerity drive.

'These are dangerous times,' he announced, eyes not twinkling
because, let's face it, if he allowed twinkling then he'd also have to
allow sparkles. It's a slippery slope to smiles.

'It has been hard,' he announced. But we'd already guessed
that. He told us he had regrets (again, not a surprise).

The Government – i.e., George Osborne – should have
clamped down more on bank pay and bonuses. 'A bad message
was sent that unrestrained greed is acceptable,' he said. 'We now
know where that leads.'

Yes we do: to depression, to feeling down, to not smiling.

'Cutting is a thankless and unpopular task,' he told us.

Vince cannot believe how ridiculous some people are. 'Some
believe government is Father Christmas,' he said (ho-ho-hos also
have to go, as I understand it). 'They draw up lists of tax cuts and
giveaways and assume that Santa will pop down the chimney and
leave presents under the tree.' Vince looked disgusted. 'This is
childish fantasy.'

My, but it's glum in Brum. I was wondering if this was, actually, black-sky thinking when, out of the blue (not banned yet but
on the list), Vince made a joke. 'Banks operate like a man who
either wears his trousers round his chest, stifling breathing, as
now,' he said. 'Or round his ankles, exposing his assets.'

The hall burst into laughter. Vince added: 'If he has some.'

The woman in front of me was laughing so hard I feared that a stretcher might be necessary. That's what happens in austerity: you get so used to nothing that even one relatively mild joke can send you totally berserk. Still, it was good to know that jokes have not gone the way of smiles in Vince's Grim New World.💔

22 September
Quoting Mill is a Boon for this love-in

I was looking for John Stuart Mill throughout Nick Clegg's pep talk to the troops

I was told beforehand that, hidden inside Nick Clegg's speech, was a reference from John Stuart Mill. This is the kind of game that Lib Dems absolutely love. Spot the J. S. Mill quote will never quite make it to 'Where's Wally?' type popularity but if there is one thing that the Lib Dems have proven, it is that they don't care if anyone likes them.

By mistake, I found myself seated deep in Lib Dem territory. Nick had chosen to give his speech in the middle of a doughnut of Lib Dem love. I ended up as part of the dough. These are the hard-core. The man next to me was reading a new Nick Clegg biography. A hardback! Another man tried to pay £1,800 for a bottle of Lib Dem whisky to raise money for the party. Everyone was in yellow. It was like a cult.

So there I was deep in dough, listening for J. S. Mill. We were told not to look at the autocue but at Nick who has, I can report, put on quite a bit of weight. The chin is not quite double but it's certainly in trouble. When you listen so intently, you hear all sorts of things. Here is my list:

- His theme was 'not easy, but right'. He said it about twenty times, it was the bass riff, the thing that made the speech work. It was all about hard choices, hard times. Of course Nick is on the right and so it fitted. I noticed immediately that it wasn't 'not easy, but left'. J. S. would never have said that anyway.

- Nick hates Labour more than he used to. Listening to him castigate Ed Miliband and Ed Balls, it sounded like there was no chance, ever, of a coalition there. 'The Two Eds, behind the scenes, lurking in the shadows, always plotting, always scheming, never taking responsibility.' (Responsibility, now that's a Mill word but is one word enough?) 'This is no time for the backroom boys,' eschewed Nick, echoing Gordon Brown's 'this is no time for a novice' taunt. Not easy but, certainly, right-wing.
- Nick likes brandy. He went off-script (OK, so I peeked at the autocue) only once when he told us how he'd got it wrong when he and the French Prime Minister exchanged gifts. 'He'd done his research, found out what year I was born in, and presented a beautiful bottle, a rare bottle, of 1967 brandy. I was told he liked hiking so what did I give him? A bar of Kendal mint cake!' The doughnut chuckled though, surely, Kendal mint cake is very close to the Lib Dem heart. This whole joke was too easy and not right.
- J. S. will feel let down. Apparently the reference to him was the words 'uphill struggle' or, to be precise, this: 'For liberals, the only struggles worth having are uphill ones.' That was it. Not easy, I thought, and not right.

When Nick ended, the doughnut jumped up as one. Nick ran over to Miriam, looking amazingly lovely in a floaty yellow dress, and they embarked on a double-kiss-a-thon that true Europeans love. My verdict? Not easy but, on the day, right.♥

28 September
Ed insists he's not Tony, Iain or Charles…

Labour met in Liverpool where Ed tried to resolve an identity crisis

The best bit of Ed Miliband's speech was when it was over. Justine joined him on stage, eyes wide. The pair of them looked like two baby birds (he a magpie, she a wren) who had just flown the nest, having learnt to fly. The crowd was on its feet, clapping like mad, as Florence and the Machine pumped out *You've Got the Love*.

They had the love! Ed and Justine pecked (as lovebirds do). Then they embarked on a journey, as they like to say in politics, wending their way through the crowd. But instead of exiting at the side through the curtain, they decided to climb the stairs at the back which, as shown by the boom camera, looked positively Machu Picchu-ish. At the top, someone had opened the double doors and we could see that, outside this dark, subterranean, netherworldly conference hall there was indeed a place of light and air. Ed and Justine turned to wave, light flooding round them, infusing them, turning them into strange-looking beings. It looked quite religious, a modern William Blake painting entitled *Ed and Justine Ascend to Heaven*. Then they turned and, poof, were gone.

It was the perfect ending for a speech that was more of a sermon anyway, with its moral capitalism in which the good are rewarded because they want something for something and the bad are not because they want something for nothing. How to tell good from bad? What about those of us who will settle for anything at all? These are all questions we will have to ask Ed when he gets back from heaven.

Ed looked impossibly young, with his sticky-up hair, his long blink, his unlined face. 'I'm not Tony Blair,' he said to boos and then anti-Blair cheers. How strange. Somehow I can't quite imagine TB ever defining himself by saying, 'I'm not Ed Miliband'.

Ed (not Tony, remember) embarked on the first political joke ever about a deviated septum. The day of his nose job was known as Ed Nose Day. This got titters. 'It needed repositioning,' he said, adding that some might say this was typical of a new Labour leader: 'He gets elected and everything moves to the centre.' Ha! Except it's not true: Red Ed may have been wearing a grey tie (why?) and standing on a white set, but that is just all camouflage. This was a speech that Tony Blair (yes, we know Ed, you aren't him) would never have given.

Ed told us that we were in the middle of a 'quiet crisis'. Worryingly, this made me think of Iain Duncan Smith when he was Tory leader which, frankly, can only be a bad thing. Perhaps Ed would soon be saying: 'I am not IDS'.

Ed says that in the twenty-first century we all have to make a choice. 'Are you on the side of the wealth creators or the asset strippers?' he demanded. 'The producers or the predators?'

Oh, a quiz! I immediately felt drawn towards the predators: raptors, lions, wolves. After all, what did producers do other than make films? But now Ed jumped in: 'Producers train, invest, invent, sell.' Aha. 'Predators are just interested in the fast buck.' So producers good, predators bad. I had not realised that, in addition to reinventing capitalism, Ed was reordering the natural world.

What would Darwin say? ('I am not Charles Darwin,' Ed would protest). For surely, if we know anything, it is that everyone is a predator of something. David Cameron certainly is. Except, it seems, Ed, who is a baby bird just learning how to fly.♥

4 October 2011
By George, he's got the answer: it's graphene

In Manchester, George Osborne indulges in some magical thinking as he unveils Plan G

George Osborne famously says that he has no Plan B. Yesterday we found out why. What he's got – and it's so secret that even people hearing his speech yesterday may not have realised it – is a Plan G. Yes, that's right, G. It doesn't stand for George or growth (don't be silly). Instead it stands for something more exciting: graphene.

What is it? At first, we only knew it rhymed with Norene. Until the graphene moment, I was worried that George was going to give an entire speech without even one big idea.

George arrived looking sombre. If we had mood music, it would have been a dirge. It was a speech about pain, a blueprint for his signature economic policy of sadomonetarism. He told us that we were anxious, worried, losing our jobs, our careers, our hopes. There was a crisis in Europe, our banks, our deficit. Then, hilariously, he chirped: 'But we should be careful not to talk ourselves into something worse.' It was like a horseman of the apocalypse wheeling round in mid-gallop to trill: 'Let's have some fun…'

Every once in a while, with Tourettian bouts of optimism, he would cry: 'Together, we will ride out this storm!' He made fun of Ed Balls, the man he loves to hate. 'Economic adviser to Gordon Brown,' he scoffed. 'I'm not sure I'd put that on my CV if I were Ed Balls. It's like "personal trainer" to Eric Pickles!' Everyone laughed: George loves a fat joke, cruel to be unkind, that's our horseman of the apocalypse, riding out the storm.

He told us a series of rather smallish things he's trying out, like lowering carbon targets and making it easier to sack people. He's going to do something called 'credit easing' – no one had any idea what it was but everyone clapped anyway.

So where was the big idea? Now, suddenly, George told us we were in Manchester. 'The city where the first computer was built, where Rutherford split the atom.' The crowd was looking at each other. Was this *University Challenge*? George said that only this morning he'd met two 'brilliant' scientists who'd won the Nobel Prize for Physics. 'Their prize was for the discovery of a substance called graphene.'

The word 'graphene' was met by silence, the crowd too baffled even to applaud. You could see the empty thought bubbles over their heads. Graphene, a thingymajiggy whatsit that sounded like the name of a country singer. George explained it was the strongest, thinnest, best conducting material known. More blank stares. Actually, with the help of Wikipedia, I can report that it is an allotrope of carbon, whose structure is one-atom-thick planar sheets of sp^2-bonded carbon atoms. So, really, almost exactly like a country singer.

George says that graphene is going to be used in everything from aircraft wings to microchips. It's the Coca-Cola of allotropes. We are inventing a national research programme to take graphene 'from the British laboratory to the British factory floor'. Do you remember Gordon Brown's 'British jobs for British workers'? Well this was British jobs for British allotropes. 'We are going to get Britain making things again!' he cried.

So there you have it. Plan G. Allotropes riding to our rescue, conquering the horsemen, saving us from the storm. The crowd clapped, they knew not why. ❦

5 October 2011
It's Hush Puppies v Kitten Heels

Catfight! The Tory party conference finally came alive when Theresa May got her claws out

Manchester became a dog eat cat world yesterday. Thank goodness, because it was all seeming just a bit dull. But then we had Theresa May trying to blame the immigration crisis on a cat (meow!), only to be kerpowed by the man wearing Hush Puppies. Plus there was Boris peddling highly suspect stories about rhubarb and, oh yes, something about broccoli.

First, catgate. Can I just say that Theresa May looks more like her personal style model Cruella de Vil every day? The only thing missing is the floor-length fur coat. Yesterday she had on leopardskin shoes with, yes, kitten heels. Strictly speaking, the shoes should be dalmatian print but, given what was to come, I could see why she went jungle.

'We all know the stories about the Human Rights Act. The

illegal immigrant who cannot be deported because,' she said icily, 'and I am not making this up, he had a pet cat.' She looked disgusted. 'That is why the Human Rights Act needs to go.'

Cruella should know: never pick on a cat. Within minutes, Ken Clarke had thrown his considerable weight – not to mention his cuddly shoes – against the Home Secretary. 'I will have a small bet with her that no one has ever been refused deportation on the grounds of ownership of a cat,' he barked.

The next thing I knew, Theresa's special adviser, who was wearing snakeskin shoes (the whole damn animal kingdom was at the conference yesterday), came around the press section with a cat briefing paper explaining why Maya (the feline in question) was, indeed, crucial to the deportation case. Meanwhile, the world had gone puntastic. Was it a Claws Four moment? Did the story have nine lives? It was the purr-fect catfight.

It was a relief, frankly, to move on to vegetables. In recent years Boris has been entertaining but damped down, for he was trying to be a serious politician. Now, with an election looming and at odds with the Treasury over the 50p tax rate, he doesn't care. From the moment he walked on stage, papers in disarray, hair helicoptering, he was full of fun. 'Down!' he cried as the audience gave him an instant ovation. 'Down!'

He told us of the 'Capone Principle': when you crack down on the small stuff, the big stuff starts to take care of itself. Untaxed cars were going to be crushed and sent back to the owners for Christmas, small cubes, with notes: 'From the Crusher, with love.'

Boris moved on to the Olympics, shouting out names: Wolverhampton had contributed the security fencing, Northampton the kerbs, Oldham the piling. 'Poole!' he shouted. 'Poole! Poole is supplying the decking!' Then, suddenly, he announced: 'I should mention that the velodrome is rubbed. You know it has a beautiful rosy hue. The velodrome is rubbed with English rhubarb. There's jobs created for English rhubarb growers and rubbers!'

Rhubarb, rhubarb, as they say. Could it be true? Later David

'Two Brains' Willetts revealed that we have invented a life-saving broccoli. Meanwhile catgate – now christened cat-flap – rumbled on. Do you ever get the feeling (sorry, feline) that the world has gone crazy? It was yesterday in Madchester.♥

6 October 2011
Dave does the can-do can-can

David Cameron, beaming like the sun, wants us all to be great and not in any way soggy

This was the speech that put the Great back into Great Britain. It was a bulldog speech, a definitive stand against sogginess and an attack on people who don't stand up. It was a pep talk with so much energy that it was practically sprinting around the convention hall. It was marvellously upbeat and, probably, a little bit bonkers.

Actually, strike out that 'probably'. 'You're not just winners,' he cried. 'You're doers!' The crowd of winning doers looked back at Dave, thrilled to be winning doers. Dave beamed back. I got the feeling he'd prepared by watching inspirational training videos, full of crazed types shouting at him: 'You can do it! Stand up! Be great! Be you! You are you! YES YOU ARE!'

You think I exaggerate but it was just like that. 'Some say to succeed in the world, we need to become more like India or China or Brazil. I say: we need to become more like us!' The winning doers who want to be more like themselves clapped wildly.

You know that story about the fight between the wind and the sun to get a man to take off his coat? The wind gusts hard but the man just wraps the coat tighter. Then the sun shines so brightly that the man has to take it off. Well, yesterday in Manchester, Dave was that sun. This speech has been five years in the making. In his 2006 conference, in Bournemouth, Dave cried: 'Let sunshine win the day!' But then he was just a sunbeam, a dancing ray in training. Now he is a glowing orb of optimism.

So here, then, is the Little Book of Dave, inspirational guidance taken from his speech which, true to his 'yes we can' spirit, he delivered despite a bad throat:

- Can-can is the new national dance. 'Let's bring on the can-do optimism!'
- Small dogs are great dogs. 'Britain has never had the biggest population, the largest land mass, the richest resources but we had the spirit. Remember, it's not the size of the dog in the fight, it's the size of the fight in the dog!'
- Our airports are hell. 'When you step off the plane in Delhi or Shanghai or Lagos, you can feel the energy, the hunger, the drive to succeed! We need that here.' I thought of Heathrow and felt pessimistic which is, of course, banned.
- So is sogginess. 'Frankly, there's too much "can't do" sogginess,' barked Dave. When he said this, I actually sat up straighter. This speech was like boot camp.
- Armbands are for sissies. The other day Dave became aware that highlighter pens come with various warnings including instructions for 'hand and eye protection'. This disgusted him. 'This isn't how a great nation was built! Britannia didn't rule the waves with armbands on!'
- Circular sentences are inspiring. 'It's not complicated but not easy either!'
- Standing up is the new sitting down. 'Let's turn this time of challenge into a time of opportunity. Not sitting around, watching things happen and wondering why. But standing up, making things happen and asking why not!'

It was inspiring but, frankly, exhausting. I can hardly wait to start putting the Great back in Britain but first I need a little lie down. Don't tell Dave.💔

Post-conference postscript: Final notes from the marriage

Ihave always thought that, for Dave and Nick, given their chemistry and sheer compatibility, any real problems with their marriage were likely to come from the kids and grandparents – i.e. their MPs, Lords and Ladies, aides (not to mention the voters).

Thus it was when, without warning, in Birmingham, Tim Farron, the ambitious President of the Lib Dems, pre-announced the divorce. Tim, young and cheeky, bestrode the stage. 'If the coalition is a marriage, well it is a good-natured one but I am afraid it is temporary,' he said. 'I don't want to upset you and it is not going to happen for three or four years but I am afraid divorce is inevitable.'

I quite like that 'I don't want to upset you' line. No, of course not Tim. I've heard of pre-nups but not a pre-post-nup.

Andrew Marr, not for the first time, was left to act as a marriage counsellor when, before the Tory conference, he had David Cameron on his BBC show.

Andrew: 'But will there be a divorce eventually?'

Dave: 'Well we're not married, so I mean there won't be…' He laughed. 'I mean I don't… You know I don't…'

Andrew: 'You haven't signed the papers; you didn't get around to it?'

Dave: 'No, no, I am happily married, but to my wife, not to Nick Clegg if I can put it that way.' (Andrew Marr laughs though I'm not sure if Nick would have joined him.) 'But no, it's not a marriage, so it doesn't end in divorce. It is a coalition where two parties have put aside some of their own interests for the good of the country.'

But actually, Dave, those of us who were at the wedding know that it is a marriage and that is what makes it all so very interesting.💔

Index

There are two people who you will not find in the index because they appear on so many pages that to list them would be like the maddest phone number in the world. They are David Cameron and Nick Clegg.